Virtual & Augmented Reality

by Paul Mealy

for dummies®

A Wiley Brand

Virtual & Augmented Reality For Dummies®

Published by: **John Wiley & Sons, Inc.**, 111 River Street, Hoboken, NJ 07030-5774, www.wiley.com

Copyright © 2018 by John Wiley & Sons, Inc., Hoboken, New Jersey

Published simultaneously in Canada

No part of this publication may be reproduced, stored in a retrieval system or transmitted in any form or by any means, electronic, mechanical, photocopying, recording, scanning or otherwise, except as permitted under Sections 107 or 108 of the 1976 United States Copyright Act, without the prior written permission of the Publisher. Requests to the Publisher for permission should be addressed to the Permissions Department, John Wiley & Sons, Inc., 111 River Street, Hoboken, NJ 07030, (201) 748-6011, fax (201) 748-6008, or online at http://www.wiley.com/go/permissions.

Trademarks: Wiley, For Dummies, the Dummies Man logo, Dummies.com, Making Everything Easier, and related trade dress are trademarks or registered trademarks of John Wiley & Sons, Inc., and may not be used without written permission. All other trademarks are the property of their respective owners. John Wiley & Sons, Inc., is not associated with any product or vendor mentioned in this book.

LIMIT OF LIABILITY/DISCLAIMER OF WARRANTY: WHILE THE PUBLISHER AND AUTHOR HAVE USED THEIR BEST EFFORTS IN PREPARING THIS BOOK, THEY MAKE NO REPRESENTATIONS OR WARRANTIES WITH RESPECT TO THE ACCURACY OR COMPLETENESS OF THE CONTENTS OF THIS BOOK AND SPECIFICALLY DISCLAIM ANY IMPLIED WARRANTIES OF MERCHANTABILITY OR FITNESS FOR A PARTICULAR PURPOSE. NO WARRANTY MAY BE CREATED OR EXTENDED BY SALES REPRESENTATIVES OR WRITTEN SALES MATERIALS. THE ADVICE AND STRATEGIES CONTAINED HEREIN MAY NOT BE SUITABLE FOR YOUR SITUATION. YOU SHOULD CONSULT WITH A PROFESSIONAL WHERE APPROPRIATE. NEITHER THE PUBLISHER NOR THE AUTHOR SHALL BE LIABLE FOR DAMAGES ARISING HEREFROM.

For general information on our other products and services, please contact our Customer Care Department within the U.S. at 877-762-2974, outside the U.S. at 317-572-3993, or fax 317-572-4002. For technical support, please visit https://hub.wiley.com/community/support/dummies.

Wiley publishes in a variety of print and electronic formats and by print-on-demand. Some material included with standard print versions of this book may not be included in e-books or in print-on-demand. If this book refers to media such as a CD or DVD that is not included in the version you purchased, you may download this material at http://booksupport.wiley.com. For more information about Wiley products, visit www.wiley.com.

Library of Congress Control Number: 2018942938

ISBN 978-1-119-48134-8 (pbk); ISBN 978-1-119-48152-2 (ebk); ISBN 978-1-119-48142-3 (ebk)

Manufactured in the United States of America

V086328_061318

Contents at a Glance

Table of Contents

Introduction

Around 25 years ago, I visited the Forest Fair Mall in Cincinnati, a large, sprawling mall that has since closed down. One of the greatest features of this particular mall (to an 11-year-old kid) was the basement arcade. Running the full length of the mall, it had everything you could want: a Ferris wheel, bumper cars, mini golf, laser tag.

But the *pièce de résistance* was a pair of Virtuality pods, a virtual reality (VR) experience created by the Virtuality Group. The Virtuality 1000 featured a stereoscopic head-mounted display helmet (HMD), an exoskeleton touch glove and gun, and a waist-high ring used to track a player's movement within the enclosure. This specific VR experience was a local user multiplayer experience: Take on all comers in a high-energy laser battle!

My father patiently waited in line with me and handed over the $10 for me to play. By the time I reached the front of the line, I was bouncing off the walls with excitement. As the helmet was lowered onto my head, I closed my eyes, mentally preparing myself for the wonders of the virtual world I would be entering. Where would I be transported to? A lush, Amazonian jungle? A gleaming futuristic metropolis? Surely my imagination could not prepare me for the wonders I was about to behold.

Thus prepared, opening my eyes, I found . . . a mostly empty, boxy world populated by pixelated characters. Confused and disoriented, I glanced around the crudely rendered environment, the tracking barely keeping up with my movements. I was being assailed with lasers (really, blocky lines), but the resolution of the headset was so limited, I couldn't even determine where I was being shot from. I was quickly eliminated from the game, and the headset came off. My less than two-minute experience in VR had left me (and my father's wallet) deflated.

Fast forward to 2013, and I found myself working in the emerging technology field. The industry was abuzz with the "next big thing": the Oculus Rift Development Kit (DK1), a VR headset originally launched via Kickstarter. Still sporting the scars of my previous VR experience but determined to see what the buzz was about, I sorted through the mess of cables in the development kit, hooked it up to my computer, and put the headset on with trepidation, preparing myself to be let down once again by the promise of VR versus the reality of VR.

Instead, all the things I hoped to experience in that Forest Fair mall years ago were delivered. The Rift tracked my head movements accurately! The visuals were convincing! Instead of floating in a vaguely 3D-ish landscape populated by blocks, I could wander about a Tuscan villa, watch butterflies flutter by, stand by a roaring fire, gaze out the windows . . . 3D audio tying it all together. It all felt so *real*. With little to actually accomplish in the demo scene (no monsters to fight or riddles to solve), I (and everyone I showed the scene to) could spend hours just wandering about the villa, for the first time truly immersed within VR.

What was little more than a simple demo scene for a Kickstarter startup became the headset that launched a thousand companies. In one fell swoop, consumer-grade VR was re-introduced to the world, and upon seeing just how far this trans-formative technology has come, hundreds of thousands have jumped into this burgeoning industry to help shape its future.

About This Book

VR, which was once only a plaything in tech laboratories or a research-and-development (R&D) experiment in large technology companies, has entered the mainstream consciousness. VR, and its technological cousin augmented reality (AR), are quickly proving to be the next pieces of transformational technology. Esti-mates vary wildly on just how big these markets might become, but many estimates place business revenue of VR and AR at over $100 billion by 2021, if not sooner.

Despite these eye-popping numbers, the VR and AR wave is still in its early stages. There is still ample time for consumers, content creators, even those with just a passing interest in learning how these technologies will affect their lives, to brush up on these technologies before the wave of mass consumer adoption hits.

In this book, I arm you with broad knowledge of the VR and AR fields, their histo-ries, and where they appear to be headed in the future. VR and AR are vast areas of study, and many Fortune 500 companies are currently waging war to try to ensure that *their* interpretation of VR/AR is the winner. As such, I don't try to make you an expert in one singular facet of the technology. Instead, I provide you with a broad knowledge base so you can confidently move forward into the fields of VR and AR as best fits your goals. I hope that the potential of these technologies will excite you enough to go out to experience and create content for them on your own.

Perhaps more than any technology wave in recent memory, the fields of VR and AR are in a state of constant flux. As such, much of the technology mentioned in this book is early-generation technology, and some might not even be released by time of publication. I've taken care to be as thorough as possible while generally focusing on technologies with an already released consumer product, but I would be remiss not to mention certain technologies that might or might not be widely available by the time this book reaches you. When covering the various hardware/

software options, I take care to mention upcoming technologies, but I give preference to technology that is already available to consumers.

While both VR and AR have a number of enterprise-level options available, I try to focus mainly on consumer-grade devices, as these devices are what the majority of consumers will interact with. However, as many current AR devices are targeted more towards enterprise consumption, I discuss those options in a bit more detail.

Finally, I try to keep things simple and clear in this book. For those who would like to explore the technologies in greater depth, I have included some more technical information within sidebars and marked with Technical Stuff icons scattered throughout the book. Those aren't required reading, so feel free to skip them if you want to ignore the more in-depth technical pieces.

Foolish Assumptions

Without any knowledge of you, the reader, any assumptions I can make are most likely wrongheaded and foolish. However, I've thrown caution to the wind and assumed the following in order to outline the type of reader this book may appeal to.

The book assumes that you have at least a passing familiarity with VR and AR. You may have heard the terms being tossed about at work, or seen someone trying out a VR experience at a mall or retailer, or even had the chance to try out a headset yourself. You may have heard of Apple's and Google's recent forays into the AR space for mobile devices (ARKit and ARCore, respectively), and maybe you're curious how you can try these experiences yourself.

The book also assumes you have an open mind regarding these technologies and are curious about where they're headed in the future. Both VR and AR are very much emerging technologies in their (mass consumer) infancy. Some of the experiences and form factors available for both are very experimental and not always the polished experiences you may be accustomed to on your personal computers or mobile devices. Getting in on these technologies in their infancy allows you to follow their growth, missteps and all, which makes it all the more exciting when they succeed!

Icons Used in This Book

As you read through this book, you'll see icons in the margins that call out blocks of information you may find important.

TIP

The Tip icon marks helpful advice for saving time and money or enhancing the experience as you begin to explore VR and AR.

REMEMBER

The Remember icon calls out a key piece of information to retain or a summary of the points just made. If you remember nothing else from the section you just read, remember the material marked here.

WARNING

Warning icons point out hazards, drawbacks, or gotchas.

TECHNICAL STUFF

Anything called out by this icon takes a deeper look at a particular technical detail. Feel free to skip this information if it doesn't interest you.

Beyond the Book

In addition to what you're reading right now, this product also comes with a free access-anywhere Cheat Sheet that includes some abbreviated explanations of the current state of VR and AR, use cases for VR and AR, and where VR and AR are headed in the future. To get this Cheat Sheet, simply go to www.dummies.com and type **Virtual & Augmented Reality For Dummies Cheat Sheet** in the Search box.

Where to Go from Here

You can jump to any chapter that interests you, and come back to revisit sections later as needed. If you're an absolute beginner, I suggest reading Chapter 1 to establish a baseline for definitions of what the terms I use mean when discussing VR and AR. If you're only interested in how you can use VR and AR today, Chapters 4 and 5 are a good starting point. And if you're looking to take the step of creating your own VR or AR content, Chapter 6 should help guide your choice for further reading.

VR and AR have often been called the "fourth wave" of transformative technology after the personal computer, the Internet, and mobile computing. Each of those previous waves has uniquely shaped our lives to the point where we can't imagine our lives without them. In this book, I help you examine how this "fourth wave" might change your life with the same effect as the first three waves. I hope you'll walk away from this book excited about this new "fourth wave" of technology, with a strong knowledge base that you can use to make your own informed decisions on the technology or apply to your own projects as you create.

1

Getting Started with Virtual and Augmented Reality

Understand the various terms, types, and histories of virtual and augmented reality.

Explore the current state of virtual and augmented reality's form factors and features.

Review virtual and augmented reality's adoption rates.

Chapter **1**

Defining Virtual and Augmented Reality

When you picture "technology of the future," what are the first things that come to mind? In ten years, how will technology be affecting your life differently than it does today?

Some people may picture self-driving electric cars that at a word automatically whisk them off to their desired destinations. Others no doubt envision an artificial intelligence (AI) utopia in which robots perform the menial labor tasks humans have had to do in the past, freeing people up to tackle life's tougher problems.

Finally, many people may foresee a future where they're able to create their own realities. They could be sitting on a couch at home but put on a headset and feel as if they're at a soccer stadium thousands of miles away. They could put on a pair of high-tech glasses and have a fully realized holographic avatar of a friend appear to chat with them. They may even picture an entire room they could step into and dial up an environmental simulation as if they were actually there.

The average person may not have had a chance to experience this just yet, but nearly everyone can envision virtual reality (VR) and augmented reality (AR) as part of humanity's future. And with good reason. For years, entertainment such as movies, TV shows, and books have been selling us on the promise of VR — the VR OASIS of *Ready Player One*, the VR real-world simulations of *The Matrix*, the full-blown environmental re-creation of the holodeck from *Star Trek*. . . . All types of entertainment have their take on what has, up until very recently, been the stuff of magic and imagination.

The ideas of VR and AR themselves seem outlandish. Within the comforts of my own home, I can put on a headset and be anywhere? Experience anything? Be anyone? Attend live concerts or sporting events as if I were there? Fly across the sea and explore other countries? Travel through entire solar systems in minutes, jumping from planet to planet? These are the kinds of VR and AR that the public has long been promised. But until recently, that promise has fallen short of, well, *reality*.

Within the past few years, however, computing and manufacturing technologies have begun to catch up with the promises of VR and AR. What was once the purview of science-fiction has been brought to life. Science-fiction writer Arthur C. Clarke once claimed, regarding the wonders of new technology, "Any sufficiently advanced technology is indistinguishable from magic." If you were to travel back in time and show an iPhone to a medieval peasant, he would think you were a wizard with a magical picture box. And today, many first-time users of high-end consumer VR headsets often describe the experience as nothing less than "magical."

Within the next decade, we can expect massive changes in how we work, how we're entertained, and how we communicate, all due to VR and AR. These technologies will fundamentally change where we're headed as a society. But in order to do so, they need creators — dreamers, innovators, and magic makers — to help them reach their potential.

Before you dive into all the details of VR and AR, you need a basic overview of these technologies. This chapter helps you recognize the different types of VR and AR and provides you with some basic vocabulary for differentiating and discussing them. This chapter also provides a brief historical overview, so you can understand how we arrived at this current place in technological history. Finally, it explains the Gartner Hype Cycle, a way of understanding how technological innovations tend to grow and change, and how the Gartner Hype Cycle applies to emerging technologies such as VR and AR.

Introducing Virtual Reality and Augmented Reality

Virtual reality is often used as an umbrella term for all manner of immersive experiences, including many related terms such as *augmented reality*, *mixed reality*, and *extended reality*. In this book, however, when I refer to *virtual reality*, I generally mean an immersive computer-simulated reality that creates a physical environment that does not exist. VR environments are typically closed off from the physical world in the sense that the environments they creates are wholly new. Although the digital environments could be based on real places (such as the top of Mount Everest) or imagined ones (such as the underwater city of Atlantis), they exist apart from the current physical reality.

Figure 1-1 shows an example of a VR environment. It's a screen shot of Wevr's VR experience, *The Blu*, which allows users to explore undersea coral reefs and ocean depths, including an encounter with an 80-foot whale.

FIGURE 1-1:
A VR screen
shot of *The Blu*
by Wevr.

Augmented reality is a way of viewing the real world (either directly or via a device such as a camera creating a visual of the real world) and "augmenting" that real-world visual with computer-generated input such as still graphics, audio, or videos. AR is different from VR in that AR *augments* (adds to) a real-world or existing scene instead of creating something new from scratch.

By strict definition, in AR, the computer-generated content is an overlay on top of the real-world content. The two environments have no way of communicating with or responding to one another. However, AR's definition has been somewhat co-opted in recent years to also include a more blended hybrid called *mixed reality*, in which interaction can occur between the real world and digitally augmented content.

REMEMBER

In this book, when I refer to *augmented reality*, I use it as a blanket term that includes mixed reality as well. The two terms are often used synonymously within the industry as well, with *mixed reality* rapidly gaining favor as the more descriptive term for the combination of analog and digital realities.

Figure 1-2 shows an example of one of the most popular recent examples of AR, Pokémon Go, which places a digital Pokémon character within your real-world environment.

THE THIN YELLOW LINE

For the past 20 years, millions of people have been exposed to a flavor of AR every Saturday and Sunday, although they may not realize it. In 1998, the 1st & Ten line was introduced by a company called Sportvision to digitally visualize the first-down line for the casual football fan.

In order to achieve this effect, Sportvision creates a virtual 3D model of the football field. While capturing video of the game, each real-world camera also transmits its location, tilt, pan, and zoom values to powerful networked computers. Using these values, the computers can determine exactly where each camera sits within the virtual 3D model of the field and can use a specialized graphics program to draw the line on top of the video feed.

Drawing that line is more complicated than you may think. If the line were simply overlaid on top of the video feed, any time a player, referee, or ball passed over where the line was overlaid, the person or object would appear "under" the digital representation of the line. This would lead to a very poor viewing experience.

In order to make the digital line appear to display under various people and objects, the software uses one color palette for colors that should appear as part of the field and another color palette for colors that should appear on top of the line. When it draws the digital line onto the video feed, the field color palette colors are converted to yellow where the line should appear, whereas colors in the other color palette are not converted, leading the people and objects to appear on top of the digital line.

This encompasses AR in a nutshell — a real environment (the football field) has been augmented with digital information (the yellow line) to enhance users' viewing experience in a way that feels natural to the viewers.

Looking at Some Other Types of Virtual and Augmented Reality

VR and AR are still in their relative infancy, so it's difficult to know which terms will fall out of favor over time and which terms will stick around. The terms *virtual reality* and *augmented reality* may have staying power, but you should also be aware of some of the other terms out there.

Mixed reality

Mixed reality (MR) may take your view of the real world and integrate computer-generated content that can interact with that view of the real world. Or it may take a fully digital environment and connect it to real-world objects. In this way, MR can sometimes function similarly to VR and sometimes function similarly to AR.

In AR-based MR, the content of the digital world is no longer passively laid on top of the real world; instead, it can act as if it were a *part* of the real world. Digital objects appear as if they existed in the physical space, and you can even interact with some digital objects as if they were actually there. For example, you might be able to drop a digital rocket onto your coffee table and watch it blast off, or bounce a digital soccer ball off the real-world walls and floor.

A ROSE BY ANY OTHER NAME . . .

You may hear terms used in ways that seem misaligned with the rest of the industry. Sometimes it's because terminology has changed since the naming occurred — which does happen, because the technologies are still very young. However, it can also be due to branding.

For example, Microsoft recently released a line of Windows Mixed Reality headsets. But by nearly any current metric, the headsets would more properly be referred to as *virtual* reality headsets, because they allow only a closed-off virtual environment similar to other VR headsets. Many people believe that Microsoft intends to merge its current batch of VR headsets with AR interaction, but the current naming can make things confusing for consumers.

As long as you understand the definitions described in this section, you should be able to evaluate products according to their actual feature set, and not necessarily how they're marketed.

Apple's ARKit and Google's ARCore, while described as AR, actually straddle the line between AR and MR and reveal the naming discrepancy occurring within the industry. Although they project a digital layer on top of the physical world, they're also able to scan the environment and track surfaces within the real world. This enables users to place digital objects in the real world, cast digital shadows on real-world items, affect digital lighting according to the real world's lighting conditions, and so on — all things that lean more toward the definition of MR.

Another example of a current AR-based MR headset is the Microsoft HoloLens (shown in Figure 1-3), a headset that scans the physical environment to mix in digital objects. This technology, which is also found in Microsoft's Meta 2, takes things a step further than the current tablet-based offerings from Apple and Google. It projects the digital environment onto translucent visors and enables your hands to interact with those digital objects as if they were physically there.

FIGURE 1-3: Microsoft HoloLens headset hardware.

Used with permission from Microsoft

In other MR instances, you may only see a completely digital environment with no view of the real world, but that digital environment is connected to real-world objects around you. In your virtual world, real-world tables or chairs may digitally appear as rocks or trees. Real-world office walls may appear as moss-covered cave walls. This is VR-based MR, sometimes called *augmented virtuality*.

REMEMBER

Following their strict definitions, AR provides no interaction with the augmented digital world, whereas MR does allow such interaction. However, these strict definitions are becoming blended in the industry. Often *mixed reality* and *augmented reality* are used as synonyms within the industry. Their meaning over time will likely grow and change. In this book, I use AR and MR synonymously, unless otherwise noted.

Augmented virtuality

A term that has yet to gain much traction within the industry, *augmented virtuality* (AV), also sometimes called *merged reality,* is essentially the inverse of typical AR. Whereas AR refers to predominantly real-world environments that have been augmented with digital objects, AV refers to predominantly digital environments in which there is some integration of real-world objects. Some examples of AV include streaming video from the physical environment and placing that video within the virtual space or creating a 3D digital representation of an existing physical object.

Figure 1-4 shows an example screenshot of AV through Intel's recently defunct Project Alloy. Using 3D cameras, Intel was able to bring in interactive imagery of physical real-world objects (such as your hands) into its virtual environments.

FIGURE 1-4:
An example
of AV from
Project Alloy.

Extended reality

Extended reality (XR) is the umbrella term for the entire spectrum of technologies discussed thus far (including VR, AR, and AV).

The *virtuality continuum* is a scale used to measure a technology's amount of realness or virtualness. On one end of the scale is the completely virtual, and on the other end is the completely real. XR spans the full spectrum of this scale, from end to end.

Figure 1-5 shows where these terms fall on this scale developed by technology researcher Paul Milgram in the 1990s. Remember, though, that MR and AR, while separated in this chart for definition's sake, are often used synonymously to refer to the spectrum that MR is shown covering here.

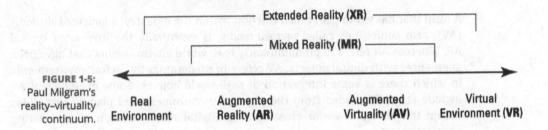

FIGURE 1-5:
Paul Milgram's
reality–virtuality
continuum.

In this book, I mainly focus on two terms — *virtual reality* and *augmented reality* — and the technological areas that they cover. Those two terms encompass most scenarios. I use *virtual reality* to refer to any hardware/software combination that creates a mostly or entirely digital experience. I use *augmented reality* to refer to any real/physical environment to which digital elements have been added (which may or may not interact with the real environment).

Taking a Quick History Tour

In 1935, a short story called "Pygmalion's Spectacles" by American science-fiction writer Stanley G. Weinbaum told the tale of a professor who invented a pair of goggles that enabled a user to trigger "a movie that gives one sight and sound . . . taste, smell, and touch. . . . You are in the story, you speak to the shadows (characters) and they reply, and instead of being on a screen, the story is all about you, and you are in it." Weinbaum's writing predates computers and nearly predates the invention of television. If Weinbaum were to travel to the present and see just how closely his vision of VR resembles that of the emerging technology of today, he would probably be shocked.

Both VR and AR have an incredibly rich and diverse history, far too deep to fully cover here. However, a general overview of some of the various incarnations of these technologies may provide some insight into where the technologies may be headed in the future.

The father of virtual reality

In 1955, a cinematographer named Morton Heilig, considered the father of VR, imagined a multisensory theater called "The Cinema of the Future." Heilig created the Sensorama (see Figure 1-6), an arcade-style mechanical cabinet built to stimulate the senses, for which he then developed a number of short films. It included many of the features prevalent in modern-day VR headsets, such as a stereoscopic 3D display, stereo speakers, and haptic feedback through vibrations in the user's chair.

FIGURE 1-6:
The Sensorama.

*Courtesy of Minecraftpsycho (https://en.wikipedia.org/wiki/
Sensorama#/media/File:Sensorama-morton-heilig-
virtual-reality-headset.jpg) under a Creative Commons license
(https://creativecommons.org/licenses/by-sa/4.0/)*

Shortly after inventing the Sensorama, Heilig also patented the Telesphere Mask, the first-ever head-mounted display (HMD), which provided stereoscopic 3D visuals and stereo sound. This (relatively) small HMD more closely resembles today's consumer VR headsets than the bulky seated form factor of the Sensorama.

The patent image shown in Figure 1-7 bears a striking resemblance to many of the headsets available today.

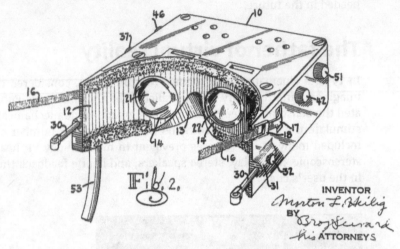

Source: https://patents.google.com/patent/US2955156A/en

FIGURE 1-7:
The Telesphere
Mask patent.

Augmented reality gets a name

In 1990, Tom Caudell, an employee at Boeing Computer Services Research, was asked to create a replacement for Boeing's current system of large plywood boards with wiring instructions for each aircraft being built. Caudell and his co-worker David Mizell proposed a head-mounted display for construction workers that superimposed the position of cables through the eyewear and projected them onto multipurpose, reusable boards. Instead of having to use different boards for each aircraft, the custom wiring instructions could instead be worn by the workers themselves. Caudell and Mizell coined the term *augmented reality* for this technology.

Early virtual reality failures

In 1993, Sega, a videogame company riding high on the release of its massively popular Sega Genesis, announced the Sega VR headset for the Sega Genesis at the Consumer Electronics Show (CES). Sega originally intended to deliver the device for $200 in the fall of 1993, a moderately affordable price point at the time. However, the system was plagued by development difficulties and was never released to the public. Sega's CEO at the time, Tom Kalinske, said that the Sega VR was shelved due to testers developing painful headaches and motion sickness — an unfortunate first foray into consumer gaming VR.

INDUSTRIAL-STRENGTH AR

Tom Caudell and David Mizell not only coined the term *augmented reality*, but also kicked off the use of AR in an industrial setting.

Industrial manufacturing is poised to be one of the most significant areas of AR expansion in the near future. Whereas companies developing consumer-facing AR applications must deal with a number of complications (including an unknown user base and unknown environments to perform in), those variables can be managed or even removed within the tightly controlled environment of an industrial manufacturing workspace. Manufacturers can develop targeted hardware and applications that can help their workforce train more quickly, work faster, access data more easily, and help avoid errors. All these benefits can lead to massive improvements in a company's bottom line, making AR usage within industrial settings a match made in heaven.

At the same time, another gaming industry veteran decided to release its take on VR gaming. The Nintendo Virtual Boy was released as the first portable unit capable of displaying stereoscopic 3D graphics. With the Virtual Boy, Nintendo had hoped to capture a unique technology and cement Nintendo's reputation as an innovator by encouraging more creativity in game development outside the traditional 2D screen space. However, development issues also plagued the Virtual Boy. Initial tests of color LCDs were said to have caused jumpy images, leading to Nintendo retaining the red LEDs that the Virtual Boy was eventually released with. Additionally, the Virtual Boy started as a head-mounted system including tracking. However, with concerns about motion sickness and the risk of developing lazy-eye conditions in children, Nintendo changed the head-mounted system to a tabletop format. Critics panned the system. It was never able to meet sales targets and disappeared from the market within a year.

These early failures, coupled with other failed attempts at creating mass-consumer VR devices, pushed VR advances back into research laboratories and academia for a few decades.

Virtual reality breaks through

In 2010, a tech entrepreneur named Palmer Luckey was frustrated with the existing VR head-mounted displays on the market. Almost all were expensive, extremely heavy, had a small *field of view* (the total viewing area a user can see), and high *latency* (delays between user interaction and the display refreshing to reflect those interactions) leading to a very poor end-user experience.

Channeling these frustrations, Luckey built a series of prototype HMDs, focusing on creating a low-cost, low-latency, large-field-of-view, and comfortably weighted headset. His sixth-generation unit was named Oculus Rift, and he offered it on the project funding website Kickstarter as Rift Development Kit 1 (DK1), as shown in Figure 1-8.

The Kickstarter campaign was a massive success, raising $2.4 million, almost 980 percent of the original target. More important, the Kickstarter campaign served to propel interest in VR in the consumer market to an all-time high.

Augmented reality hits the mainstream

AR was treated to a surprise surge in popularity from a rather unexpected source: the mobile phone. Similar to VR, AR had trudged along in relative obscurity for a few decades since its inception. Interest had increased slightly with the rise of VR in recent years, and new developments from companies such as Microsoft, Meta, and Magic Leap had shown promise, but nothing was available for mass consumption, and it was unclear when anything would be.

In 2017, AR underwent its largest boost in public awareness since its inception, as both Apple and Google released their own takes on AR for their various handheld mobile devices running either iOS or Android. Though neither has released exact numbers, estimates place the number of users with ARKit- or ARCore-capable devices to have reached over a quarter billion by the end of 2017.

THE FOURTH WAVE

Large-scale technology revolutions rarely occur in linear progressions of innovation and adaptation. Instead, they come in waves. No one can predict how large a wave will be, how fast it will occur, how disruptive the technology will be, or which way the wave will break.

VR and AR are often regarded as the fourth wave of emerging technological change. (The first three waves were the personal computer, the Internet, and mobile devices.) A wave is beginning to crest that could shape the future of humanity. Recognizing where we are in the wave and how we can best be a part of it means that we, too, can help shape the future.

With such a small sample size of life-altering technologies, it can be difficult to make predictions on how these waves will play themselves out. However, evaluating the first three waves and their development can help paint a picture of how the wave of VR and AR might break.

Perhaps the biggest takeaway from the previous waves was that each successive technological wave has been shorter than the last as far as consumer adoption. Internet adoption was quicker than personal computer adoption, and the mass adoption of cellphones was quicker still. Most current predictions for VR have VR ubiquity occurring no later than 2022, with AR coming a few years behind (2025 or so). By that time, experts predict VR and AR will have woven themselves completely into our daily lives, and picturing our lives without them would be akin to picturing our lives today without mobile phones or the Internet.

AR, long toiling in relative obscurity, suddenly had an enormous market of consumers to create content for, and developers began racing to create content for that market. Some examples include AR gaming applications, utilities that place 3D objects within a real room for interior decorating planning, map utility applications that overlay the real world with turn-by-turn directions or points of interest, and apps that can translate foreign language signs simply by pointing a mobile device camera at them.

Evaluating the Technology Hype Cycle

Technological waves also go through various peaks and troughs before they reach mass consumer adoption. Information technology research firm Gartner once proposed what it called the *Gartner Hype Cycle*, a representation of how the expectations around transformative technologies play out upon release (www.gartner.com/technology/research/methodologies/hype-cycle.jsp). The Gartner Hype

Cycle can help predict how a technology will be adapted (or not) over time. Both the Internet (with the dot-com crash) and mobile pre-2007 went through similar (if not exactly analogous) market curves.

In the beginning, an *Innovation Trigger* kicks off interest in the new technology, triggered by early proof-of-concepts and media interest.

Next is the *Peak of Inflated Expectations.* Buoyed by the early work and media buzz, companies jump in with higher expectations than the technology can yet deliver upon.

What follows is the *Trough of Disillusionment*, where interest in the technology begins to dip as implementations of the technology fail to deliver on the lofty expectations set by the initial Innovation Trigger and media buzz. The Trough of Disillusionment is a difficult space for technology, and some technologies may die out in this space, never fulfilling their initial promise.

Those technologies that are able to weather the storm of the Trough of Disillusionment reach the *Slope of Enlightenment,* as second- and third-generation products begin to appear and the technology and its uses are better understood. Mainstream adoption begins to take off, often paying dividends for the early adopters able to see their way through the trough with their ideas and executions intact.

Finally, we reach the *Plateau of Productivity*, where mass adoption truly begins, and companies able to weather the stormy waters of the hype cycle can see their early adoption profit.

Determining where VR and AR are in this cycle can be useful in making your decisions on how to approach these technologies. Does it make sense for your business to jump into these technologies now? Or are things not ready for prime time, and should you perhaps hold off for a few more years?

Gartner claims that VR is just leaving the Trough of Disillusionment and headed into the Slope of Enlightenment at the end of 2017, with a payoff of mass adoption within two to five years. AR, on the other hand, is listed by Gartner as currently wallowing in the Trough of Disillusionment, putting mass adoption for AR at a more conservative five to ten years out.

REMEMBER

Though the Trough of Disillusionment sounds like an ominous place for AR to be, it's a necessary phase for technology to pass through. Innovative technology, before hitting consumers' hands, needs to go through the grind of establishing an identity and determining where it fits in the world. Manufacturers need to figure out what problems it solves well and what problems it does *not* solve well. That often requires numerous trials and failures to discover.

AR as a mass consumer device is in its adolescence. Manufacturers and developers need time to figure out what form factor it should exist in, what problems it can solve, and how it can best solve them. Rushing a technology to market before these questions can be answered can often cause more problems than it solves, and is something that manufacturers of any emerging technology, including VR and AR, should be wary of.

Further, Gartner released this Hype Cycle report for VR and AR less than one month after Apple's ARKit announcement and a full month ahead of Google's ARCore announcement. An argument could be made that those two releases technically triggered mainstream adoption purely by the install base of ARKit and ARCore. However, that feels slightly disingenuous. Installed base alone does not automatically equal mainstream adoption (though it is a large piece of the puzzle).

When using a technology becomes frictionless and nearly invisible to the end user, when using that technology becomes as second nature as starting up your web browser, checking your email on your mobile device, or texting a friend, *that* is when a technology has truly hit mainstream adoption. Neither technology has yet reached this level of ubiquity, but both are looking to hit their stride. The long run of VR and AR holds the same promise of technological waves as the personal computer and the Internet.

The time for you to take action on these technologies is now, whether it's to simply research what they can do for you, to dive into purchasing a device for your own consumption, or even begin creating content for VR and AR.

IN THIS CHAPTER

» Reviewing the various form factors for virtual reality

» Comparing the features of current virtual reality hardware

» Surveying the available types of virtual reality controllers

» Exploring some of the current issues with virtual reality

» Assessing virtual reality adoption rates

Chapter **2**

Exploring the Current State of Virtual Reality

With virtual reality (VR) developments in a state of constant flux, it's an exciting (and frenetic) time to be involved with VR. Stopping and taking stock of where these developments are headed is important. Are we racing toward mass adoption of VR, propelling us to the peak of the fourth wave of technological change within the next year or two? Or, as some critics have suggested, is the current VR cycle just another misstep in VR's development cycle? A promising rise of the tide, followed by a washout leaving companies high and dry, leading to another decade of VR wallowing in the "Trough of Disillusionment?"

Many experts believe that VR will begin to see mainstream adoption by 2021 to 2023. By that time, VR headsets will likely be on their third or fourth generation of technology, and many of the issues that exist in 2018 will have been solved.

This chapter takes a look at the current state of the technology (as of this writing). Many first-generation devices have been released, with many second-generation (or first-and-a-half generation) devices announced as well. Understanding where VR is now will help you make your own predictions about where the technology is headed, and decide for yourself where we are in the VR cycle.

Looking at the Available Form Factors

Most VR hardware manufacturers seem to be driving toward a similar form factor, generally a headset/integrated audio/motion controller combination. That form factor may indeed be the best base setup for VR experiences, but it could also speak to a lack of innovation that there is not more variety in hardware executions for mass consumer devices. Perhaps years down the road, VR's form factor will change entirely. For now, most VR form factors are executed as a headset, but every company has designed its own version of how that form factor should look and feel.

To keep the focus of this book somewhat manageable, I mainly focus on the consumer head-mounted displays (HMDs) with the largest consumer base. Currently, those are the Oculus Rift, HTC Vive, Windows Mixed Reality, Samsung Gear VR, PlayStation VR, Google Daydream, and Google Cardboard. These are the first-generation consumer VR headsets with the broadest reach at this time, though the list will change in the future. Even if another headset comes along, it will likely share many of the same evaluation criteria I include here. Many of the upcoming second-generation devices (see Chapter 4) can be evaluated against the same criteria. Becoming familiar with the various options, benefits, and drawbacks of various hardware executions will enable you to evaluate any new entries into the market, not just the hardware mentioned here.

For consumer-grade VR, HTC Vive and Oculus Rift currently sit at the high end of our VR experience graph. Without a doubt, they offer some of the most realistic experiences of any VR hardware to date. Those experiences come at a cost, however — both for the headsets themselves and for the separate hardware required to power them.

Microsoft's Windows Mixed Reality VR headsets, a new addition to the VR market, are in the same high-end tier of VR experiences as the Vive and the Rift. Don't let the name fool you, though. Mixed Reality is just how Microsoft is branding its VR headsets — there is nothing "mixed reality" about them at this time — though the name could point to a convergence of VR and AR in the future. Will the products eventually function as both a VR headset and as an augmented reality (AR) headset via a camera pass-through image of the surrounding environment? That could be the direction Microsoft would *like* to take it, but that capability doesn't fully exist yet in its current batch of headsets.

REMEMBER

Windows Mixed Reality is not a brand of hardware; instead, it's a mixed reality platform that includes specifications that hardware providers can follow to create their own Windows Mixed Reality Headsets. (Google Cardboard, discussed later in this chapter, functions in a similar fashion.) To use a personal computing metaphor, you might think of the HTC Vive or Oculus Rift as Apple, in that each manufacturer creates and markets its own headset hardware, controlling all aspects. On the other hand, Microsoft controls only the software specifications for Windows Mixed Reality; it doesn't necessarily create its own hardware. Various manufacturers can create their own headsets and sell them under the Windows Mixed Reality name, provided they meet Microsoft's specifications. However, the AR headset Microsoft HoloLens (which Microsoft does produce) also technically falls under the Windows Mixed Reality platform. It can all get very confusing. In this chapter (and throughout the book), when I discuss Windows Mixed Reality, it is generally in relation to the line of immersive VR headsets. When discussing the Microsoft HoloLens, I typically refer to it directly by name.

Without one definitive Windows Mixed Reality VR headset to use as a baseline, it can be difficult to compare apples to apples for evaluation purposes. For example, the Acer Windows Mixed Reality headset may have different baseline specs than, say, the HP Windows Mixed Reality headset. That said, the specifications of most Windows Mixed Reality VR headsets generally place them toward the higher end of VR experiences.

The PlayStation VR offers a take on VR by a game console manufacturer. Sony's PlayStation VR doesn't require a separate PC to run it, but it does require a Sony PlayStation gaming console. Reviewers have praised the PlayStation VR's ease of use, price point, and game selection, but they've knocked the lack of a room-scale experience, the slightly underperforming controllers, and the lower resolution per eye versus the higher-end headsets listed here.

Table 2-1 compares some of the available desktop VR headsets. For legibility, I provide separate tables for the higher-end "desktop" VR experiences, which require external devices to power them, typically computers or game consoles, and the lower-end mobile VR experiences, which work with mobile devices such as smartphones. (The mobile device info is coming up later in the chapter, in Table 2-2.) This is not to say that one experience is necessarily a better choice than the other. Both have different sets of strengths and weaknesses. For example, you may require the most powerful or most immersive experience you can buy — in which case, externally powered "desktop" VR experiences are for you. Or, perhaps image fidelity is not as much of a concern and you require mobility for your VR headset, making the mobile VR headsets a better fit for your personal needs.

REMEMBER

Although this evaluates the first generation of VR devices, it is important to remember that all this can change quickly. The second generation of devices that will see its release within the next year or two (see Chapter 4) includes high-end devices that remove the need to be powered by external hardware, or at the very least removes the wires from the experience. This "untethering" of users from their machines will be a great step toward making VR more accessible.

There are many different variations of Windows Mixed Reality Headsets with varying specifications. I include specs for the Acer AH101 Mixed Reality Headset, a popular Windows Mixed Reality Headset.

TABLE 2-1   Virtual Reality Desktop Headset Comparison

	HTC Vive	Oculus Rift	Windows Mixed Reality	PlayStation VR
Platform	Windows or Mac	Windows	Windows	PlayStation 4
Experience	Stationary, room-scale	Stationary, room-scale	Stationary, room-scale	Stationary
Field of view	110 degrees	110 degrees	Varies (100 degrees)	100 degrees
Resolution per eye	1,080 x 1,200 OLED	1,080 x 1,200 OLED	Varies (1,440 x 1,440 LCD)	1,080 x 960 OLED
Headset weight	1.2 pounds	1.4 pounds	Varies (0.375 pound)	1.3 pounds
Refresh rate	90 Hz	90 Hz	Varies (60–90 Hz)	90–120 Hz
Controllers	Dual motion wand controllers	Dual motion controllers	Dual motion controllers, inside-out tracking	Dual PlayStation move controllers

TIP

You may hear stationary experiences referred to a few different ways — standing, seated, stationary, desk-scale. . . . They all mean the same thing: You can't move about in physical space in the VR experience.

TECHNICAL STUFF

OLED stands for *organic light emitting diode.* Known for its ability to display absolute blacks and extremely bright whites, OLED generally compares favorably to LCD in its contrast ratios and power consumption.

Slightly lower on the first-generation consumer VR devices performance and features scale are mobile-powered VR devices such as the Google Daydream and Samsung Gear VR. These devices require little more than a relatively low-cost headset and a compatible higher-end Android smartphone, making these devices a good entry-level choice for the curious first-time user.

At the low end of the first generation of consumer VR headsets are mobile-powered headsets such as the Google Cardboard, so named for the fact that the original Cardboard was little more than a few specially designed lenses and a folded cardboard container for your mobile device. Google Cardboard relies on little more than some inexpensive parts and your mobile device to create a VR headset, and almost any newer mobile device — iOS or Android — can run the required Google Cardboard software. However, due to its lack of specialization, the Google Cardboard VR experience doesn't provide the level of experience offered by dedicated headsets.

As with Windows Mixed Reality headsets, Google doesn't necessarily manufacture all Google Cardboard headsets. The Cardboard specifications are freely available on Google's website. Other manufacturers have also produced a number of Google

Cardboard variations, such as Mattel's View-Master VR and DodoCase's SMARTvr. All the Cardboard variations use similar technology and offer similar levels of support.

TIP

Don't be fooled by the name — not all Google Cardboard devices are made out of cardboard. Many of the Google Cardboard devices are, but others, such as the Homido Grab and View-Master VR, are constructed from much sturdier materials. These viewers are generally touted as "Google Cardboard Compatible" or "Google Cardboard certified," meaning they meet the Google Cardboard specifications set out by Google.

Table 2-2 compares some of the available options for mobile VR headsets. It can be difficult to provide direct specifications for the mobile executions because each headset may support multiple mobile devices and, thus, not have a single specification it adheres to.

TABLE 2-2

Virtual Reality Mobile Headset Comparison

	Samsung Gear VR	Google Daydream	Google Cardboard
Platform	Android	Android	Android, iOS
Experience	Stationary	Stationary	Stationary
Field of view	101 degrees	90 degrees	Varies (90 degrees)
Resolution	1,440 x 1,280 Super AMOLED	Varies (Pixel XL 1,440 x 1,280 AMOLED)	Varies
Headset weight	0.76 pound without phone	0.49 pound without phone	Varies (0.2 pound without phone)
Refresh rate	60 Hz	Varies (minimum 60 Hz)	Varies
Controllers	Headset touchpad, single motion controller	Single motion controller	Single headset button

Keeping those general categories in mind, let's take a look at the total sales and reach of the VR headsets mentioned so far. All companies have remained relatively quiet concerning their true sales numbers, but the figures in Table 2-3 are the reported forecast via Statista as of November 2017 (www.statista.com/statistics/752110/global-vr-headset-sales-by-brand/). You'll notice Google Cardboard figures are higher than those listed by Statista. That's because Cardboard has been around longer than the two years tracked here. Google self-reported more than 10 million Cardboards having shipped worldwide as of February of 2017.

TABLE 2-3

Virtual Reality Headset Units Sold

Device	Units Sold
HTC Vive	1.35 million
Oculus Rift	1.1 million
Sony PlayStation VR	3.35 million
Samsung Gear VR	8.2 million
Google Daydream	2.35 million
Google Cardboard	More than 10 million

Surprisingly, the lower-quality experience offered by Google Cardboard appears to have not adversely affected its adoption numbers, making it appear to be the clear winner thus far in the VR headset adoption race. Samsung's Gear VR is showing strong adoption numbers for a midlevel user experience, and Google Daydream and PlayStation VR show decent numbers whose lower adoption likely aligns with being released nearly two years after Google Cardboard and a year after the Gear. HTC Vive and Oculus Rift show numbers that reflect the premium price tag associated with their experiences. Windows Mixed Reality, with its late 2017 release date, does not have sales figures available.

It shouldn't come as a complete shock that consumers are preferring to enter the VR market with an inexpensive option such as the Cardboard. With an unknown technology, consumers appear to be entering the market somewhat warily, and only the most bleeding-edge early adopters have been purchasing the more expensive, higher-end headsets.

However, it should lead you to think about what these sales numbers mean for the future of VR. The numbers show decent adoption rates, but nothing like the massive adoption seen by other technology such as gaming systems. As a comparison, the PlayStation 4 (the system that powers PlayStation VR) sold one million consoles within its first 24 hours at retail.

Additionally, there is a currently steep drop-off between the lower- and higher-end headsets, and you should consider just how many of those who first experience VR on one of the lower-end headsets will end up converting to a higher-end headset. Could mobile VR sales actually be cannibalizing higher-end VR sales for this generation and unintentionally harming future VR sales?

The lower-end VR headsets offer (predictably) a lower-end experience. Cardboard has a noble goal (democratizing the VR experience by getting it into the hands of as many users as possible), but it may also lead to users who believe that their VR experience within Cardboard is representative of the current generation of VR, which is not the case. Even some of the midlevel systems, such as Daydream and

Gear VR, do not offer the same level of immersiveness that the higher-end VR headsets, such as Vive or Rift, do. I take a deeper look at this potential problem later in this chapter.

Focusing on Features

Besides price and headset design, there are also a number of different approaches each manufacturer is taking in regard to the VR experience it offers. The following sections look at some of the most important VR features.

Room-scale versus stationary experience

Room-scale refers to the ability of a user to freely walk around the play area of a VR experience, with his real-life movements tracked into the digital environment. For first-generation VR devices, this will require extra equipment outside of the headset, such as infrared sensors or cameras, to monitor the user's movement in 3D space. Want to stroll over to the school of fish swimming around you underwater? Crawl around on the floor of your virtual spaceship chasing after your robot dog? Walk around and explore every inch of a 3D replica of Michelangelo's *David*? Provided your real-world physical space has room for you to do so, you can do these things in a room-scale experience.

REMEMBER

Although most of the first-generation VR devices require external devices to provide a room-scale experience, this is quickly changing in many second-generation devices, which utilize inside-out tracking, discussed later in this chapter.

A *stationary* experience, on the other hand, is just what is sounds like: a VR experience where the experience is designed around the user remaining seated or standing in a single location for the bulk of the experience. Currently, the higher-end VR devices (such as the Vive, Rift, or WinMR headsets) allow for room-scale experiences, while the lower-end, mobile-based experiences do not.

Room-scale experiences can feel much more immersive than stationary experiences, because a user's movement is translated into their digital environment. If a user wants to walk across the digital room, she simply walks across the physical room. If she wants to reach under a table, she simply squats down in the physical world and reaches under the table. Doing the same in a stationary experience would require movement via a joystick or similar hardware, which pulls the user out of the experience and makes it feel less immersive. In the real world, we experience our reality through movement in physical space; the VR experiences that allow that physical movement go a long way toward feeling more "real."

Room-scale is not without its own set of drawbacks. Room-scale experiences can require a fairly large empty physical space if a user wants to walk around in VR without bumping into physical obstacles. Having entire rooms of empty space dedicated to VR setups in homes isn't practical for most of us — though there are various tricks that developers can use to combat this lack of space (see Chapter 7).

Room-scale digital experiences must also include barriers indicating where real-world physical barriers exist, to prevent users from running into doors and walls, displaying the boundary in the digital world of where the physical-world boundaries exist.

Figure 2-1 illustrates how the HTC Vive headset currently addresses this issue. When a user in headset wanders too close to a real-life barrier (as defined during room setup), a dashed-line green "hologram wall" alerts the user of the obstacle. It isn't a perfect solution, but considering the challenges of movement in VR, it works well enough for this generation of headsets. Perhaps a few generations down the road, headsets will be able to detect real-world obstacles automatically and flag them in the digital world.

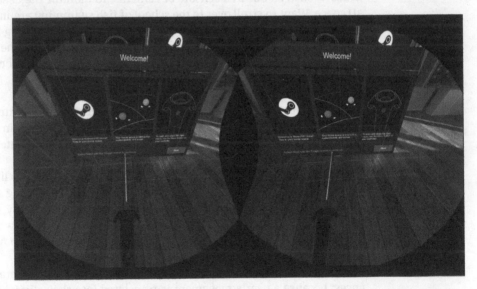

FIGURE 2-1:
The "hologram wall" border as seen in HTC Vive.

Many room-scale VR experiences also require users to travel distances far greater than their physical space can accommodate. The solution for traveling in stationary experiences is generally a simple choice. Because a user can't physically move about in her stationary experiences, either the entire experience takes place in a single location or a different method of locomotion is used throughout (for example, using a controller to move a character in a video game). Room-scale experiences introduce a different set of issues. A user can now move around in the virtual world, but only the distance allowed by each user's unique physical setup. Some users may be able to physically walk a distance of 20 feet in VR. Other users' physical VR play areas may be tight, and they may only have 7 feet of space to physically walk that can be emulated in the virtual environment.

VR developers now have some tough choices to make regarding how to enable the user to move around in both the physical and virtual environments. What happens if the user needs to reach an area slightly outside of the usable physical space in the room? Or around the block? Or miles away?

If a user needs to travel across the room to pick up an item, in room-scale VR he may be able to simply walk to the object. If he needs to travel a great distance in room-scale, however, issues start to arise. In these instances, developers need to determine when to let a user physically move to close-proximity objects, but also when to help a user reach objects farther away. These problems are solvable, but with VR still in its relative infancy, the best practices for VR developers regarding these solutions are still being experimented with (see Chapter 7).

Inside-out tracking

Currently only the higher-end consumer headsets offer room-scale experiences. These high-end headsets typically require a wired connection to a computer, and users often end up awkwardly stepping over wires as they move about in room-scale. This wired problem is generally twofold: Wiring is required for the image display within the headset, and wiring is required for tracking the headset in physical space.

Headset manufacturers have been trying to solve this wired display issue, and many of the second generation of VR headsets are being developed with wireless solutions in mind. In the meantime, companies such as DisplayLink and TPCast are also researching ways to stream video to a headset without the need for a wired connection.

On the tracking side, both the Vive and the Rift are currently limited by their externally-based *outside-in* tracking systems, where the headset and controllers are tracked via an external device. Outside of the headset, additional hardware (called *sensors* or *lighthouses* for Rift and Vive, respectively) are placed around the room where the user will be moving around while in VR space. These sensors are separate from the headset itself. Placing them about the room allows for extremely accurate tracking of the user's headset and controllers in 3D space, but users are limited to movement within the sensor's field of view. When the user moves outside that space, tracking is lost.

Figure 2-2 shows setup for the first-generation HTC Vive, which requires you to mount lighthouses around the space you want to track. You then define your "playable" space by dragging the controllers around the available area (which must be within visible range of the lighthouses). This process defines the area you're able to move in. Many first-generation room-scale headsets handle their space definition similarly.

Measure your space.

Next we will measure your available space. This space should be free of any obstacles that you might collide with while wearing the Headset.

Click Next to continue.

BACK   NEXT

FIGURE 2-2:
HTC Vive room
setup.

In contrast, *inside-out* tracking places the sensors within the headset itself, removing the need for external tracking sensors. It relies on the headset to interpret depth and acceleration cues from the real-world environment in order to coordinate the user's movement in VR. Windows Mixed Reality headsets currently utilize inside-out tracking.

WARNING

Inside-out tracking has been a "holy grail" for VR; removing the need for external sensors means users may no longer need to be confined to a small area for movement. Just like every technology choice, however, it comes at a cost. Currently, inside-out tracking provides less accurate environmental tracking and suffer from other drawbacks, such as losing track of the controllers if they travel too far out of line-of-sight of the headset. However, manufacturers are focused on ironing out these issues, with many second-generation headsets utilizing inside-out tracking for physical movement in VR. Inside-out tracking may not fully relieve you of having to define a "playable" space for VR. You still will need a method of defining what area is clear for you to move about in. However, solid inside-out tracking will allow for wireless headsets without external sensors, a big leap for the next generation of VR.

Even though most high-end first-generation VR headsets still require tethering to a computer or external sensors, companies are finding creative ways to work around these issues. Companies such as the VOID have implemented their own innovative solutions that offer a glimpse of what sort of experiences a fully self-contained VR headset could offer. The VOID is a location-based VR company offering what they term *hyper-reality*, allowing users to interact with digital elements in a physical way.

The cornerstone of the VOID's technology is their backpack VR system. The backpack/headset/virtual gun system allows the VOID to map out entire ware-houses worth of physical space and overlay it with a one-to-one digital environ-ment of the physical space. The possibilities this creates are endless. Where there is a plain door in the real world, the VOID can create a corresponding digital door oozing with slime and vines. What might be a nondescript gray box in the real world can become an ancient oil lamp to light the user's way through the fully digital experience.

The backpack form factor the VOID currently utilizes is likely not one that will see success at a mass consumer scale. It's cumbersome, expensive, and likely too complex to serve a mass audience. However, for the location-based experiences the VOID provides, it works well and gives a glimpse of the level of immersion VR could offer once untethered from cords and cables.

Both Vive and Rift appear to be gearing up to ship wireless headsets as early as 2018, with both the HTC Vive Focus (already released in China) and Oculus's upcoming Santa Cruz developer kits utilizing inside-out tracking.

Haptic feedback

Haptic feedback, which is the sense of touch designed to provide information to the end user, is already built into a number of existing VR controllers. The Xbox One controller, the HTC Vive Wands, and the Oculus Touch controllers all have the option to rumble/vibrate to provide the user some contextual information: *You're picking an item up. You're pressing a button. You've closed a door.*

However, the feedback these controllers provide is limited. The feedback these devices provide is similar to your mobile device vibrating when it receives a noti-fication. Although it's a nice first step and better than no feedback whatsoever, the industry needs to push haptics much further to truly simulate the physical world while inside the virtual. There are a number of companies looking to solve the issue of touch within VR.

Go Touch VR has developed a VR touch system to be worn on one or more fingers to simulate physical touch in VR. The Go Touch VR is little more than a device that straps to the ends of your fingers and pushes with various levels of force against your fingertips. Go Touch VR claims that the device can generate a surprisingly realistic sensation of grabbing a physical object in the digital world.

Other companies, such as Tactical Haptics, are looking to solve the haptic feedback problem within the controller. Using a series of sliding plates in the surface handle of their Reactive Grip controller, they claim to be able to simulate the types of friction forces you would feel when interacting with physical objects. When hitting a ball with a tennis racquet, you would feel the racquet push down against your grip. When moving heavy objects, you would feel greater force pushing against your hand than when moving lighter objects. When painting with a brush, you would feel the brush pull against your hand as if you were dragging it over paper or canvas. Tactical Haptics claims to be able to emulate each of these scenarios far more precisely than the simple vibration most controllers currently allow.

On the far end of the scale of haptics in VR are companies such as HaptX and bHaptics, developing full-blown haptic gloves, vests, suits, and exoskeletons.

bHaptics is currently developing the wireless TactSuit. The TactSuit includes a haptic mask, haptic vest, and haptic sleeves. Powered by eccentric rotating mass vibration motors, it distributes these vibration elements over the face, front and back of the vest, and sleeves. According to bHaptics, this allows for a much more refined immersive experience, allowing users to "feel" the sensation of an explosion, of a weapon recoil, or the sensation of being punched in the chest.

HaptX is one of the companies exploring the farthest reaches of haptics in VR with its HaptX platform. HaptX is creating smart textiles to allow you to feel texture, temperature, and shape of objects. It's currently prototyping a haptic glove to take virtual input and apply realistic touch and force feedback to VR. But HaptX takes a step beyond the standard vibrating points of most haptic hardware. HaptX has invented a textile that pushes against a user's skin via embedded microfluidic air channels that can provide force feedback to the end user.

HaptX claims that its use of technology provides a far superior experience to those devices that only incorporate vibration to simulate haptics. When combined with the visuals of VR, HaptX's system takes users a step closer to fully immersive VR experiences. HaptX's system could carry through its technology to the realization of a full-body haptic platform, allowing you to truly feel VR. Figure 2-3 shows an example of HaptX's latest glove prototype for VR.

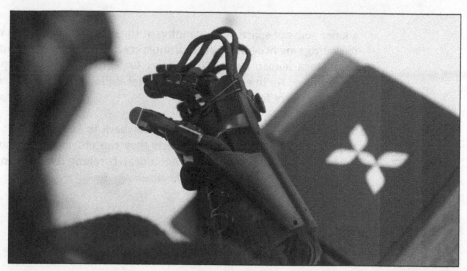

Audio

As VR seeks to emulate reality as closely as possible, it must engage other senses besides sight and touch. Smell and taste simulation are (perhaps thankfully) likely far off from reaching the mass consumer adoption, but 3D audio is ready for its day in the sun. Engaging the user's sense of hearing plays an important role in creating a realistic experience. Audio and visuals work together to provide a sense of presence and space for the user and help to establish the feeling of being there. Directional audio cues, alongside visual cues, can also be vital in guiding users through a digital experience.

Human hearing itself is three-dimensional; we can distinguish the 3D direction that a sound is coming from, the general distance from the source, and so on. Simulating that effect is necessary for a user to feel as if she's experiencing audio as she would in the real world. 3D audio simulation has existed for a while, but often as a solution without a problem. With the rise of VR, 3D audio has found itself a market that can help propel it forward (and vice versa).

Most current headsets (even lower-end devices such as Google Cardboard) have support for spatial audio. *Spatial audio* takes into consideration the fact that the user's ears are on opposite sides of the head and adjusts sounds appropriately. Sounds coming from the right will reach the user's left ear with a delay (because the sound wave travels slower to the ear farther away from the audio source). Before spatial audio, apps simply played sounds coming from the left in the left speaker, or coming from the right in the right speaker, cross-fading between the two.

Standard stereo recordings consist of two different channels of audio signal, recorded with two microphones spaced apart. This recording approach can create a loose sense of space, with panning of the sound between each channel. *Binaural* recordings are two-channel recordings created by using special microphones that simulate a human head. This allows for extremely realistic playback through headphones. For live audio in VR, binaural audio recordings can create a very realistic experience for the end user.

TIP

Spatial and binaural both have one drawback to keep in mind: Headphones are required to experience the 3D effects they can provide. Headphone use is typical for most VR headsets, so this is not a deal-breaking requirement, but something to consider when evaluating VR headsets.

Considering Controllers

Early virtual experience users discovered that, although the visuals are important, the experience quickly falls flat if you don't have a system of input that matches the visuals in fidelity of experience. Users may be fully immersed in the visuals of a VR experience, but as soon as they try to move their hands or feet and find those movements not reflected in the virtual world, the immersion crumbles.

"The virtual reality experience is not going to be complete with just the visual side," Oculus Rift founder Palmer Luckey told *The Verge*. "You absolutely need to have an input and output system that is fully integrated, so you not only have a natural way to view the virtual world, but also a natural way to interact with it."

The following are various input devices and features you will come across as you delve into the world of VR. Some are very simple, and some are incredibly complex. Each offers a vastly different take on how interaction in the virtual world should occur. Sometimes the simplest input solution may serve the experience the best, such as a gaze to trigger an action. Other times, nothing fills out the immersion experience better than a fully realized digital hand mimicking the movements of a user's physical hand.

Toggle button

The toggle button is so simple it barely warrants an entry here. However, it's also currently the only physical input method for the virtual world on the best-selling VR headset, the Google Cardboard. (Based solely on number of devices sold at the time of this writing.)

Little more than a simple on/off tap switch (or magnetometer toggle), the humble button rarely needs much of an introduction for anyone to learn how to use (beyond perhaps pointing them to where it's located). Click, and actions are triggered.

Integrated hardware touchpad

Some hardware manufacturers, such as Samsung (on the Gear VR), have taken the idea of an integrated hardware button a step further by incorporating a full touchpad on the side of their headsets. Figure 2-4 shows Samsung's integrated touchpad (1) used for tapping, swipes, and clicks, as well as an integrated Home button (2) and Back button (3).

FIGURE 2-4:
Samsung Gear VR's integrated touchpad.

Courtesy of Oculus

The touchpad allows for better interaction than the simple toggle button. The touchpad gives the user the freedom to swipe horizontally or vertically, tap on items, toggle volume, and back out of content as needed. The touchpad also provides a backup means of control if the user misplaces a device's motion controller.

One drawback is that integrated control solutions need ways to communicate with the device running the experience. For example, mobile VR headsets using integrated hardware controls may require a micro-USB (or similar) connection to the mobile device. In addition, because the touchpad may not have a natural integration with the virtual world (simulating the controller in the virtual world), it can pull the user out of the experience.

Gaze controls

Gaze controls can be baked into any VR application. They are a popular means of VR interaction, especially in applications that may seek to provide a user interaction method that can be more passive than active. (Think of gazing at a control for a set period of time to trigger that control versus actively using a touchpad or motion controller.) Applications such as video applications or photo viewers, where a user may be more passively engaged with the content, are good examples of applications which often utilize gaze controls.

And gaze controls are not for passive interaction alone. Gaze, in combination with other methods of interaction (such as hardware buttons or controllers), is often used in VR to trigger interactions. As eye tracking (discussed later in this chapter) becomes more popular, gaze controls will likely see even more usage.

REMEMBER

Gaze controls monitor the user's gaze direction and often include a reticle (or cursor) and a timer. To select an item or trigger an action, the user simply gazes at it for a certain number of seconds. Gaze controls can also be utilized in conjunction with other methods of input for even deeper interactions.

A *reticle* in VR is any graphic used to help indicate where a user is gazing. For headsets that do not include eye tracking, this is typically the center of a users vision. Often just a simple dot or crosshair, the reticle typically sits on top of all elements as a way to help visualize what a user will currently be selecting. A reticle directly in the center of view offers a simple solution until more sophisticated eye tracking in headsets becomes mainstream.

Figure 2-5 shows an example of a reticle in use in VR. The reticle helps a user know where his gaze is focused within a virtual scene.

FIGURE 2-5:
A reticle in
use in VR.

Keyboard and mouse

Some VR headsets utilize variations of a standard mouse and/or keyboard for interaction. The problem with such setups can be that there is no way to see the keyboard from inside the headset. Even the best touch typists have trouble typing when unable to at least glance down at the keyboard.

Using a mouse can also be problematic. In standard 2D digital worlds, such as on desktop PCs, the mouse has long been the standard tool for shifting the view to "look around." In the 3D world, though, the headset gaze should control what a user is seeing. In a few early applications, both the mouse and gaze controls could shift a user's view, but this interaction had the potential to be very disorienting, as the mouse pulled the gaze one way and the user's physical gaze pulled another.

Some VR apps still support keyboards and mice, but those input methods have mostly fallen out of fashion as the main input in favor of more integrated input solutions. However, these new integrated solutions can come with a drawback of their own. With a keyboard no longer available as the main input device, how can long-form text be entered into applications?

A number of different control options have been put forth to solve that problem. Logitech has created a proof-of-concept VR accessory that allows HTC Vive users to see a representation of its physical keyboard in the virtual space. Connecting a tracker to your keyboard, Logitech creates a 3D model of its keyboard in your VR space right on top of the physical version of the keyboard, an interesting execution that could help the touch typists of the world.

Fully digital text input solutions exist as well. Jonathan Ravasz's Punch Keyboard is a predictive keyboard that enables users to type using motion controllers as drumsticks. Figure 2-6 shows the Punch Keyboard in use. Moving forward, VR application developers will need to find and standardize on better text input methods if they are to see mass consumer adoptions.

FIGURE 2-6: Jonathan Ravasz's Punch Keyboard in use.

Standard gamepads

Many headsets and controllers support standard gamepads or videogame controllers, a familiar input solution for many gamers. The original Oculus Rift even shipped with an Xbox One controller, a gamepad many gamers were already familiar with (see Figure 2-7).

Used with permission from Microsoft

FIGURE 2-7:
The Xbox One controller.

However, gamepads in VR as an input solution typically don't feel as integrated as some of the other input options. They are, however, a familiar input method for many VR users who are also gamers, and it was a good first step away from keyboard and mouse. Most VR headsets seem to be moving away from relying on standard gamepads as the main source of input for VR, preferring instead more integrated motion controllers.

TIP

The main issue with standard gamepads was the lack of integration with the digital world. The difference between the physical experience of using the gamepad and the digital experience can pull the user out of the immersion of the VR experience. This is likely why most headsets preferred to develop their own, more integrated motion controllers.

Motion controllers

Motion controllers, once mainly a slightly gimmicky device for 2D PC games, have quickly become the de facto standard for interaction in VR. Nearly all the larger headset manufacturers have released a set of motion controllers compatible with their headsets.

Figure 2-8 displays a pair of Oculus Touch motion controllers, the latest set of controllers packaged with the Oculus Rift. HTC and Microsoft both have similar variations on the same theme, both offering a pair of untethered motion controllers.

FIGURE 2-8:
A pair of Oculus Touch motion controllers.

A controller ideally should be nearly invisible to the end user. When utilizing many of the input methods previously discussed in this chapter, users must make conscious decisions outside of the VR experience to do so: *I am now clicking a button on the side of the headset. I am now hunting/pecking for the W key on the keyboard.* Motion controllers take a step in the direction of eliminating the issue of input being separate from your VR experience. Motion controllers are typically visualized within the VR experience, and can begin to feel like a natural extension of your hand. Many of the higher-end VR controllers also offer six degrees of freedom of movement, allowing even deeper immersion of these methods of input.

TECHNICAL STUFF

Six degrees of freedom (6DoF) refers to the ability of an object to move freely in three-dimensional space. In VR, this typically refers to the ability to move forward/backward, up/down, and left/right with both orientation (rotational) tracking and positional (translation) tracking. 6DoF allows realistic tracking of the controllers in VR space to their actual position and rotation in physical space.

Not to be left behind from the higher-end headsets, first-generation mid-tier mobile headset options (Gear VR and Daydream) have included motion controls of their own. These options have been simplified from the higher-end headsets. Typically realized as a single controller with a variety of features (a touchpad, volume controls, Back/Home buttons, and so on). The controller also has a representation in the digital world, allowing the user to "see" what his hand is doing in the real world. Unlike the higher-end motion controllers, these controllers typically only offer three degrees of freedom (only tracking their rotation in the virtual space).

Figure 2-9 displays what a user would see in VR when using the Samsung Gear VR controller. There's a virtual representation of the real device, enabling the user to target items in VR.

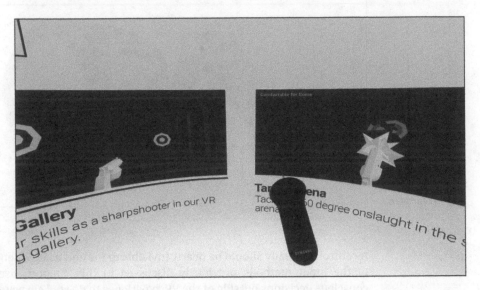

FIGURE 2-9:
Samsung Gear VR
controller in VR.

WARNING The tracking of controllers on the Gear VR and Daydream headsets, though impressive for mobile devices, does not achieve the same level of accuracy as the higher-end, tethered headsets. Plus, without a second motion controller (one for each hand), it can sometimes feel as though the motion control is just a glorified TV remote.

However, although it's less sophisticated than the higher-end motion control options, even these simple one-handed control representations can provide much more of an integrated experience for VR than the previously discussed options. The ability to "see" the controller in the virtual space and track its physical movement is an enormous step toward immersing the user into the virtual world and incorporating a user's physical movements into the virtual space.

The higher-end headset options (such as the Rift, Vive, and Windows Mixed Reality) have a pair of wireless motion controllers. The motion controllers have some slight differences (a touchpad on each Vive wand, shown in Figure 2-10, versus the analog joysticks of the Oculus Touch), but they share many similar qualities overall.

FIGURE 2-10:
A pair of HTC Vive "wand" motion controllers.

These high-end controller pairs allow for incredibly precise (sub-millimeter) object detection. Being able to look down and see a visual representation of the controllers moving in tandem with your physical body is another important step in making the VR experience truly immersive.

Many VR applications have started to target only motion controllers as their main input device moving forward. Motion controls appear to be the standard for interaction in VR for now. However, a plethora of other options is available for interacting in VR, with many more being developed.

Hand tracking

Hand tracking enables headsets to track the user's hands in VR without any additional hardware worn on the extremities. And some people consider hand tracking the next evolutionary step from motion controllers.

A number of companies are exploring this avenue for both VR applications. In AR applications, this method of control is seeing even more development. Companies such as Leap Motion have been working on hand tracking extensively, both inside and outside of VR, for years. Leap Motion initially launched its hand tracking controller in 2012, intended for use with 2D screens. With the rise of VR, the company pivoted its technology to cover VR as well, seeing the potential its technology could have for interaction in that space.

Unlike motion controllers, where the visual in VR is typically a controller, wand, virtual "fake" hand or similar model, hand tracking typically brings a representation of your actual hand into the virtual space. You pinch your fingers, and your digital hand pinches. You flex your thumbs, and your digital hand flexes its thumbs. You give the peace sign, and your digital hand does as well. Viewing a digital representation of your physical hands in VR, with full finger tracking, is a bit of a mind-bending experience. It can feel as if you're trying on a new body. You may find yourself staring at your hand in VR, opening and closing your fist, just to watch your digital representation do the same.

WARNING

Visually, hand tracking can be an amazing experience, but it's still lacking in some areas. Unlike with motion controllers, the interaction possibilities in the virtual space can be somewhat limited. With a motion controller, numerous hardware interactions are available. Physical hardware on the motion controller such as buttons, trackpads, triggers, and so on all can fire off different events in the virtual world. There are no such options with hand tracking alone. An application that utilizes hand tracking as the main method of interaction will likely need to solve for a multitude of scenarios requiring input. With only the hand providing input, this can be a tall order.

Another drawback of hand tracking is that, although the tracking itself can be impressive, it lacks the tactile feedback a user would expect if interacting in the real world. Picking up a box in VR using hand tracking alone does not give the tactile feedback of picking up a box in the real world, which can feel awkward to many users.

Hand tracking will likely continue to take a back seat to motion controllers for standard consumer VR experiences for the near future. However, hand tracking will eventually find a place in VR. It's too special an experience to not eventually find a way to be utilized within the digital world.

Eye tracking

In 2016, a company called FOVE released the first VR headset with built-in eye tracking. Facebook, Apple, and Google also all acquired eye-tracking startups for their various VR and AR hardware devices, signaling eye tracking as a field to watch.

Eye tracking has the potential to make a user's experience in VR much more intuitive. Most of the current generation of headsets (outside of entries such as the FOVE) determine only where the user's head is turned, not necessarily where the user is actually looking.

As discussed earlier in this chapter, most headsets use a reticle that sits directly in the middle of a user's view to inform the user where her gaze is centered. However, in the real world, people often focus their vision somewhere else besides directly in front of their faces. Even using a computer screen, often directly in front of your gaze, your eyes are often straying to the bottom or top of the screen to select various menus, or down to your keyboard or mouse, even though your head may remain stationary.

TECHNICAL STUFF

An auxiliary benefit of eye tracking will be the ability to add foveated rendering to applications. *Foveated rendering* renders only the area a user is gazing directly at in full definition and reduces the image quality of the picture everywhere else. Current headsets must render the entire viewable area in full definition at all times, because they don't "know" where the user's gaze may actually be. Foveated rendering fully renders only a small area at a time. This reduces the processing power necessary to render complex VR environments, which in turn enables lower-powered computers or mobile devices to run complex experiences, making VR more accessible to all.

Figure 2-11 shows an example of how foveated rendering would play out in VR. With the eye focused on one area, the center foveated region would remain at full resolution. The secondary blended region would create a step between the full-resolution area and the much lower-resolution peripheral region.

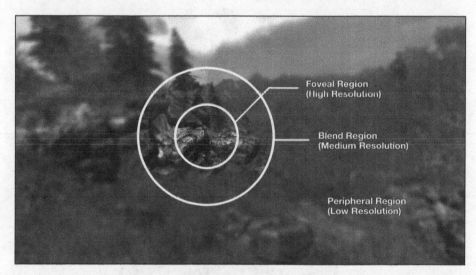

Foveal Region
(High Resolution)

Blend Region
(Medium Resolution)

Peripheral Region
(Low Resolution)

FIGURE 2-11: An example of foveated rendering at work.

Although FOVE is focused on eye tracking within its own headset, other developers such as Tobii and 7invensun are focusing on creating foveated rendering hardware that can be added to existing VR consumer devices.

With most major headset manufacturers remaining mum on their plans for adding eye tracking to their next generation of devices, it's likely that onboard eye tracking for headsets may be a generation or two out, though it's definitely a development to keep an eye on.

. . . and much more

Voice control and speech may begin to see deeper uses as an interaction method with VR. Windows Mixed Reality headsets already allow speech commands, and most headsets with integrated microphones can support voice recognition as well. Plus, speech recognition and conversational user interfaces (UIs) are fields that are currently seeing heavy development and investment outside of VR/AR. Although speech recognition wasn't a clear area of focus for some of the first generation of VR headsets, it's a natural method of input that will likely see heavier development in the VR space in the near future.

On the hardware front, there is no lack of innovation in the methods of input space for VR. Some of the specialty options range from a vast collection of VR gun controllers, to foot controllers such as the 3D Rudder or SprintR, to full-blown platforms walking or running in VR such as the Virtuix Omni treadmill, shown in Figure 2-12.

FIGURE 2-12:
Virtuix's Omni treadmill for locomotion in VR.

Courtesy of Virtuix

Many controller options may find their way filling niche spaces in arcades or other one-off experiences. The real trick is finding which peripherals will be the next big thing in VR, and which will end up falling by the wayside.

The VR controller landscape is nothing if not extremely large and ever expanding. And for good reason: No one has yet to discover the "one true way" to mimic our physical experience in VR. Perhaps human perception of reality is so complex that there will never be one true way to mimic our interaction with the physical world. Or perhaps VR will reveal input methods we only *wish* we could incorporate into our physical world.

Now and in the near future, the standard VR experience appears to be rallying around a combination of gaze interaction and motion controllers for the broad set of interactions VR hopes to emulate. But who knows what the far future holds?

Recognizing the Current Issues with VR

Consumer-grade VR is steadily getting lighter, cheaper, and more polished, but it still has a number of technical hurdles to overcome to truly reach its mass consumer potential. Fortunately, renewed interest in VR the past few years has led to an influx of investments in the field, which should accelerate uncovering solutions. The following section explores some of the major issues facing VR today and how some companies are working to resolve them.

Simulator sickness

Early HMD devices generated widespread user complaints of motion sickness. This issue alone was enough to derail early VR mass consumer devices such as Sega VR and Nintendo's Virtual Boy. It's an issue that modern headset manufacturers still grapple with.

Motion sickness can occur when there are inconsistent signals between your inner ear's vestibular sense of motion and what your eyes are seeing. Because your brain senses these signals are inconsistent, it then assumes that your body is sick, potentially from a toxin or some other affliction. At that point, your brain may decide to induce headaches, dizziness, disorientation, and nausea. VR headset use can induce a type of motion sickness that doesn't necessarily involve any real motion; researchers have dubbed it *simulator sickness.*

There are a number of ways to combat simulator sickness, including some unconventional approaches. One study by Purdue University's Department of Computer Graphics Technology suggested adding a "virtual nose" to every VR application to add a stabilizing effect for the user. Virtualis LLC is commercializing this virtual nose, naming it *nasum virtualis.* Embedding the nose in the user's field of view acts as a fixed point of reference to ease VR sickness. Your physical nose appears in your line of sight in real life, but you often don't perceive it there. Similarly, most users in Virtualis's studies didn't even notice the virtual nose in VR, but they reported a 13.5 percent drop in severity of sickness and an increase of time spent in the simulator.

Figure 2-13 displays how a virtual nose may appear to users in VR.

FIGURE 2-13:
Using a virtual
nose to prevent
simulator
sickness.

The most effective way that VR developers can combat simulator sickness, however, is to minimize latency between a user's physical motion and the headset's response. In the real world, there is no latency between the movement of our heads and the visual response of the world around us. Reproducing that lack of latency in headset is of paramount importance.

With the proliferation of VR on low-powered mobile devices, it's more important than ever to keep the frames per second (FPS) each headset can display as high as possible. Doing so enables the visuals in the headset to stay aligned with the user's movement.

Here are some other suggestions for avoiding simulator sickness when creating or using VR apps:

>> **Ensure the headset is properly adjusted.** If the virtual world seems blurry when trying on your headset, most likely the headset needs adjustment. Most headsets enable users to tweak the device's fit and distance from their eyes to eliminate any blurriness. Be sure your headset is properly adjusted before going into any VR experience.

>> **Sit down.** For some people, the sense of stability that being seated provides helps them overcome their motion sickness.

>> **Keep text legible.** Avoid reading or using small-font text in VR, and keep text use to a minimum (just a few words at a time).

>> **No unexpected movement.** When developing, never move the camera programmatically without reason. The user should feel motion occurs due to his own motion or triggered via interaction.

>> **Avoid acceleration.** It is possible to move virtual cameras without triggering simulator sickness, but that motion needs to be smooth. Avoid accelerating or decelerating a user when motion in the virtual space needs to occur.

>> **Always track the user's movements.** Do not reverse the camera against a user's motion or stop tracking the user's head position. A user's view must update with her head movement.

>> **Avoid fixed-view items.** *Fixed-view items* (items that do not change when the view changes, such as a pop-up to inform the user of something in the middle of the screen or a heads-up display [HUD]) are fairly common in 2D gaming today. This mechanic does not work well in VR, however, because it isn't something users are accustomed to in the real world.

As devices become more powerful, simulator sickness due to low FPS should, in theory, become less common. The more powerful the device, the better the ability to keep the visuals and movement of the virtual world tracked to the user's physical movement, reducing the main cause of simulator sickness.

However, although we have far surpassed the processing power of computers of old, we still run into software that often runs slower than games of 20 years ago. In general, the more powerful our hardware gets, the more we tend to ask of it. Better visuals! More items on screen! Larger fields of view! More effects! Knowing the potential causes of simulator sickness should help you navigate these issues should they appear.

The screen-door effect

Put on any older VR headsets, or some of the current smartphone-powered VR headsets, and look closely at the image produced in the headset. Depending on the resolution of the device you're using, you may notice "lines" in between the displayed pixels. As a child, you may have noticed the same thing if you sat too closely to your older TV set. This issue is called the *screen-door effect,* for its resemblance to looking at the world through a screen door. Although this problem has long been solved for televisions of today with extremely high resolutions, it has been reintroduced in some VR headsets.

Figure 2-14 displays an example of an exaggerated screen-door effect example as seen in VR. (An actual screen-door effect would occur on a pixel-by-pixel basis, not shown here.) With the display so close to a user's face, the grid of space between pixels can begin to become apparent.

This effect is most noticeable in displays with lower resolutions, such as older headsets or some smartphones, many of which were never intended to be used primarily as VR machines, held inches from your nose and magnified via optic lenses.

Various proposals have been put forth to solve this issue. For example, LG has suggested placing a "light diffuser" between the screen and lenses, though most people agree the real fix will be higher-resolution displays. High-definition displays should alleviate the screen-door effect, as they have for TV, but they'll require more processing power to run. As with simulator sickness, the hope is that the better the hardware, the less likely this effect will be to occur. With a little luck, the screen-door effect should become a relic of the past within the next generation or two of VR headsets.

Movement in VR

Moving through the digital environment of VR is still an issue. Higher-end headsets, such as Vive and Rift, allow users to be tracked throughout a room, but not much farther than that. Anything more requires some sort of movement mechanic built into the application itself, or specialized hardware beyond what most consumers likely have available (as discussed in the "Considering Controllers" section earlier in this chapter).

Movement over large distances in VR will likely be an ongoing logistical problem for application developers. Even utilizing some of the solutions listed previously, movement in VR that does not correspond to physical motion can trigger simulator sickness in some users. And even if you could guarantee an omni-directional tread-mill for every user to track his or her movement, there are often large distances users will not want to cover walking. Plus, users with limited mobility may be unable to traverse distances on foot. Movement is an issue that hardware and software developers will need to work together to solve. And there are solutions available. I discuss some of the potential solves for movement in VR in the Chapter 7.

Health effects

Health risks are perhaps the largest unknown on this list. The Health and Safety guidelines for Oculus Rift caution against use if the user is pregnant, elderly, tired, or suffering from heart conditions. They also warn that users might experience severe dizziness, seizures, or blackouts. Scary-sounding stuff! There are also big unknowns as to the long-term health effects of VR. Researchers have yet to thoroughly study the impact of long-term use of VR headsets on eyesight and the brain.

Initial studies have generally shown that most adverse health effects are short-term, with little lasting effect on the user. However, as users begin to stay in VR space for longer stretches at a time, further studies would be required to discover any long-term effects of VR usage.

In the meantime, VR companies seem to be erring on the side of caution regarding the potential long-term effects. As Sarah Sharples, president of the Chartered Institute of Ergonomics and Human Factors, said in an interview with *The Guardian*, "Absolutely there are potentially negative effects of using VR. The most important thing that we should do is just to be cautious and sensible. But we should not let that stop us from taking advantage of the massive potential this technology offers as well."

Cannibalization of the market

One final worry has to do with the VR market as a whole. The mobile market (and specifically the cheapest implementation, Google Cardboard) holds a massive adoption advantage over the higher-end headsets (refer to Table 2-3). And perhaps for good reason. It's easier for a consumer to stomach a $20 purchase of a low-end mobile VR headset than to save up a few hundred dollars for a higher-end model.

Predictably, low-end headsets tend to offer lower-end experiences. A user may dismiss a low-end VR system as little more than a toy, believing it represents the current level of VR immersion, when nothing could be farther from the truth.

However, perception can often become reality. Could the proliferation of low-end VR implementations serve to harm VR's adoption in the long run, cannibalizing its own market?

The sales figures of lower-end devices have likely made some companies sit up and take notice. Many manufacturers appear to be focusing on a multi-tiered strategy for their next generation of headsets, offering experiences ranging from low end to high end for consumers. For example, Oculus co-founder Nate Mitchell claimed in an interview with *Ars Technica* that Oculus would focus on a three-headset strategy for its next generation of consumer headsets, with the stand-alone Oculus Go, set to be released in 2018, as its lower-end standalone device, followed by the Oculus Santa Cruz, a mid-tier headset experience. Similarly, HTC has released the HTC Vive Pro as a higher-end device, with the standalone HTC Vive Focus (released in China), focused more on the mid-tier market. For a more in-depth discussion of the various market segments of upcoming hardware, see Chapter 4.

In the long run, there is likely a broad enough market base to support all varia-tions of VR. With the advent of the next generation of headsets, it will be interest-ing to see which devices make the biggest inroads with consumers. The near future will likely bring a rise in midrange mobile device headsets, while the higher-end, external PC-based headsets cater to those going all-in on high-end devices. The latter is a smaller demographic, but one that is willing to spend more to get the best-in-class experience that VR can offer.

Assessing Adoption Rates

Research firms such as Gartner Research estimate that mass adoption of VR will occur by 2020 to 2023. Based on the current state of VR hardware, features, and issues explored in this chapter, that estimate feels appropriate — though it will need to see strong adoption of the upcoming second-generation consumer devices (releasing soon) to get there.

The adoption rate of headsets, especially the low- to mid-tier headsets such as Google Cardboard and Gear VR show that the public is ready to dip its toes into the water of VR. Manufacturers are still trying to determine what sort of headsets the public wants, and this first round of headsets has given them figures to work with and make decisions against.

Today's consumers only have access to the first-generation mass consumer VR headsets. Some companies (such as Oculus, Google, and HTC) have announced plans for their next generation of headsets, but other companies (like Microsoft) are just now getting their first generation of devices into the VR market (in the case of Microsoft, the Windows Mixed Reality VR headsets launched in late fall of 2017).

Although many of these first-generation headsets offer impressive immersive experiences, it's clear that within this first generation, no manufacturer has completely figured out what will work best for mass consumer adoption in the VR space. For each headset version released, each VR app created, more and more knowledge is gained and companies are able to adjust their road maps and home in on creating truly great (and commercially viable) VR devices.

Mark Zuckerberg, Facebook CEO, recently announced a goal of "getting one billion people into virtual reality." That's an incredibly lofty goal. For comparison, the Internet, which most people would consider ubiquitous throughout the globe, has 3.2 billion users worldwide. For VR to reach close to that number of users would take a massive level of adoption.

However, many corporations have a vested interest in VR's success, and many consumers want it to succeed. The next few years will be pivotal for the development of VR. This time period will likely paint a picture of the type of growth we can expect to see for VR, as it strives to hit mass consumer adoption. When headset manufacturers are able to fully dial in the experience aligning with consumers' affordability sweet spot, Zuckerberg's goal may not be out of reach.

IN THIS CHAPTER

» Reviewing the various form factors
for augmented reality

» Looking at the different types of
consumer experiences offered by
augmented reality

» Exploring some of the current issues
with augmented reality

Chapter **3**

Exploring the Current State of Augmented Reality

ugmented reality (AR) has lately enjoyed a renaissance of sorts. Because of the rich history of virtual reality (VR), AR had seemingly taken a backseat to VR in terms of general public recognition. Whether the concepts were more nebulous to grasp or VR was seen as the "sexier" technology, AR has always seemingly played second fiddle to VR in consumer mindshare.

In no period was this more pronounced than that of 2013 to mid-2017. VR headsets re-entered the public consciousness with a bang, and AR took a back seat yet again.

However, a funny thing happened in the fall of 2017. Apple and Google announced ARKit and ARCore, respectively, making it much easier for developers to write AR applications for the iOS and Android platforms. This announcement was huge, because it immediately vaulted the number of AR-compatible devices to nearly half a billion devices (the installed base of compatible iOS and Android devices). Not every user on every iOS or Android mobile device will utilize AR-based applications, but those who want to try it out no longer have to purchase additional hardware to do so.

Figure 3-1 shows the growth rate for ARKit- and ARCore-enabled devices over the next few years, as predicted by ARtillry Intelligence. ARtillry predicts nearly 4.2 billion handheld AR devices will be in consumers' pockets by 2020, a massive market and an incredible rate of growth. Apple is predicted to lead the charge at first of mobile AR, with Google and Android catching up and surpassing iOS as replacement cycles for Android devices kick in a few years out.

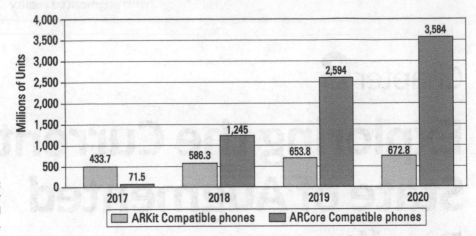

FIGURE 3-1:
Install base for ARCore and ARKit.

Just as AR shares some ancestral traits with VR, it also appears to be sharing some of its current issues. Much in the same way that Google Cardboard introduced VR to the masses, both ARKit and ARCore are proving to be a boon to AR's consumer name recognition. However, they provide what could be considered an inferior experience compared to some of their more advanced wearable counterparts, such as Microsoft's HoloLens, the Meta 2, or Magic Leap.

Perhaps most interesting is where researchers place AR's adoption rates. Research firm Gartner, utilizing its Technology Hype Cycle, claims that VR has begun its trip on the Slope of Enlightenment, putting mass adoption for VR within the range of two to five years (2020 to 2023). AR, it claims, is currently wallowing in the Trough of Disillusionment, putting mass adoption more conservatively at five to ten years out (2023 to 2028).

This chapter describes some of the consumer-facing AR devices available today, to help you make your own informed decision about when this technology will begin to see mass consumer adoption. It also outlines some of the pitfalls AR must overcome in order to pass through the Trough of Disillusionment and begin climbing the Slope of Enlightenment for consumer consumption.

Looking at the Available Form Factors

Unlike VR, where manufacturers have generally been building toward a single form factor (a headset that covers the head/eyes, headphones, and a pair of controllers), AR is still trying to find the form factor that suits it best. From glasses to headsets, from large tablets to mobile phones to projectors and heads-up displays (HUDs), AR is available today in a number of different forms.

It's entirely possible that any or all of these form factors will work well for AR executions. It's also possible that *none* of these is the right form factor for AR, and that some other execution will be released and reign as the "best" way to experience it. (AR wearable contacts, perhaps?) Only time will tell, but in the meantime, we can evaluate some of the more popular executions available currently.

Because of the variety in AR form factors, AR experiences can't be clearly separated into high/middle/low-end experiences as I do in Chapter 2 for VR headsets. The current AR experience is vastly different across each form factor, and each form factor serves a different market. In the following sections, I explain the most common form factors and their intended uses and audiences.

Mobile devices

Although arguably on the low end of AR experiences, mobile devices currently cover the largest market segment for AR. Applications such as Snapchat, Instagram, Yelp, and Pokémon Go have all offered rudimentary forms of AR for some time now, though most users may not have realized it. Every time you found yourself adding bunny ears to your image on Snapchat or found Pikachu cavorting in your local park, you were using a primitive form of AR on mobile. Figure 3-2 displays a user video (the real world) augmented with a digital overlay within Instagram.

Though building AR experiences on mobile devices was possible in the past, the release of ARKit and ARCore made doing so much easier for developers. ARKit and ARCore are the underlying development packages for building AR-based applications for iOS and Android, respectively. They have a similar feature set focused around making the digital holograms placed into a user's environment simple for developers, and making these holograms appear more *real* to the end user — features such as *plane detection* (to allow objects to be placed correctly in space) or *ambient light estimation* (which detects the lighting of the real world and allows developers to mimic that lighting on their digital holograms).

FIGURE 3-2:
AR at use in
Instagram.

REMEMBER

ARKit and ARCore are not hardware devices; they're software development packages that developers use to write applications for specific hardware. They interact with iOS and Android devices, but neither technology is hardware itself, and that's a good thing. Instead of having to purchase a separate device to experience Apple's and Google's AR mobile implementations, you can experience it using your existing mobile device, provided it meets ARCore or ARKit minimum technical requirements.

AR headsets

Mobile is the entry point for many AR users, but it offers arguably the lowest-end experience. The form factor of mobile can make for an awkward user experience. A user is required to constantly hold a device and capture the image of the physical world, onto which the digital augmentation is overlaid. Plus, the form factors of current mobile devices provide only a small window (the size of the screen) into the combined real and digital world, far smaller than a user's full field of view.

A headset can provide a much more immersive user experience for AR applications. Some examples include the Microsoft HoloLens, the Meta 2, and the Magic Leap. This brings us to our first hiccup regarding AR headsets — and speaks to just how far behind AR headsets are in their development cycle compared to VR headsets as of this writing.

Although those three devices are probably the three most well-known AR headsets, none of them is truly a mass consumer device just yet. The HoloLens is available now, but it's marketed to businesses and enterprises, not consumers. The Meta 2 (shown in Figure 3-3) is available now, but only as a developer kit, not a full release. And though much has been made of Magic Leap and its impressive team and investor group, as of this writing, the Creator Edition of its headsets have yet to ship to developers (though Magic Leap has announced a ship date of 2018).

FIGURE 3-3:
A user navigating
Meta 2 digital
holograms via
hand gestures.

Courtesy of Meta

At a high level, many AR headsets appear to be taking the form of large headbands or helmets with a translucent visor attached to the front, as in Figure 3-3. The headset projects images onto the surface of the goggles to overlay reality with digital content. The Magic Leap One takes a slightly different approach; the form factor of a pair of goggles and light fields to display content to its users. Some headsets (such as HoloLens) are entirely self-contained units, offering much more freedom of movement at the cost of processing power. Others (such as Meta 2) keep you tethered to a computer to power the experience, sacrificing movement for the processing power a desktop PC can offer. The Magic Leap One exists as a bridge between the two, requiring tethering to a Lightpack (a small wearable computer) to power its Lightwear goggles.

Windows Mixed Reality headsets could be an interesting addition to this group. With its approach to VR and AR, Microsoft seems to be pointing to the belief that the experience of VR and AR will eventually blend together. Instead of projecting onto a translucent lens, as the HoloLens and Meta 2 do, the current Windows

Mixed Reality headsets include front-facing cameras that could conceivably function as a pass-through for an AR experience. However, such functionality is not yet in place. As of this writing, the Windows Mixed Reality headsets function only as VR devices, with no AR features. Microsoft's naming and positioning seem to signal that these devices will eventually function as more than just VR headsets, but only time will tell if that is, indeed, the case.

Table 3-1 compares the "big three" headsets in AR. As you can see, as of this writing, we don't have hard specs for Magic Leap's final form factor versus the more established headsets of Microsoft and Meta.

TABLE 3-1   **Augmented Reality Headset Comparison**

	Microsoft HoloLens	Meta 2	Magic Leap
Platform	Windows	Proprietary	Lumin (proprietary)
Standalone	Yes (wireless)	No (wired to PC)	Requires wearable Lightpack computer
Field of view	Unknown (35 degrees)	90 degrees	Unknown
Resolution	1,268 x 720	2,560 x 1,440	Unknown
Headset weight	1.2 pounds	1.1 pounds	Unknown
Refresh rate	60 Hz	60 Hz	Unknown
Interaction	Hand gestures, voice, clicker	Hand gestures and positional tracking sensors, traditional input (mouse)	Control (handheld 6DoF controller), others

REMEMBER

The current generation of AR headsets offers the best AR experience available at the moment, but they're interim solutions. No one is quite sure what the end form factor of AR will look like. That title could perhaps belong to a combined headset, as Windows hopes with Windows Mixed Reality, or perhaps a form such as AR glasses.

AR glasses

In the near future, the best way of experiencing AR may be a simple pair of glasses. Both HoloLens and Meta 2 are currently more along the lines of large visors; there has yet to be a convincing release of AR glasses. Magic Leap One gets us closer, but it's still a fairly bulky pair of goggles. Google Glass and the recently released Intel Vaunt are the best-known examples of a simple AR glasses execution. However, the current execution of glasses such as Google Glass are little more than a wearable HUD. They lack the large field of view, graphical capabilities, and ability to "place" digital content in the physical environment, and they have extremely limited resolution and very little interactivity. Figure 3-4 depicts someone using the touchpad on the side of his Google Glass to swipe through a timeline of content displayed onscreen, contained in the small mirror in front of the user's eye.

Courtesy of Loic Le Meur (https://en.wikipedia.org/wiki/Google_Glass#/ media/File:A_Google_Glass_wearer.jpg) under a Creative Commons license (https://creativecommons.org/licenses/by/2.0/)

FIGURE 3-4:
Google Glass
Explorer Edition.

REMEMBER

Although interesting in their own right, HUDs like Google Glass are often not considered true AR devices. With the release of ARKit and Apple CEO Tim Cook's praise of AR as the future of technology, speculation abounds about Apple's plans to produce its own pair of AR glasses. This has yet to be confirmed by Apple. For the time being, AR content availability is limited to mobile-device AR and a small number of AR headsets.

Considering Controllers

AR/mixed reality (MR) controllers typically have a very different set of problems to solve than VR controllers. Whereas most VR headsets completely obscure a user's vision to the outside world, many AR form factors enable a user to see the world around her either via video feed or via a translucent visor. This can simplify some problems traditional headsets may experience. A user can see into the real world and is not blindly fumbling around for real objects.

On the other hand, this enhanced view can make other technical problems far more complex. Because the user can view the real world, it can be awkward having to use a controller to interact with digital holograms that appear to exist in the real world. This calls for developers to create a system for interacting with these digital objects using only your hands.

The following sections describe some of the methods of interacting with objects in AR.

Touch

Touch interaction in AR is mainly used in mobile implementations of AR. AR's use in popular consumer apps such as Snapchat on mobile devices has moved AR quickly into mainstream consciousness. However, implementation on devices not specifically designed for AR (such as smartphones) has brought some baggage along with it.

One of the challenges is just how to utilize mobile device input methods in AR applications. Users are accustomed to navigating mobile device screens through a series of taps, swipes, and similar gestures to the screen, but those actions may not be sufficient to navigate and control an AR experience.

The mobile implementations of AR do not introduce new hardware, and as such, they do not directly implement any new system of interaction. Instead, they have to conform to current mobile device interactions. How AR input is handled on mobile devices is typically up to the application developer to define. Most developers use a combination of gaze controls (covered next) and standard mobile interactions to allow users to interact with AR content. For example, a user may position his gaze cursor/reticle over a digital hologram in 3D space, tap the mobile screen to select it, and then drag to move the digital hologram once selected.

Figure 3-5 illustrates how Apple's User Interface Guidelines suggest to developers how to guide users while interacting with digital holograms in the real world. In this instance, a virtual object is being placed in the real world. In the left pane of Figure 3-5, note the corner markers around the rug to indicate that plane (flat surface) detection is in progress. The center pane of Figure 3-5 shows a focus square (a solid outline) around the rug, indicating that the screen is ready for user touch and displaying where a touch will place the object. After the user places the object, the focus square disappears, leaving only the virtual object placed in the "real" world, as displayed in the final image on the right.

FIGURE 3-5:
Placing virtual
objects via touch
in mobile AR.

Gaze

As in VR, gaze control is a popular means of AR interaction. Often used in conjunction with other interactions such as gesture or controller clicks, gaze controls build off of what the user is already doing, turning her head or device to look around in the environment, and trigger interaction based on what the user chooses to focus on.

Mobile gaze controls often include a grid following the user's gaze, to indicate where a digital hologram may be placed in the real world. Figure 3-6 displays how Android handles this scenario. A virtual grid is overlaid on top of the real-world scene to help visualize to the end user just where Android's bugdroid mascot hologram will be placed.

Some headset-based AR applications include a *reticle* (a cursor or crosshair) placed in the center of the user's vision to help the user know what she's about to interact with. Applications can then determine where a user's attention is, as well as where the user's attention is not. If an app needs a user to focus on an important object, it can trigger cues to focus the user on the important object in the scene.

Gaze controls work fairly well in AR today, but they'll truly come into their own when built in conjunction with eye tracking. In current implementations, gaze in both VR and AR forces the user to turn his entire head to look at items in the digital space. Upcoming eye tracking implementations promise to make this method of selection much more natural. In the real world, when you want to focus on something, rarely do you turn your entire head and center it directly on what you would like to focus upon. Instead, you likely focus on items via a combination of head and eye movement. Eye tracking will allow AR headsets to take into account not just head positioning for selection, but eye positioning as well. When eye tracking hits the mainstream, expect the use of gaze tracking to explode in popularity within AR.

Keyboard and mouse

When we picture the future, it's easy to imagine a world wholly removed from keyboard and mouse, as we fly through a fully digital landscape, molding our digital environments through futuristic control input methods.

The reality of the matter is there are still many actions where a keyboard or mouse may be the best current method of input. Current AR implementations take this into account. The Meta 2, for example, accepts both keyboard and mouse input. And, although Meta 2 designers picture the need for a mouse dissipating over time as hand tracking evolves, there are still instances where a keyboard may be the simplest method for input for the foreseeable future, such as long-form text entry. However, with the rise of voice as a control option (discussed next), perhaps the need for a keyboard for input will diminish as well.

Voice

Conversational user interface (UI), or the communication between a human and machine using language familiar to us humans, is one of the fastest-growing emerging technology fields. From Amazon Alexa to Google Home to Apple's Siri, conversational UI combined with artificial intelligence are quickly finding their place in society.

It's only natural that voice and speech will find their way as an input control mechanism for VR and AR. Voice is a natural way to communicate, and it has a very small learning curve compared to that of more traditional, hardware-based controls. Voice seeks to remove the friction of learning a new system to control AR applications, attempting to make the interface between human and machine as natural as possible.

Magic Leap has demoed voice control for its AR implementation, and both Google and Apple have their own digital assistants built into their mobile devices. Microsoft has also chosen to go all in on voice commands with its AR headsets, making it a core method of interaction for both the HoloLens and Windows Mixed Reality headsets.

Setting the stage for what could become the standard for voice interaction in AR, Microsoft includes a set of speech commands for standard controls (such as *select*, *go to start*, *teleport*, *go back*, and so on). It also enables developers to use custom audio input options to build their own voice controls. Best of all, it includes a dictation option to enable users to input text into apps, bypassing the awkward digital keyboard that many VR and AR apps struggle with.

Although voice will likely never become the only method of input for AR applications, expect it to play a very significant role for input in the near future for most AR devices.

Hand tracking

One of the major ways AR differs from VR is the ability to see the environment around you. This includes being able to see the most common tools you use to physically interact with the world around you currently: your hands. This visibility makes hand tracking much easier and less problematic in AR than in VR.

Some AR headsets use gesture input via hand tracking as part of their device's core experience. Though hand tracking has been treated as nice to have but not essential by most major headsets in the VR space, hand tracking is a first-class citizen in AR. What the mouse is to traditional two-dimensional screens, hand tracking will likely become to AR headsets and glasses. Both the Meta 2 and HoloLens support a series of standardized gestures for their respective headsets, allowing interactions with the digital holograms they display.

Figure 3-7 displays the Meta 2's real-world hand tracking technology and a user performing a two-handed grab gesture.

FIGURE 3-7:
Meta 2 hand
gestures.

Source: https://devcenter.metavision.com/design/
user-interface-guidelines-interaction-inputs

Similarly, external companies such as ManoMotion seek to bring gesture analysis and recognition further into the AR space. ManoMotion is particularly notable for support of mobile AR, allowing developers to add this more "natural" method of interaction via gestures to their mobile applications, where a better method of AR input is sorely needed.

WARNING

One major problem that most AR headsets suffer from is the inability to track your hands when they're outside the interactive tracking region — which typically means the headset's or mobile device's line of sight. In other words, any interaction via gestures, hand motions, and so on will typically require you to bring your hands directly in front of your line of sight. This is not a show stopper, but you're likely fairly adept at navigating the real world without needing your hands directly in front of your face. (Think touch typing, using a mouse, using a video game controller, steering a car, and so on.) Although there are ways to track users' hands when outside the line of sight, doing so requires another piece of hardware, which can defeat the purpose of implementing the friction-free hand tracking option in the first place. Look for future AR headsets to make improvements on the ability to track hands farther outside of line-of-sight than the current generation.

Motion controllers

On the low end, headsets such Microsoft's HoloLens include very simple peripherals such as the HoloLens Clicker (see Figure 3-8), a device configured to enable users to click and scroll with minimal hand motion as a replacement for the air-tap gesture.

Recognizing the Current Issues with
Augmented Reality

FIGURE 3-8:
The HoloLens
Clicker.

Simple controllers like the Clicker seek to bridge the gap between natural non-hardware controls such as voice and gestures and full-blown motion controllers. Often used in conjunction with gaze, the Clicker allows simple interaction for users, such as gazing at a hologram and then clicking it to select, or scrolling by click and hold, and then rotating the Clicker up or down. The Clicker does solve some of the issues discussed regarding hand tracking. It can be used casually, without the need to keep your hands within headset line of sight for selecting items.

On the higher end of the spectrum are devices such as Microsoft's motion controllers for its current generation of Mixed Reality headsets or Magic Leap's six-degrees-of-freedom "Control" controller. Motion controllers in AR will likely closely resemble their counterpart in VR. Just as our motion controllers in VR seek to emulate the natural experience of using our hands/gestures, motion controllers in AR will attempt to do the same thing.

Using motion controllers in AR could make certain features possible that gestures alone cannot, such as adding more options for hologram selection and movement.

Overall, fewer controller options are available today for AR than for VR. VR has a head start on consumer devices, and AR hardware has some catching up to do. However, you can begin to see some patterns emerge. AR is focused on merging the physical and the digital. The most important step will be creating that frictionless relationship between the physical environment and digital content. Creating that frictionless relationship can mean adhering to a "less is more" philosophy regarding hardware solutions for users, opting instead for the most natural user interaction implementations (hand tracking, voice input) possible.

Users in AR in the near future will most likely find themselves interacting with their AR holograms via a combination of touch, gaze, voice, and hand tracking.

Recognizing the Current Issues with Augmented Reality

It has long seemed like AR exists in VR's shadow. The idea of visiting fully virtual worlds separate from our own has long captured the public's imagination and taken precedence over the "augmenting" of our existing world. On the other hand, AR has long held many practical applications in enterprise environments, such as industrial manufacturing. This could lead to users familiarizing themselves with the technology on the job, potentially leading to an upsurge of consumer AR usage at home.

As discussed in Chapter 1, technology research firm Gartner predicts that VR will reach mass adoption by 2020 to 2023, whereas it predicts mass adoption of AR a few years beyond that. That means it will potentially be a decade before we see large-scale adoption of AR, which seems a logical conclusion. Both VR and AR have technical issues to solve. AR shares almost all the same issues VR experiences but has the additional issues to solve of computer vision for detecting real-world objects, unique display form factors on transparent displays (if not using a video camera as pass-through), digital object placement, locking digital holograms in place within the real world, and much more.

Form factors and first impressions

AR's biggest attempt to catch up to VR and step into the limelight of public consciousness may also prove to be one of the biggest issues it has to contend with. To experience VR, users must buy extra peripherals, such as costly headsets and computers to power them. The addition of AR to standard mobile devices immediately puts a form of AR into hundreds of millions of users' hands.

However, that experience of AR is far less than optimal. The engineers at Apple and Google have done an astounding job of bringing an AR experience to devices not built primarily for that purpose, but most consumers' initial experience with AR will be one that is limited to what a mobile device can deliver.

As the saying goes, you never get a second chance to make a first impression. If users have a low-quality AR experience on their mobile devices, they may broadly associate that experience with AR in general and dismiss the technology entirely as only as advanced as what a mobile AR experience can provide. They may then dismiss the myriad of other form factors that exist to deliver a potentially superior AR experience.

Cost and availability

The solution to the "first impression" issue is an issue of its own. Although a number of AR headsets and glasses appear to be in development, only a select few are available for purchase as of this writing, and most are targeting enterprise, are "developer editions," or in general are not ready for public consumption.

Plus, unlike VR, for which a number of low-cost headsets are available, AR headset/glasses hardware can easily cost thousands of dollars, which puts them out of the reach of all but the most dedicated innovators or early adopters. This cost differential can help explain why AR's mass adoption is estimated to be a few years farther out than that of VR.

This issue is illustrated in Figure 3-9, which displays the technology adoption life cycle, a model that helps describe how the general public adopts new products and technology. AR, and AR headsets specifically, exist very much within the early stage of adoption, the Innovators stage. It can be challenging for technologies to overcome the hump of Early Adopters and cross the chasm to reach the Early Majority consumer adoption stage.

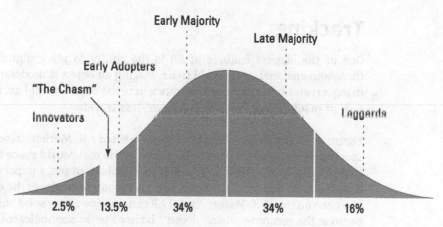

FIGURE 3-9: The technology adoption life cycle.

Perceived usefulness

The best hardware in the world means nothing if it isn't accompanied by amazing software. The public seems intrigued by the promise of AR, but many are not quite sure what they would use it for. Many people understand the benefits of VR, because being able to put yourself in a fully virtual world has been explored in relative depths by popular media. AR, on the other hand, has remained a bit more under the radar, making it hard for the public to envision how it will be used.

This can be a chicken-or-the-egg scenario. Software developers don't want to build software for hardware that hasn't reached certain consumption levels, and consumers don't want to purchase hardware that doesn't have a broad base of applications for them to use. Users need a compelling reason to purchase these devices.

It will likely take a few enterprising software developers creating some "must-have" applications that will drive consumer adoption. Although the road for those software developers will not be well traveled, the ones to create the first "killer applications" for AR will be handsomely rewarded.

There already exist a number of AR applications that show off just what AR is good at. I discuss some current use cases of AR in Chapter 11, as well as cover a number of intriguing AR applications you can download today with your AR-compatible mobile device in Chapter 16.

Tracking

One of the biggest features of AR is the ability to place digital objects in the three-dimensional, real-world space. Placing an object is moderately simple to do using a real-world marker to indicate where the object should go, but the ultimate goal of many AR applications is marker-less tracking.

Figure 3-10 shows an example of *marker-based* AR. Marker-based AR requires a specifically designed marker to be placed in the real-world space for the cameras/computer vision to orient themselves to. In this example, a paper printout of a QR code has been placed on the table, and the AR software places the digital hologram of a cube on top of it. Marker-based AR can provide a very solid base to track from, because the computer vision doesn't have to be as sophisticated as marker-less tracking. It just has to recognize the marker.

TECHNICAL STUFF

One of the terms you'll hear thrown around when discussing AR is *computer vision*. Computer vision is a broad field of study, but in the context of AR it typically describes how a computer can understand the environment it's seeing via digital image or video.

FIGURE 3-10:
Marker-based AR.

Computer vision that can handle *marker-less* AR is technologically difficult because it requires a complex understanding of real-world 3D space. Our brains can view a scene and easily distinguish among a wall, a window, and a doorway, but a computer will just see a collection of pixels, with no one pixel more meaningful than the other. Computer vision describes how a computer can take a collection of pixels and understand what they mean. For example, given an image of a table, computer vision would allow the application to not only recognize it as a collection of pixels, but also identify it as an object in 3D space with a height, width, and depth.

Even on systems that can do the processing required for marker-less AR, there can be delay while the processing occurs. Some AR devices are quicker than others at processing the environment (with HoloLens performing notably well in this regard), but many AR devices suffer from some amount of tracking *latency* (delay). Move your mobile device or change your head position quickly enough, and you may see some shifting of the digital holograms placed in physical space, even on the best of the current-generation devices. In the real world, though, if you observed a chair changing position or sliding across the floor when you turned your head, you would assume your house was haunted. These tracking issues are still a common occurrence in AR experiences today.

Getting tracking correct is one of the biggest challenges AR faces, but one that will go a long way toward maintaining the illusion of a user's digital items existing in the physical space. Expect the next generation of devices to make tracking a priority and improve upon the current generation of tracking technology.

Field of view

Field of view (FOV) refers to the space in which digital holograms can appear. For example, the FOV for mobile AR is the amount of viewable space on your device screen. The device screen acts as your window into the AR world. Look away from this window into the digital, and you would only see the real world, where no holograms exist.

REMEMBER

On some current AR headsets/glasses, the digital FOV typically covers only a very small area within the visor or glasses, not the entire viewable area. This gives the effect of gazing into the virtual world through a small window or letter slot.

Figure 3-11 demonstrates an example of how this limited FOV plays out within headsets. Similar to looking through a letter slot, the holograms would only appear in the area I've marked as *hologram visible*. Any part of the hologram that falls into the area I've marked *hologram not visible* would be cut off at that point. As you can see, a headset with a narrow FOV has a much more difficult time offering the same level of immersion as a headset with a larger FOV.

Hologram Visible   Hologram Not Visible

FIGURE 3-11:
An example of a
narrow field
of view.

Photo by Breather on Unsplash (https://unsplash.com/photos/bjhrzvzZeq4)

Obviously, a larger FOV is preferable to a smaller one. If the holographic images display only in a small window, it's easy to be pulled out of the experience as you see the holograms get cut off within your FOV. Meta 2 appears to have the largest FOV of the current batch of headsets, claiming a 90-degree FOV, but all have a long way to go before approaching the FOV of the human eye (approximately 135 degrees vertical and 200 degrees horizontal).

Improving the FOV of the AR experience figures to be one of the next big leaps for AR to make with its next generation of hardware. In fact, Microsoft has already announced that it has found a way to more than double its current FOV for its next generation of HoloLens, which would be a great step toward solving the biggest complaint most people have with the HoloLens.

Visuals

Like the current generation of VR headsets, current AR headsets struggle to meet the high-resolution demands consumers are accustomed to.

Additionally, many current AR devices suffer from poor *occlusion* (the effect of an object blocking another object). In AR, *occlusion* typically refers to physical objects obscuring digital ones. You may have noticed this issue in AR mobile apps such as Pokémon Go: Sometimes, you're able to create a very realistic scene with Zubat hovering above the ground; other times, Squirtle appears to be half-stuck inside a wall. Such visuals are due to lack of proper occlusion in AR. When occlusion is properly executed, digital objects can be accurately and realistically placed in any relationship to real-world objects — under them, partially behind them, on top of them, or whatever the simulation requires.

The HoloLens and Meta 2 devices can perform a reasonable degree of occlusion, and Magic Leap's demo videos appear to show a very high level of occlusion (though because the device has yet to ship as of this writing, it's hard to predict if the production device will be able to reach the high bar set in its video demos).

Figure 3-12 displays a screen shot of the occlusion Magic Leap displayed in one of its early demo videos. The digital hologram of a robot seamlessly is occluded by the top and side leg of a table. If Magic Leap is able to replicate this fidelity of graphics, combined with this level of occlusion in its mass-consumer device, it will be a massive step forward for AR. It may not seem like much, but think about it in terms of the marker-less orientation discussed earlier in the chapter. In order to place the robot behind the table leg, the simulation software has to understand the 3D space and not just see a collection of pixels. It needs to view the scene and be able to calculate what should be in the foreground, what should be in the background, and where the digital hologram should fit into all this. It needs to understand what "under the table" means and know which parts of the table are farther forward in space than others. That is not easy to achieve.

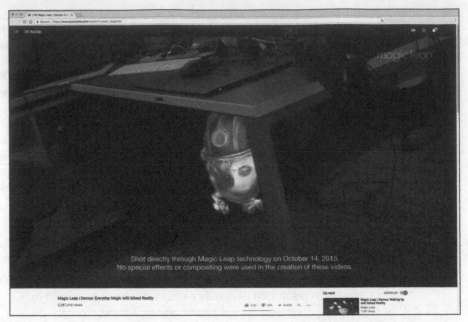

FIGURE 3-12:
Magic Leap demo video.

Source: https://www.youtube.com/watch?v=kw0-JRa9n94

For AR to deliver a quality experience on a mass consumer scale, solving occlusion for dynamic environments will be an important issue to iron out.

Assessing Adoption Rates

If you evaluated the markets solely on *install base* (users who have the capability to run VR or AR experiences), you might think AR adoption rates were far ahead of VR adoption.

However, those numbers are buoyed strictly by the releases of ARKit and ARCore for iOS and Android devices. Though a massive technological achievement, the mobile device implementation of AR often feels a bit like an appetizer to the main course, which is functional, affordable, wearable AR. We're most likely still several years out from mass consumer adoption at that level of fidelity.

Technology, especially technology that caters to a mass consumer base, is all about trade-offs. Availability of materials, performance, form factor, size, and cost must all be taken into account. Thanks to science fiction in the media, consumers have grown to believe they should be able to put on a pair of stylish, unobtrusive glasses and be whisked away to their futuristic AR world. And we're not quite there yet.

REMEMBER

AR today exists mainly in simple executions on mobile devices, in simple HUDs, or in bulky headsets with a lower resolution and smaller FOV than consumers are expecting or accustomed to. However, companies are currently investing heavily in AR/MR, experimenting with a variety of see-through optics, and the form factor and visuals of AR experiences in five years will be vastly different than those of today.

Gartner Research's prediction of mass consumer adoption being five to ten years out (2023 to 2028) seems fairly realistic, given the current limitations of the technology. However, no less an authority than Bill Gates, in his book *The Road Ahead*, proclaimed, "We always overestimate the change that will occur in the next two years and underestimate the change that will occur in the next ten." Ten years, in technological development terms, is an eternity.

Based on what we know about the advances of VR and AR, it isn't hard to imagine a merging of VR and AR into a single device that can toggle between both, removing the need for separate hardware. Perhaps Windows Mixed Reality headsets offer a glimpse of what that future could look like: a fully enclosed VR headset with a video pass-through for AR experiences. Or perhaps the future is in the transparent projected-image options such as HoloLens, Meta, or Magic Leap. And perhaps AR will benefit from VR's developments, pushing its timeline closer to the shorter five-year adoption cycle than ten years out. In the meantime, we may have to subsist on the appetizer of mobile AR, while the main course of wearable AR is still cooking.

2

Consuming Content in Virtual and Augmented Reality

Explore the various current hardware options for consuming virtual and augmented reality experiences.

Discover the potential near-future options for consuming virtual and augmented reality experiences.

Chapter **4**

Consuming Content in Virtual Reality

The virtual reality (VR) market is very young, but already packed with choices for consuming content. Consumers have a number of headsets to choose from — from simple, mobile-powered devices to high-end headsets run by powerful external computers. Often, there isn't a simple way to compare all these choices side-by-side to find out what works best for your particular consumption needs. Determining what's available now, what's coming out next, and when the right time to enter the market may be confusing.

In this chapter, I discuss the available first-generation versions of VR headsets and hardware as of early 2018. I take a look at the upcoming second generation of VR headsets, many aiming to be released within 2018 or early 2019. Finally, I touch upon some things to keep in mind when comparing the current and upcoming generations of devices.

Exploring Consumer-Grade Virtual Reality

Consumer-grade headsets have experienced an explosion of growth since the initial offering of the Oculus Rift DK1 in 2013. A field that had been quiet for decades on the consumer front suddenly experienced a massive jump in growth, inviting numerous tech giants to fund their own headsets to capture the potential of VR.

As of this writing, we're currently between generations of VR hardware. The first generation of consumer-grade VR headsets has been released, and companies are in the midst of planning their next generation. They're watching the various trends in the hardware markets to see which direction the winds seem to be blowing in regard to consumer purchasing habits. The first generation has established baseline expectations in consumers' minds for quality and price point. Headsets released in the second generation of hardware will have to surpass the current generation in these benchmarks in order for consumers to consider this second generation a success.

In this section, I establish a baseline to help you evaluate the upcoming generation of headsets. If you're in the market for a VR headset or you're just interested in comparing existing and future models, this should help you in your evaluations. For a deeper comparison of the available form factors, refer to Chapter 2.

When you make decisions based on first-generation hardware and software adoption, keep in mind who the drivers of that market are. Emerging markets with higher price points, such as VR, can often find themselves driven by early adopters who may or may not be indicative of your actual market.

High-end devices

The current high-end VR headsets are almost all powered by an external computer. Nearly all the current generations high-end devices offer a room-scale experience, enabling users to move about in physical space and have those movements reflected in the VR world. Nearly all the current generations high-end headsets work with a pair of motion controllers. These devices all feature a wide field of view (FOV) and generally very high-resolution displays. Most of these first-generation devices are tethered via cable to the computer powering them.

The high end is made up of headsets such as the HTC Vive, Oculus Rift, Windows Mixed Reality headsets, and, to a lesser extent, the PlayStation VR. The PlayStation VR is a bit of an outlier because it doesn't offer the same room-scale experience of the other headsets. However, it does offer a more premium VR experience than many of the mid-tier choices.

If you're serious about getting a premium VR consumption experience that includes the best games and the highest-end graphics and applications, you'll likely want one of the headsets that fall into the high-end range. The bigger question may be whether to get a model from this generation or hold out for the next generation of high-end devices, all of which come with their own set of notable improvements on current-generation devices.

Figure 4-1 shows the first-generation HTC Vive and its associated controllers and "lighthouse" sensors.

FIGURE 4-1:
HTC Vive, controllers, and sensors.

Mid-tier devices

The Google Daydream and Gear VR are the main serious mid-tier competitors for the first generation of headset. Both require an Android device with decent specs in order to run their VR experience. Their FOV is slightly less than that of the higher-end headsets, and they have a slower refresh rate, so the screen images are refreshed fewer times per second.

Both come with a single motion controller that offers three degrees of freedom of movement, loosely tracking (but not fully tracking) the controller's movement in space. Neither offers any room-scale experience or tracks the user's position outside of head rotation and orientation.

TECHNICAL
STUFF

Three degrees of freedom (3DoF) in relation to VR headset controllers typically means the controller has rotational tracking only. It's essentially paired to the position of your headset. Unlike with the higher-end headsets such as the HTC Vive or Oculus Rift, if you were to leave your controller on the floor and walk away from it while wearing these 3DoF headsets, the controller wouldn't retain its position in 3D space.

If you're interested in exploring simple VR executions, you have an existing supported Android device, and you aren't willing to spend what it costs to get a high-end device, these middle-tier devices can be a good entry-point experience for VR consumption. Your consumption options will be more limited in this middle tier, but plenty of applications are targeted toward this level of experience.

Figure 4-2 shows the first-generation Google Daydream along with its motion controller.

FIGURE 4-2:
Google Daydream
and controller.

Low-end devices

The current low end of the VR headset market is occupied by Google Cardboard and its variants. Like the mid-tier VR headsets, Google Cardboard experiences are all powered by a separate mobile device, such as a smartphone. Unlike with the mid-tier experiences, however, Google Cardboard experiences can run on many different mobile devices including lower-end ones.

Any manufacturer can produce a Google Cardboard viewer by following the Cardboard specs that Google provides. This flexibility has led to the existence of a multitude of form factors. The only things these devices have in common are that they're all powered via a separate mobile device, they all have similar lenses, and almost all rely on a single, on-headset button for any interaction within the virtual world. The limited interaction that Google Cardboard offers limits it to being little more than a VR "viewer," offering users a far more passive consumption experience than the mid-tier and high-end headsets.

Google Cardboard may be a good entry point if you have little more than a passing interest in VR, you don't have an Android device, and you aren't willing to invest in a more immersive experience. Although Cardboard is popular for its low cost, the VR experience it delivers pales in comparison to either the higher-end or mid-tier experiences. Your consumption choices will be limited at this level. The devices themselves limit what can be run in Google Cardboard, and many content creators prefer to build for higher-level experiences.

Figure 4-3 shows Mattel's View-Master, a Google Cardboard–powered update of its classic toy.

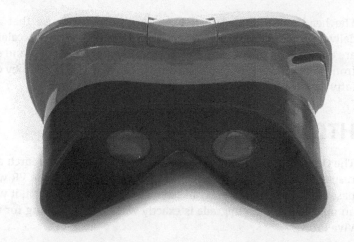

FIGURE 4-3:
Mattel's
Google
Cardboard-
powered
View-Master.

REMEMBER

There is a market for nearly any type of VR headset. What Cardboard may lack in features, it may make up for in price or availability. Providing a classroom of elementary-school students a Google Cardboard experience may be far more palatable than providing them all high-end headsets. Cardboard's experience may not be able to match the immersiveness of high-end headsets, but you may still find Google Cardboard is the best fit for your particular consumption needs.

Identifying Near-Future Hardware

With the levels set for the first generation of VR hardware, we can now take a look at the upcoming generation of VR devices and see how they compare. As you'll see, these headsets' offerings vary considerably in experience quality, just like the first-generation offerings did, but the quality scale has been moved forward from the first generation. The high-end devices of the current generation will be blown away by some of the higher-end next-generation devices, and what may be considered low end in this second generation exceeds the first generation's mid-tier devices. The future looks very bright for the next generation of VR head-mounted displays (HMDs).

WARNING

A number of companies have announced VR consumer headset releases in the near future. However there is a vast ocean between announcement and a mass consumer-scale release. That ocean is littered with companies both large and small that have tried and failed to navigate the treacherous waters from announcement to final release. Failure often comes through no fault of the company or product itself. Be it competing products, a fickle customer base, or any number of potential issues, the evolution from ideation to release is a difficult climb for any product.

The headsets discussed in this section represent those that appear poised to deliver on their promise of release within the 2018 and 2019 calendar years. There are entries from manufacturers with a proven track record, and some new entries from competitors trying to break into the market. Whether they can deliver on the lofty expectations they all strive to meet has yet to be seen.

HTC Vive Pro

The Oculus Rift and HTC Vive had consumer releases in March and April of 2016, respectively. That may not seem that long ago, but in the VR world, where time passes akin to dog years, it can seem like a lifetime. As such, it was about time for an upgrade. And an upgrade is exactly what HTC is aiming for with its new HTC Vive Pro.

The original Vive was widely touted as one of the best consumer VR experiences you could buy. Instead of trying to create an entirely new headset, HTC has instead focused on addressing some of the complaints fans had with the original Vive. The Vive Pro will increase the resolution of the original Vive from 1,080 x 1,200 per eye to 1,440 x 1,600 per eye. By all accounts, the change is akin to moving from standard-definition television to HD television.

The second feature that stands out with the Vive Pro is the new Vive Wireless Adapter. This adapter, which will work with the original Vive as well, features Intel's WiGig technology to offer a wireless experience that operates in the 60 Ghz band. This should lead to lower latency and better performance. Note, however, that unlike experiences that feature inside-out tracking, the Vive will still need its light-house sensors to positionally track users in space. Vive's current headset, which offers six degrees of freedom tracking for its headset and controllers, has generally been regarded as one of the best in the consumer market. And early reviews point to the wireless adapter being able to retain that experience — a big step forward.

TECHNICAL STUFF

Six degrees of freedom (6DoF) refers to the ability of an object to move freely in three-dimensional space. In VR, this typically refers to the ability to move forward/backward, up/down, and left/right with both orientation (rotational) tracking and positional (translation) tracking. 6DoF allows realistic movement in VR worlds and increases the immersiveness of the VR experience. Devices that only offer 3DoF will never feel as immersive as 6DoF devices.

This is one of the major differentiators to be aware of for VR headsets. Higher-end headsets such as the HTC Vive allow full 6DoF, while the current-generation low-end and mid-tier devices mostly do not. Current mid-tier mobile options such as Google's Daydream and Samsung's Gear VR allow only 3DoF of movement — the three rotational movements (pitch, yaw, and roll). They don't, however, allow for the translational movements, a big differentiator between the high-end headsets and the rest.

HTC also chose to integrate headphones into its new headset. (A common complaint of the original Vive was having to supply your own.) The Vive Pro also has an additional front-facing camera (in addition to the existing camera) in the headset. No word yet from HTC as to what these cameras could be used for, though rumors abound about their potential for environmental depth-sensing, for AR applications, or the potential to make the Vive Pro compatible with Windows Mixed Reality experiences.

HTC seems to be positioning the Vive Pro as an item for those looking for a high-end VR experience, similar to the existing HTC Vive. Think enterprise-level, high-end gaming or entertainment users. The Vive Pro likely won't pull in consumers who are more price sensitive, but the creators appear to want to target the premium-tier market for those pushing the envelope with their experiences. HTC shipped the Vive Pro in April 2018.

HTC Vive Focus

The HTC Vive Focus is HTC's upcoming mid-tier headset. We already know the details about the features of the HTC Vive Focus because it has been released in China (and the Internet being what it is, word gets around).

The Vive Focus is a standalone headset (not powered by an external computer or mobile device). The headset itself contains the computer powering the experience. It claims to be the world's first standalone VR headset available to consumers with 6DoF tracking.

The onboard cameras of the Vive Focus provide world-scale inside-out tracking. This means no external tracking devices are required for the user to be able to move about in the physical world and have her movements tracked in the virtual world. Early reviews of the positional tracking of the Focus have been very favorable, a good sign for the potential of untethered headsets in general.

The Focus is powered by a rechargeable battery that provides up to three hours of active use time. It comes with a single Vive Focus controller that supports 3DoF for the controller itself, similar to the controllers of the current-generation mid-tier experiences.

The Vive Focus currently sells in China for about $630. At a higher price point than some of the other upcoming headsets, the Vive Focus, much like the original Vive before it, seems to be targeting a higher-end market that is looking for a premium experience. Speaking in an interview with Antony Vitillo at `https://skarredghost.com`, HTC's China Regional President of Vive had the following to say: "We don't want to be the price leaders. We don't want to sell a product that costs $200 with minimal features. Everyone that puts on a Vive should expect the best experience possible." Vive seems less concerned with competitors than with trying to find what works for mainstream adoption.

Vive has stated that the headset's reception in China will determine whether the headset will see a further international release. It will be very telling to see how the Chinese market receives the Focus and what it could mean for a larger-scale release.

Lenovo Mirage Solo

The Lenovo Mirage Solo is similar to the HTC Vive Focus. It's an all-in-one stand-alone headset that doesn't require any extra computers or mobile devices to power it. Similar to the Vive Focus, the Mirage Solo will allow 6DoF via a pair of front-facing cameras, allowing inside-out positional tracking. This setup enables you to wirelessly move about the virtual worlds the same way you navigate the real world. With a built-in display, a 3DoF controller, and positional tracking using Google's WorldSense technology, the Mirage Solo eliminates the need for any external sensors. The headset is also built on top of Google Daydream technology, allowing the headset to tap into Google's existing Daydream ecosystem of applications.

The Mirage is set to release sometime in the second quarter of 2018. The original price point was set above $400, but Lenovo has since adjusted this and is looking to aim at a price below $400. As of this writing, final pricing has not been announced. It will be interesting to see where the price finally lands. It's clear, however, that companies such as Lenovo are keeping an eye on the casual market to try to determine the correct price point to target that market.

Oculus Santa Cruz

The Oculus Santa Cruz was originally announced at Oculus Connect 3 in 2016. Oculus seems to be positioning this new product as a mid-tier headset similar to the Vive Focus and Lenovo Mirage Solo. However, it promises a higher-end VR experience than current mobile VR models such as the existing Gear VR or upcoming models such as the Oculus Go (discussed later in this chapter). However, it doesn't quite deliver the same level of experience as the PC-powered Oculus Rift. Oculus co-founder Nate Mitchell has confirmed this to Ars Technica, framing the Santa Cruz as the mid-tier product in Oculus's three-headset strategy for VR hardware.

Like the Focus and Solo, the Santa Cruz is a self-contained headset. Instead of being powered by any external device, it contains everything you need in the headset itself. No more tripping over external wires or cords leading to your device. It purportedly will allow 6DoF for motion and positional tracking via the headset's inside-out tracking. Similar to tethered headsets that rely on sensors, Santa Cruz will display a virtual grid if you come too close to a physical barrier such as a wall.

The Santa Cruz also appears to be designed to utilize a pair of 6DoF wireless controllers, which could put its motion controls a cut above other mid-tier current- and next-generation wireless headsets whose controllers only allow for 3DoF. Santa Cruz's four arrayed cameras around the edges of the headset allow for a very large area in which to track the controllers' position. Some current-generation headsets that utilize inside-out tracking for their controllers can cause tracking to be lost if the controllers move too far out of the line of sight of the headset sensors. Oculus appears to have taken steps in order to solve this issue with the Santa Cruz.

The Santa Cruz appears to be following other headsets in regards to audio as well. The Go and Santa Cruz both utilize a new spatial audio system that, instead of relying on headphones, will place speakers onto the sides of the headset, allowing audio to be broadcast not only to the HMD wearer but the rest of the room as well. There is still a 3.5mm audio jack for those who prefer headphones, but the convenience of speakers is a nice touch.

On the surface, the Santa Cruz sounds like a promising device. The biggest question marks surrounding the Santa Cruz at the moment are timeline and final specs. Oculus has been silent on final product specifications, release date, and so on, so no final product specs can be listed. Oculus is shipping devices to developers in 2018; this would lead most to believe that the final hardware specifications are close to being locked in. Based on previous products' timelines between developer release and final release, a good estimate for consumer release date for the Santa Cruz would likely be early 2019, though only Oculus knows its final release date.

REMEMBER

With the current generation of VR headsets, audio consumption has often been cited as one of the reasons VR experiences feel like solitary experiences. Most current-generation headsets come with or require a set of headphones to experience what's happening in VR. This can lead to a very immersive experience for the wearer but effectively shuts the wearer off from the outside world, completely covering his eyes and ears. Many of the newer headsets appear to be leaning toward implementing speakers on the headset itself alongside headphone audio ports. This will enable the headset wearer to still have at least an auditory connection to the outside world, as well as let others hear what the wearer is currently experiencing.

Oculus Go

Oculus appears to be targeting a different crowd with its Oculus Go standalone headset. Whereas the Mirage, Focus, and Santa Cruz all appear to be positioned as mid-tier options between the existing desktop and mobile VR markets, the Go looks to take over (while up-leveling) the current mobile VR experience.

The Go is a standalone headset that doesn't require a mobile device. It offers 3DoF, providing rotational and orientation tracking but not the ability to move backward or forward physically in space. This makes the Go more suited to seated or stationary experiences.

Although the Go doesn't appear to offer a number of the features that the Mirage and Focus do (most notably the addition of 6DoF tracking), Oculus likely hopes to use a lower price point (around $200) to lure in those entry-level VR users who may have previously considered purchasing a Gear VR or Google Daydream for mobile VR experiences.

Figure 4-4 depicts the new form factor of the standalone Oculus Go headset.

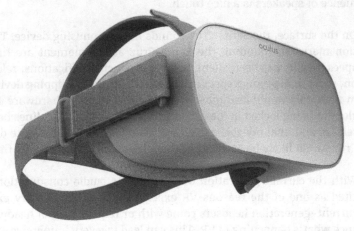

FIGURE 4-4:
The standalone
Oculus Go.

Courtesy of Oculus

Similar to other standalone headsets such as the Mirage and Focus, the Go controller will provide 3DoF tracking. Much simpler than the current Rift motion controllers, the Go controller aligns itself more closely with the current Daydream or Gear VR options. The Go will have its own library of games but will also offer support at launch for many of the existing Gear VR titles.

Figure 4-5 displays the new Oculus Go controller. The Go controller will be slightly different in form but offer the same functionality as Samsung's current Gear VR controller.

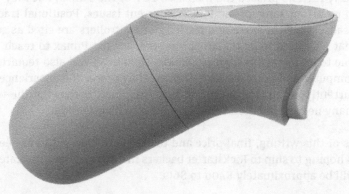

Courtesy of Oculus

FIGURE 4-5: The Oculus Go controller.

Pimax 8K

Pimax is a Chinese startup that appeared on Kickstarter in 2017 and surprised many with a claim that the company had plans to release the world's first 8K headset. While the "8K" claim is a bit of a marketing trick (in that its two 3,840-x-2,160-pixel displays don't actually make the headset 8K), many have been impressed with the visuals offered by its two 4K displays. The Kickstarter offering was a roaring success, with an original goal of $200,000 being obliterated as pledges shot past $4.2 million.

The human eye's natural FOV is around 200 degrees. Pimax's claim of a 200 degree FOV has yet to be verified, but by all accounts the FOV of the headset stands well above the FOV of almost every other current-generation and even most next-generation HMDs. Early reviews indicate that the unique lenses and insanely high-resolution screens give the feeling of the world wrapping around you as you would experience in real life.

FOV aside, Pimax also offers a number of other unique modules the group hopes to bring to its headset, such as *eye tracking* (the ability of the headset to monitor your eye movement and adjust based on where you're looking), inside-out tracking, hand tracking, and even scent enabling (yes, just what it sounds like). It also offers a number of the things you would expect to exist in the current generation of headsets — positional tracking via base stations, motion controllers, and so on. Pimax is compatible with OpenVR as well, meaning it can be used by other items that follow the OpenVR specification (such as the Vive controllers).

TECHNICAL STUFF

OpenVR is a software development kit (SDK) and application programming interface (API) built by Valve for supporting SteamVR (powering the HTC Vive) and other VR headsets.

Early reviews praised the increased FOV of the Pimax, but they were also careful to point out some of the Pimax's current issues. Positional tracking of both the headset itself in space and tracking of controllers are cited as some of the kinks that may need to be ironed out in order for the Pimax to reach its full potential. Due to its incredibly high resolution, the Pimax will also require a very high-end computer and graphics card to adequately power the experience. The Pimax also currently requires tethering to that computer, eschewing the wireless direction many next-generation headsets appear to be targeting.

As of this writing, final price and release date have yet to be seen, though Pimax is hoping to ship to Kickstarter backers in 2018 and have indicated the price range will be approximately $400 to $600.

Technology releases at mass-consumer scale become a numbers game of finding the price point consumers will pay. This price point can often determine the features and specifications you build into your headset. Although it may be possible to manufacture a true 8K headset with a full 200-degree FOV and full inside-out tracking (and, in fact, such a headset may exist already in the enterprise world), a consumer-scale release of such a headset is cost-prohibitive at this time, and the market for purchasing it likely does not exist.

It remains to be seen whether Pimax will be able to iron out the issues that currently exist with the headset while retaining what makes the headset unique. But companies such as Pimax that seek to push the envelope are a good thing for the industry as a whole. Regardless of whether the Pimax 8K becomes a success, it does signal a next step forward for VR in attempting to remove yet another barrier between the medium and full immersion.

REMEMBER

The list of headsets in this chapter is far from exhaustive. There are any number of VR headsets that are coming out (or even already released) that could be compared to the headsets on this list. For example, StarVR is a headset with similar specs to the Pimax 8K in terms of FOV and refresh rate. Currently StarVR is enterprise-level hardware whereas Pimax is looking to target the mass consumer market. If you're developing VR applications, especially targeted for enterprise level customers, be sure to research all the potential options available.

LooxidVR

Looxid Labs is a startup responsible for the LooxidVR system, a phone-based VR headset created to capture insights into human perception within VR. The

LooxidVR headset incorporates both EEG sensors to measure brain waves and eye-tracking sensors to determine what a user is looking at. Combining this data could allow for better understanding of users' emotional reactions to various stimuli and could lead to more immersive experiences.

Individual consumers are not Looxid's current target. You likely won't find yourself buying a LooxidVR device for single-use consumption anytime soon. However, by selling its system to researchers and businesses, Looxid could begin to have a deep impact on the VR industry as a whole. The Looxid system could find a great deal of use in the healthcare industry, particularly in therapy and in measuring users responses to mental trauma. It could also be used in gaming, with games modifying their gameplay based on your biometric response. Is a certain area of the game causing you stress as measured by Looxid? Perhaps the game will modify itself to make that area easier. Playing a horror game and one section of the game elicits elevated responses? The game could modify itself to include more of whatever it is that seems to be triggering that response from you, making it even more intense.

With its incorporation of both eye tracking and brain monitoring, the Looxid system could also find uses as a powerful tool for advertising and user analytics. Advertising is a field that VR has yet to unravel, but many are attempting to do so, as the payoff could be huge. Google has begun to experiment with what advertising in VR could look like. Unity has started to experiment with VR ads as well, putting forth the idea of "Virtual Rooms," which would provide separate branded experiences included in users' main applications.

With Looxid's system, it will be possible to capture analytic data from these advertisements deeper than any current VR offering, including how well these ads succeed with their target markets.

TECHNICAL STUFF

Unity's "Virtual Room" ad technology is Unity's answer to how advertising in VR should look. The Virtual Room is a VR native ad format Unity is creating in conjunction with the Interactive Advertising Bureau. The Virtual Room will be a fully customizable mini application that appears within your main VR application. A user can choose to interact with the Virtual Room or ignore it.

Varjo

Varjo is notable in its claim that its current headset can offer an effective resolution of 70 megapixels (human eye resolution) in VR, whereas most current generation headsets sit at around 1 or 2 megapixels.

Varjo aims to accomplish this utilizing eye tracking to follow where a user is looking and render the highest resolution only for that space, with items in the user's peripheral vision rendered at a lower resolution. (See Chapter 2 for more on foveated resolution.)

The Varjo headset is still in prototype mode, but the company hopes to release a beta version of its headset to the professional market in late 2018 and follow up with a consumer-market release. Things like production volume and final design are yet to be determined, though as of this writing, the company lists the professional headset as "under $10,000." That price doesn't inspire confidence just yet, but you'd be wise to keep an eye on the technology and see if other manufacturers take note and begin incorporating foveated rendering techniques within their own headsets.

Comparing Current and Future Options

Looking to both the existing and future options for headsets, patterns begin to emerge about the direction VR is headed in the near future, the markets it appears to be targeting, and the solutions you can expect on the horizon.

The current generation of VR headsets can be split into three main groups: desktop headsets, mobile headsets, and mobile "viewers." The desktop headsets are generally the higher end, almost all powered by (and tethered to) external hardware devices, whereas mobile headsets are powered by separate mobile devices that are inserted into headset hardware. This allows the mobile headsets to run untethered from any external hardware, but it has generally led to lower-quality experiences. Mobile "viewers" such as Google Cardboard are a step down from the mobile headsets, offering even less interactivity.

With the upcoming generation of hardware, the waters begin to get murkier. The desktop/high-end headset class still exists (with entries such as the Vive Pro, Pimax 8K, and so on), but dropping below that is where things can start to get confusing. A number of standalone headsets have appeared that no longer require separate devices to power them. This will likely lead to a more frictionless VR experience. The Vive Focus, Mirage Solo, and Oculus Santa Cruz appear to be leading the charge in creating a new, up-leveled VR experience that will exist somewhere between the desktop-powered experiences and mid-tier mobile-powered experiences — all without introducing the friction of requiring a separate device to power these experiences.

Entries such as the Oculus Go are beginning to emerge in the space that was previously occupied by mobile devices. However, with hardware dedicated specifically to VR and the requirement of a separate mobile device removed, these entries should be able to improve upon the current mobile experience of VR.

The next generation of headsets may all have a slightly different approach to certain form factors, but they have a number of things in common. Almost all headset manufacturers are looking for ways to remove the need to be tethered to external hardware. Whether it's through the use of inside-out tracking or wireless adapters for display and sensors, most next-generation innovators are looking to cut the cords.

Six degrees of freedom of movement is a necessity as well for any mid-tier to high-end headsets. This first generation of mid-tier headsets may have been able to get away with a less-than-premium experience for motion tracking, but consumers have come to expect more of the next generation, and most next-generation headset manufacturers are stepping up to meet those expectations.

The same expectation for freedom of movement exists for controllers, though it appears that companies have not put as much of a premium on that experience just yet. A number of mid-tier headsets appear to be fine with only allowing 3DoF. That choice does make those mid-tier headsets that offer full 6DoF, such as the Santa Cruz, stand out from the crowd.

Higher resolution has been an area of concentration as well. Nearly all of the next generation of headsets include improvements in resolution as compared to first generation models. Interestingly, with a few exceptions — such as the Pimax or Star VR — FOV has not been addressed at the same premium. Most headsets appear to be unconcerned with improving on around a 110-degree range, far lower than our ability to perceive 200 degrees. This likely points to FOV being a prohibitively expensive problem to solve. Manufacturers have apparently decided that the current FOV range is good enough for most users at this point, and they're concentrating their resources elsewhere.

The upcoming generation of HMDs also appears to be giving at least a cursory nod to the potential of a VR/AR hybrid. The appearance or improvements of front-facing cameras and sensors to many of the new headset entries could point to the ability to merge AR capabilities into these VR headsets. Merging of the technologies probably won't occur in this next generation of VR HMDs. VR manufacturers have been mum on that particular feature, leading most to believe it is not a point of focus for VR headsets just yet.

TIP

The world of VR can seem to move very quickly. Companies you've never heard of will likely release headsets with features you can't dream of within the next few years. The most important takeaway from this chapter is not a direct comparison of one VR headset to another, but instead learning the ability to evaluate these choices on your own based on various feature sets, some of which may not even exist.

Overall, manufacturers still seem to be trying to find the right balance between performance and price point for the mass consumer market. A concentration of manufacturers appear to believe that mid-tier headsets have the most potential for growth over the next few years. With numerous mid-tier entries of standalone headsets in the $200 to $400 range, companies are betting on a large market existing at that price point. Premium experiences beyond the mid-tier devices will come at a premium price, and manufacturers are also happy to cater to that market, though generally in less numbers and with less expectation of a huge market for premium experiences. However, as more businesses begin to adopt VR, this premium market could see a rise as well.

These features can provide you a picture of an idealized headset in the near future. A standalone self-contained headset, with high resolution, untethered, and the ability to track the world around you with 6DoF via inside-out tracking without the need of sensors. Also, look for a wide FOV, controllers that are able to be tracked with 6DoF, and most important, a sub-$200 price point.

No headset in this second generation of VR HMDs appears to align fully to that criteria. But the pace and leaps in technology that have been made over the last two years are extraordinary. We're only approaching the second generation of mass-consumer VR headsets, and already there are options that are extremely close to what you might consider an "idealized" VR headset. It isn't impossible to imagine a headset releasing within the next generation that is able to meet all those requirements. We may need to start setting our expectations even higher for the third generation of devices.

It's now just a matter of determining what kind of support the market will provide for this upcoming generation. The first generation of headsets was fueled by the hype of VR, which enabled the second generation to move forward powered off of that same hype. A cool reception of the second generation of headsets could significantly slow advances in development, while a strong positive reception could power innovation for the next generations of hardware and software within the VR space for years to come.

Chapter 5

Consuming Content in Augmented Reality

ugmented reality (AR) currently finds itself at the point where virtual reality (VR) was four or five years ago. Consumer buzz around the technology has started to build, but few people have had a chance to experience it in any meaningful way.

AR has yet to experience that "a-ha" moment with consumers, when a switch is flipped in their minds to the possibilities of AR. Flipping that switch may start a "space race" of sorts, in which manufacturers will aggressively compete to see whose AR form factor will win out. Determining a winner in that contest may ultimately come down to a matter of cost. Who will be able to create a compelling experience for consumers at a price that supports mass-scale production? Up to this point, most current AR hardware solutions have chosen to focus their efforts on building enterprise-level solutions that most consumers can't afford.

As a result, at this point in AR's development, you're far less likely to be a casual consumer of AR via a dedicated device than you are with VR. Any AR consumption you may be interested in will likely be geared toward the enterprise level. However, there are exceptions. Companies like Mira (discussed later in this chapter) offer solutions for consumer-based AR at a low price point, and mobile AR experiences of this generation are widely used.

In this chapter, I discuss some of the current choices available for consuming AR experiences, as well as cast some light on potential future options that may become available within the next year or two. I also compare this current generation of hardware with the upcoming generation to paint a picture of just how big a leap you can expect from the second generation of AR devices.

REMEMBER

Besides the headsets covered in this chapter, the AR market has a number of other hardware solutions that you may want to investigate on your own. For example, the DAQRI Smart Glasses are an AR headset specifically targeted toward professional use. Certainly, headsets such as the HoloLens are focused on enterprise for now, but they're expected to reach the broader consumer market eventually. Headsets such as the DAQRI have instead proclaimed that their narrower focus is geared toward markets such as manufacturing and construction, and consumer adoption isn't a goal for them.

Exploring Consumer-Grade Augmented Reality

Consumer-grade is a bit of a misnomer for most of the current AR hardware solutions we discuss (with notable exceptions such as Mira, ARKit, and ARCore). Most of the current generation of AR headsets focus their attention on enterprise-grade solutions. Additionally, many of the current generation of AR headsets are being sold in development mode, where preorder kits are available for developers but not at a scale for mass consumption.

Furthermore, at the time this book goes to print, not all of the first generation of AR hardware will have been released. It's still very much a moving target to talk about. However, all the listed hardware devices in this section have at least reached a point in their development to be considered part of this first generation.

REMEMBER

When researching AR hardware, you may find many AR headsets released as beta or developer kits. This typically means the headsets are not currently ready for mass consumption. Hardware released in developer mode is targeted toward developers, often to create a base level of software before releasing for mass consumers. Manufacturers know that a wide-scale release of their headsets without corresponding software would likely fail. Releasing headsets to developers enables manufacturers to not only work with and solicit input from power users of their devices directly, but also begin to build their marketplace from the ground up with apps created by the developers receiving the early releases of their devices.

Microsoft HoloLens

The HoloLens is one of the higher-profile head-mounted displays (HMDs) on the market, in part due to Microsoft's marketing clout. But marketing aside, the HoloLens has proven to be one of the most impressive first-generation HMDs and has gone a long way toward setting the standard for AR headsets.

The HoloLens is a standalone headset that does not need to be connected to a desktop or laptop. Its built-in sensors map the environment around you for placing 3D holograms. It recognizes gestures and voice for user input. In the same way that visuals are overlaid on top of the real world, HoloLens has an onboard 3D speaker system instead of headphones that overlays AR audio on top of real-world audio. This helps prevent the user from being closed off from the real world. If mapped correctly, the HoloLens also allows for occlusion of digital-world holograms by real-world physical objects. A holographic ball that rolls under a real-world table could disappear from sight, as if it were real.

Although the HoloLens is undoubtedly one of the benchmark AR headsets, there are still improvements to be made. The most common complaint about the HoloLens is its field of view (FOV). The tracking and visuals of the HoloLens are extremely impressive, but the smaller FOV can sometimes cut off the hologram you're looking at, breaking immersion with the experience. FOV aside, the hardware is a bit bulky and not exactly subtle. Even with its size however, it manages to be a comfortable experience, packing an impressive amount of computing power into a wearable device.

REMEMBER

Microsoft has loftier goals for their mixed-reality devices than most imagine. In an interview with Bloomberg, HoloLens inventor Alex Kipman claimed, "The phone is already dead. People just haven't realized." Kipman holds the belief that a mixed-reality device such as the HoloLens will one day replace all mobile phones. Looking at the current bulky form factor and high cost of most AR headsets, that may be a difficult future to imagine. However, with a rumored Apple AR standalone device, Microsoft's HoloLens, and Google's mixed-reality explorations with ARCore, that future may be closer than you think.

Looking forward, expect the next generation of HoloLens to dramatically improve the FOV. Microsoft has claimed that it already has a method to more than double the FOV of the current-generation HoloLens, putting it close to being on par with current-generation VR headsets. This will be a huge step in shoring up what many consider the current-generation HoloLens's biggest weakness.

The future of the HoloLens may be mass consumption, but the current-generation price and FOV will be the main factors keeping it out of the hands of everyday consumers for now. However, the HoloLens is a good choice for any current enterprise-level AR experience. With Microsoft's lofty goals, don't be surprised by a mass consumer release of the HoloLens or similar device within a generation or two.

Figure 5-1 depicts a user's visuals while inside the Microsoft HoloLens.

FIGURE 5-1:
The Microsoft
HoloLens in use.

Meta 2

The Meta 2 is an AR headset that can develop an environmental map of the physical world in which to display its 3D holograms. It also features hand tracking and gestures for navigation and uses reflected projections in front of a semi-transparent mirror to display holograms.

Meta broke away from HoloLens in one major category: Meta chose to tether the Meta 2 to a computer. According to Meta's head of developer relations, this was a deliberate choice (see the nearby sidebar, "Exploring the Meta 2"). Although this feature removes your ability to wander as freely through your environment, it offers more computing power and a larger FOV. The Meta 2 has a 90-degree FOV, almost as large as current-generation VR headsets and nearly three times as large as the HoloLens. This larger FOV helps position the Meta 2 as a device that could one day replace your traditional 2D screen.

The Meta 2 may be a good choice for your project if you require the extra power and wider FOV of the Meta 2 over the HoloLens and if your users will likely be mostly stationary (at a desk, for example). Similar to the HoloLens, the Meta 2 of this generation is considered an enterprise-level device, because not many consumers will have a Meta 2 available to them at this stage.

EXPLORING THE META 2

David Oh is the head of developer relations at Meta, and his involvement with Meta puts him on the front lines of AR design and development. I spoke with him to get his views on where AR is now and where it's headed in the near future.

Mr. Oh acknowledges that AR is currently still in the early adoption phase:

> Our current headset, the Meta 2, is made for developers, early tech adopters, and enthusiasts. A great application can take up to a year or more to create, and developers will have the opportunity to create innovative AR experiences ahead of our consumer device release.
>
> We've learned a great deal that has surprised us while creating the Meta 2. However, first we have to address what we learned from releasing our original device, the Meta One. Meta One was a sleeker version of the Meta 2. However that sleekness came with a price, which was a smaller FOV and a lower-resolution display. We learned that our customers didn't care about the smaller form factor, but cared more about a wide FOV, to see the entire hologram, and to display higher resolution to see more details in the 3D content. We delivered this with the Meta 2 and learned from our community of developers that the advantages previously mentioned made for a better augmented reality experience. We've also doubled down on our hand tracking algorithm. There are only a handful of companies focused on hand tracking, and we learned from our customers that having integrated hand tracking lends itself to a better experience as well.

I asked Mr. Oh about where Meta is now and where it's focused on being in the future. He replied:

> Our team of neuroscientists created a set of spatial guidelines to enable developers to build better augmented reality experiences. This year we've focused our time on creating an AR ecosystem. We aim to help developers hone their AR development chops and educate our customers and partners on how AR can be incorporated into their workflows to build productivity. By next year, we will have more tools for developers to build AR applications more efficiently, and will also grow our developer app distribution system. In five years, Meron Gribetz, our CEO and founder, is laser-focused on enabling Meta's headset to simply be a strip of glass that can be readily adopted by the mass market.

(continued)

(continued)

Unlike display technology (computers, televisions), which are passive, AR is interactive. You can literally walk around a hologram, or hold it in the palm of your hands. AR is a paradigm shift in technology. The most interesting thing about AR's future will be working in conjunction with other forms of input, such as haptic feedback controllers and haptic suits that allow you to feel holograms. Other inputs that will enhance our AR experiences are EEG [electroencephalograph] wearables, which monitor brain activity and can be used to augment the augmented reality experience.

Mr. Oh closed with his final thoughts regarding the future of AR:

People will be able to weave all the benefits of technology into their everyday lives. You'll be able to speak to anyone regardless of language, never get lost, diagnose any condition or problem you may have, and most importantly have all the world's information available in your real-world environment, and in real time. It's going to be awesome.

Figure 5-2 depicts users' visuals while working collaboratively with the Meta 2.

FIGURE 5-2:
The Meta 2 being utilized collaboratively in design.

Courtesy of Meta

Magic Leap

Magic Leap has long remained in the shadows of the AR world, emerging now and again to drop an impressive new teaser video of its technology. The company's products have been hidden from sight for seven years, and in that time Magic

Leap has shown enough to investors to raise around $2 billion in funding and amass a company value of almost $6 billion. However, little was known about the final form factor of its product until the end of 2017, when Magic Leap revealed the Magic Leap One Creator Edition.

The Magic Leap One is composed of three separate components:

>> **Lightwear:** The display goggles worn on a user's head

>> **Lightpack:** A pocket computer to power the visuals and accept input

>> **Control:** A six-degrees-of-freedom (6DoF) controller to allow input and haptic feedback to and from the system

The Magic Leap One is a standalone device that can be worn freely (like the HoloLens), but still needs to be tethered to its Lightpack computer (like the Meta 2). However, the small size of the Lightpack makes it clear that the Magic Leap One is intended for a more standalone, mobile experience than the Meta 2.

Similar to the HoloLens and Meta 2, the Magic Leap One has a number of onboard sensors to detect surfaces, planes, and other objects to allow for digitally mapping your physical environment. This should allow for robust object interaction with your environment (digital balls bouncing off your physical walls, virtual robots hiding under physical tables, and so on). Input is offered through the Control, but the Magic Leap system reportedly also supports a number of input modes such as voice, gesture, and eye tracking.

Owing in part to its computing brains being worn on a user's belt or in his pocket, the Magic Leap One headset is smaller than either the HoloLens or Meta 2. Visually, it appears closer to the simple glasses many people imagine when they think of "future AR technology," though the size is still bulkier than standard glasses. The FOV of the Magic Leap likely will fall somewhere between the smaller FOV of the HoloLens and the larger FOV of the Meta 2.

The Magic Leap system should be available to developers in 2018. Without a released product, it's difficult to determine just what market the first-generation Magic Leap One may be appropriate for. However, if you're consuming or developing for AR devices in 2018, the Magic Leap is a device not to overlook.

Mira Prism

The creators of the Mira Prism are taking a different approach to offering an affordable AR experience. Eschewing other AR headsets' inclusion of an onboard computer to power their glasses, the Mira Prism instead will utilize a mobile device to power the AR experience. All you need is a compatible mobile device and the Prism headset, and you're good to go.

The Prism is a clever solution to the cost problem that plagues many existing AR headsets. Most consumers are not comfortable spending upwards of $3,000 on a first-generation AR device with little consumer content available. Because the Prism is powered by your mobile device, the developer kit pricing for the headset hardware is only $99, a cost much more palatable to everyday consumers.

Many of the first-generation VR headsets approached this problem in the same way to great success. Google Cardboard, the Samsung Gear VR, and the Google Daydream are all examples of VR headsets that provide low-cost headset hardware that can be powered by a mobile device. The sales numbers of Cardboard, Daydream, and Gear VR far outstrip those of their more powerful but more expensive counterparts.

Mira looks to fill the market space between a mobile-device-only AR experience and the high-end standalone AR headsets. That market clearly existed for the VR world; Mira hopes to prove that the same market exists for AR experiences.

Figure 5-3 depicts the Mira Prism in use.

FIGURE 5-3: The Mira Prism in use.

Courtesy of Mira

Apple ARKit and Google ARCore

Although not the sci-fi glasses we have in mind when imagining the AR of the future, the way most users will experience AR for the first time is through their mobile devices. ARKit and ARCore were Apple's and Google's AR platforms targeted toward their iOS and Android base, respectively.

RE-IMAGINING MOBILE AR

Raymond Mosco is the head of developer strategy and Gabriella Meier is director of communication at Mira. They sat down with me to discuss the origins of the Mira Prism and their plans for the AR device in the near future.

Ms. Meier explained how Mira came about:

> Our founders were part of the inaugural class of USC's Jimmy Iovine and Andre Young Academy. They were always excited about AR technology, but the cost of buying AR headsets is prohibitive, especially for college students, which they were at the time. They researched a number of directions and were able to find a solution that worked well. They launched the device at Comic-Con in July 2017 and immediately sold out of preorders.

Mr. Mosco added:

> Our research has shown that handheld mobile device AR experiences provide user fatigue around the five minute mark. With that in mind, we created a novel way to create a hands-free augmented reality experience on a device less than 1/30th the cost of many other AR headsets currently on the market. And our team is made up of VR/AR industry veterans, so they understand the space we are working in and the scale of what we are trying to accomplish.

> Our goal has always been to become a consumer device. Keeping our cost low allows us to do that. Having said that, there are a number of existing industries that cannot justify the scale and hardware cost of some of the existing AR devices, so we are actually seeing a lot of interest in the enterprise space and have existing partnerships in place on that side of the fence as well.

Mr. Mosco also spoke to Mira's plans for the Prism moving forward:

> We are proud of where we are. Our SDK [software development kit] is currently built on top of Unity, and many of our developers that have built VR experiences for Gear VR or Daydream are able to port those experiences to the Prism with ease. And we have a lot of plans for the device moving forward. Our current device supports most iPhone devices; we are looking to support Android as well. Your phone isn't docked in the current version of our headset, which leaves things like the device charging port open to third-party hardware. We currently utilize marker tracking for our environmental tracking but definitely do not want to be tied to that. Our next steps will be finding ways of improving our computer vision solution and enabling gesture tracking on our device.

(continued)

(continued)

Ms. Meier added:

For the next two to three years, we are really going to focus on software, the Internet of Things, and how we can integrate our technology into your home, work, and beyond. Microsoft and Meta have shown the power of AR and how beneficial it can be. We're hoping to capitalize on that promise at consumer scale.

Note: The *Internet of Things* (IoT) refers to any physical device that can be connected to the Internet to exchange data. Almost any device can be turned into an IoT device with the addition of networking technology. Light bulbs, thermostats, security systems, televisions, vehicles — almost anything can be an IoT device. The addition of IoT technology to these devices enables them to communicate with other IoT devices or be controlled remotely.

The baseline features of both ARKit and ARCore are similar. Both ARKit and ARCore provide motion/positional tracking for their digital holograms, environmental understanding to detect things such as horizontal planes in a scene, and light estimation to detect the amount of ambient light in a scene and adjust the visuals of their holograms accordingly. ARKit 1.5 updates include support for vertical surfaces (walls) and 2D images as well. ARCore is looking to follow suit. These features all work together to allow 3D holograms to be placed in space in a room and treated as if they exist within the environment with you. Placing a virtual chess piece on the real-world table will make it appear (when viewed through your mobile device) as if the chess piece is on the table. Walk toward it, away from it, all around it — the virtual chess piece will still appear as if it is on the physical table.

Many current AR headsets use a type of projection for their visuals. This can lead to holograms that are never fully opaque but instead appear slightly transparent to the viewer. Because ARKit and ARCore are delivered integrated into the video feed of your mobile device, full opacity of your holograms is allowed. However, unlike many headsets, neither ARKit nor ARCore support a deep understanding of your environment. Occlusion is possible on these devices, but it's far from perfect and it takes extra work to achieve.

Due to its tight control over both the hardware and software, ARKit may have some advantages between its hardware and software integration. Meanwhile, ARCore has shown a bit of an advantage in its environmental mapping. ARCore manages to store a much larger data map of its surroundings, which can lead to more stable mapping.

Deciding between ARKit and ARCore likely comes down to the hardware either you or your target market prefers. The features and limitations of both ARKit and ARCore are similar enough that neither has a distinguishable advantage over the other currently. If you or your market prefers Android devices, ARCore is the way to go. If you lean toward Apple, ARKit is your best solution.

Figure 5-4 shows what a user sees in real life and in AR, with the app ARCore Solar System running on a Google Pixel device.

TIP

Though I mainly focus on wearables and mobile phone factors in this book, augmented reality/mixed reality/extended reality experiences are not limited to those form factors alone. In Chapter 3, I discuss other ways of experiencing this content, such as the first-down marker in football broadcasts. In Chapter 11, I discuss a few other ways of experiencing AR, such as projected AR experiences.

Identifying Near-Future Hardware

With so many devices still in development mode, it can be difficult to look forward to future hardware. Near-future hardware for AR is often just current-generation hardware that has yet to see release.

Heads-up displays

A number of upcoming smart glasses are worth a mention but may not fall under our strict definition of AR (which trends more toward mixed-reality executions).

Intel's recently announced Vaunt glasses fall into this category. The Vaunt offers an intriguing look at a potential future where AR glasses could actually look like glasses instead of a bulky headset. Vaunt unobtrusively projects information to the user in a form factor nearly indistinguishable from regular glasses. What it doesn't appear to be just yet is an AR headset along the lines of a HoloLens or Meta 2.

Vaunt currently provides a heads-up information display without the environment-sensing capabilities or high-resolution 3D display of current AR headsets. Instead of focusing on realistic image projection, the Vaunt wants to provide the type of information (such as notifications) most useful to you in the simplest form factor possible. Similar to the simple notifications you receive on your phone of an incoming call or text message, the Vaunt will surface these notifications at the edge of your vision within the glasses. You can then view or dismiss the messages with a casual glance. This type of execution is similar to the type of information the original Google Glass surfaced for users. It will be interesting to see if this is the type of information that's actually most useful to users, as opposed to the full-blown environment-sensing capabilities of AR devices.

Interestingly, Vaunt is currently powered by your mobile device (Android or iPhone) over Bluetooth, pushing the heavy calculation down to your phone. This undoubtedly helps facilitate the device's smaller hardware footprint, perhaps a pointer at things to come for future generations of AR headsets.

AR devices

To see where AR headsets will be focused next, look to where companies appear to be turning their attention. Hong Kong–based Realmax presented a prototype device at the 2018 Consumer Electronics Show that aligned closely to the current generation of AR headsets but with a 100-degree FOV. This would surpass nearly all currently available AR devices' FOV. Technology company Avegant is working on a "multi-focal planar approach" to solve one of AR's current challenges: replicating human depth perception and how our eyes shift focus between objects near and far. These two companies illustrate areas the next generation of AR headsets will focus on: greater FOV and ways to better replicate depth in AR headsets.

AR also has and will exist outside of just the headset. Companies such as WayRay have presented their own take on AR experiences in different form factors. WayRay's True AR navigation system is a holographic AR in-windshield product designed to be installed directly into your windshield by the manufacturer. In the near future, your new car purchase may include a built-in AR windshield to provide you locations, directions, speed, and any other information that may be pertinent to your trip.

Perhaps the biggest elephant in the room for near-future AR devices is Apple and its future AR intentions. Rumors have long swirled around the company's development of an AR headset, and CEO Tim Cook has made no secret of Apple's interest in AR technology. During the Utah Tech Tour, he praised AR and claimed that AR use would be as common as "eating three meals a day."

He also pointed out that AR had a long road ahead of it: "AR is going to take a while, because there are some really hard technology challenges there. But it will happen, it will happen in a big way, and when it does we will wonder how we ever lived without it. Like we wonder how we lived without our phone today." Apple has also filed numerous patents around the fields of VR/AR for items such as an Optical System for Head-Mounted Display. But no one but employees at Apple know for sure Apple's unannounced plans in the VR/AR space.

WARNING

Like most things in emerging technology fields, almost everything should be taken with a grain of salt until it's in consumers' hands. Companies such as Apple often file patents to cover their bases. Many things can happen between product rumors and actual product release to change the course of hardware development. The best way to handle upcoming developments is to stay on top of news about these devices' development cycles but regard each with a dose of skepticism until the device has reached consumers.

Comparing Current and Future Options

With so many AR companies yet to release their first-generation devices, comparing our current and future options can be difficult. Unlike the VR space, AR has not seen enough devices released to understand what consumers will respond well to. And understanding what consumers will react favorably to is what drives almost all future decisions.

However, we can take a look at some of the devices that have been released and consumers' reactions to them thus far. We can also look at what features future devices purport to bring to the table that improve upon current generations, and how those features may begin to influence other devices.

Current AR experiences can be segmented into two basic categories: the more powerful "desktop" headset experiences and less powerful mobile device experiences. *Desktop* is a bit of a misnomer here. Devices like the HoloLens are completely standalone, while the Magic Leap is powered by a portable computer worn by the user. The "desktop" headset experiences could be thought to include headsets such as the HoloLens, the Meta 2, and the upcoming Magic Leap One. All these devices are powered by an onboard, pocket, or tethered computer.

So far, the mobile device experiences have far been relegated to mobile devices utilizing ARKit and ARCore. However, mimicking the VR market, the AR market is also seeing the emergence of a potential middle-tier with devices such as the Mira Prism or experiences such as Star Wars: Jedi Challenges AR (see Chapter 11). These experiences utilize a mobile device but integrate it with specially designed AR hardware to enhance the AR experience offered by your mobile device alone.

Looking to the future, we can reasonably expect the high-end AR experience headsets to focus on finding ways to pack an improved FOV and top-of-the-line tracking into a smaller form factor. Finding a way to get close to the comfort level of true AR glasses is likely on the minds of most AR headset manufacturers.

Interestingly, among the high-end headsets, there doesn't appear to have been a huge rush to bring the price down to mass-consumption levels. Perhaps due to pro-hibitive manufacturing costs or a misalignment with device capabilities and mass-consumer expectations, for the time being the companies making high-end AR headsets seem content to focus on production for enterprise-level consumption.

TIP

The HoloLens, the Magic Leap, and the Meta 2 all share similarities (they're all AR headsets, after all), but they also have some major differences in their target markets, form factors, and functionality. Because they're all AR headsets, you'll often hear them all discussed in the same breath, compared and contrasted. In reality, they're all very different devices, and as the AR headset market matures, it wouldn't be surprising to see these devices all find their own appropriate markets and co-exist.

The future for middle- and lower-end, mobile-powered AR experiences is an interesting one. ARKit and ARCore will likely continue to see improvements made to their environmental detection and occlusion capabilities. But most experts believe that the final form for AR will be a wearable device, such as a headset or glasses, not a handheld mobile device. Devices like Mira Prism are proving that a middle-tier experience, powered by your mobile device, may be able to work as a wearable AR experience. Apple's intention to manufacture AR glasses appears strong, but nothing is certain in the hardware world. Regardless, based on the state of current generation of high-end headsets, it's hard to imagine that the next generation would be able to make the giant leap necessary to bring us from where we are now directly to the "stylish, futuristic AR glasses" phase with full immersion and realism.

Could an upcoming-generation iPhone or Android device be used to power a sleek pair of AR glasses similar to the way Intel's Vaunt glasses or Magic Leaps' Light-pack functions? After all, our mobile phones are already functionally high-powered computers. And devices like Magic Leap already bet on the idea that consumers won't be too bothered by being tethered to a separate device, as long as that device is inconspicuous enough to be comfortably worn. Perhaps that's the future that will tide us over for a generation or two until we reach the point, as predicted by Alex Kipman, where mobile devices will disappear completely, hav-ing been completely replaced by AR headsets.

3

Creating Content in Virtual and Augmented Reality

Evaluate your project to determine the proper technology execution.

Discover methods to plan out your virtual or augmented reality project, from determining your audience to exploring design principles and best practices.

Learn to create content for your VR and AR projects, from options for capturing the real world to creating 3D models to development tools.

Chapter **6**

Evaluating Your Project

With all the recent hype surrounding virtual reality (VR) and augmented reality (AR), it's easy to get caught up in the hype and decide that you need to find a way to incorporate those technologies in your next project. And that's understandable — VR and AR are exciting! But it's important to remember that VR and AR are just tools that can enhance your project when used correctly — or obfuscate your project when used incorrectly.

As with any project, assessing your business goals and project needs is paramount for providing users with a satisfying experience. A project built in VR or AR because it was the "cool" thing to do is bound for failure. Be sure to evaluate your project needs as you should with any project to determine if a VR or AR execution makes sense.

 When starting any project, don't let the technology drive your decision! The technology you decide to use should always fall out of the process of discovering what best addresses your users' needs.

WARNING

Assessing Your Project's Technology Needs

Before you decide on a project's technical execution, it's important to assess what technology will best fit that project's goals by asking yourself some questions. These are the same sorts of questions you should ask when starting *any* project, whether you decide to use VR, AR, or some other technology.

There are many other questions that can help plan a successful project, but these examples should help eliminate some of the noise and narrow down your possible technical executions. You may decide that a VR or AR execution is not the way to go. And that's okay! Deciding *not* to use a technology is just as valid a choice as deciding to use a technology. With great power comes great responsibility, and that includes the ability to decide when it may not be appropriate to utilize certain technologies, no matter how shiny and exciting they may be.

REMEMBER

If you answer the following questions and decide an execution in VR or AR is right for you, remember the pros and cons of each. At this stage, the deficiencies to keep in mind for evaluating your project are higher-level. For now, concentrate on evaluating your project based on what each technology can or can't accomplish at a high level. Avoid deep dives into technical deficiencies — you can deal with them after choosing a project execution. (Some of these deeper technical issues are addressed in Chapters 2 and 3.)

What is the elevator pitch for my project?

An *elevator pitch* is a brief synopsis of what the project will set out to accomplish. It's meant to be a quick speech (20 seconds or so, or the length of a short elevator ride) that is memorable and concise.

Elevator pitches are a good barometer for whether your project idea is intriguing and worth pursuing. If you can't sell someone on your idea within 20 seconds, it probably isn't defined enough and won't capture the interest of your intended audience. Defining your elevator pitch is the first step in helping distill your idea so you can decide what technologies to use to bring it to life.

TIP

An elevator pitch should identify a specific project goal and explain how you're seeking to solve it. It should define the main takeaway or benefit of the project in a way that makes people want to have it.

Let's turn to the world of manufacturing as an example. Suppose you run a factory producing widgets. Part of your widget business requires training new employees on complicated machinery, specifically the WidgetMaker 5000. The WidgetMaker 5000 has multiple users interacting with it at once to create your widgets, requiring a good deal of specialized training for your employees. In the past, training has happened either completely removed from the factory floor on computer kiosks, or in person, requiring machine experts to run trainees through using the machinery together.

You've analyzed your current training methods and found that the computer kiosks don't provide the same "real-world" scenarios your trainees will run into when using the actual machine, and pulling your highly skilled employees out of their jobs to train future employees has been a costly undertaking. Similarly, not all your training managers have the same training style, resulting in different trainees receiving different information.

You need to come up with a solution to quickly get new trainees up to speed. In a perfect world, this solution will give trainees experience with the actual machinery and free up your highly skilled employees to concentrate on their own work. Because it will be on the factory floor, it'll need to be a portable solution that can be moved about with ease.

At this point, you should be evaluating all manners of solutions — high tech and low tech. Whatever best solves your particular problem should be the path you follow.

An example of a poor elevator pitch for your application might be something like this:

> My application will train employees.

That pitch gives no detail concerning what the project is, and it'll be difficult to do any further evaluation on the right medium for the project.

Here's a more successful elevator pitch:

> My application will provide employees hands-on training with the WidgetMaker 5000 on the factory floor. This training will replicate real-world scenarios for trainees and help analyze how well that information is retained. Finally, it will free up our machine experts to focus on their jobs instead of training future employees.

REMEMBER

Fleshing out your elevator pitch will better position you as you begin drilling down to answer more specific questions on your project execution. You can repeatedly look back to your elevator pitch to ensure your project goals are all in alignment.

What are my goals and objectives?

Goals and objectives can help further define the project. Goals help establish *where* you want to go, and objectives say *how* you plan to get there.

Using the example elevator pitch from the preceding section, you could define the goals as follows:

>> Provide real-world usage to trainees on our machines.

>> Improve comprehension and retained knowledge of how to use the WidgetMaker 5000.

>> Free up machine experts from the need to teach trainees.

Then you can begin to define more specific objectives that support these goals. The objectives for this example project might include the following:

>> Create a method for trainees to use actual machinery during training.

>> Build a hands-free, self-guided tool for trainees to step themselves through training alongside other trainees.

>> Build an evaluation method for testing retained knowledge.

>> Create an application that can be used over and over by trainees, ensuring that all trainees receive the same knowledge.

What problem does my project uniquely solve?

In answering this question, you start to see where VR and AR choices separate themselves from more standard project executions. Unlike traditional website or mobile/desktop apps, VR and AR technologies are still in their infancies, making many ideas and executions unique in their own right simply because not a lot of companies have developed applications yet using these technologies.

However, an idea's uniqueness does not necessarily mean that it should be created. A "Pet Rock Simulator" built in VR may be unique, but it doesn't stand on its merits as a good idea.

Many of the ideas you have for VR and AR executions may have already been done in more traditional media. Evaluating those traditional projects to see what they do well, where they may be deficient, and what new and better ideas your project will be bringing to the table can help establish a baseline of features you need to incorporate.

WARNING

Don't fall in love with a technology over the best fit for your project! Always evaluate your project against the merits of any technology. If a problem can be better solved using a traditional method, it's likely not the best fit for a VR- or AR-based solution.

Returning to the previous example, notice that some of the objectives could be solved with traditional 2D methods. For example, some factories already utilize 2D video or computer applications for stepping their trainees through how to use their machinery.

In the case of the WidgetMaker 5000 training, however, the 2D experience couldn't provide the same depth of experience that a VR or AR execution could provide. In this scenario, you've already tried utilizing traditional 2D methods (in this case, computer kiosks) and found that they didn't provide the same level of depth that being on the factory floor with the machines provides. Trainees who have utilized your current 2D training have had more accidents and mistakes than those who have had training on the actual machine. It seems like your current 2D training isn't able to properly replicate the harried environment of your factory floor, nor the complicated nature of interacting with your WidgetMaker 5000.

This leads you to believe that something that can provide training more closely to what real-world usage of the WidgetMaker 5000 is the better way to go. Both VR and AR could still conceivably be in the running for your project execution at this point. VR could simulate the factory environment and machine interactions virtually. AR could provide training directly on the factory floor, overlaying training on top of the machine itself. You should continue evaluating these executions as you move forward.

Who is the target market?

If you've made it this far in deciding that your project is a good fit for a VR or AR execution, defining your target market should help further narrow your project's execution.

Is your target market older? Younger? Technically savvy? Do you want to aim for the broadest market possible or a smaller, more controlled subset? Will your users be trained to use the software or will they have to learn it on their own?

Defining the target market will drive many of the other choices you make further down the line. For example, if you're aiming for the broadest possible adoption, you'll want to create applications targeting the devices with the broadest reach. It wouldn't make much sense to create an application that runs only on devices that not many users have.

WARNING

As you look to define your market, be wary of the reach of the technology you choose to execute against. Though the VR and AR markets are maturing, keep an eye on adoption rates as they relate to your project execution. Building an experience that would require millions of users to have access to AR glasses may not be the best choice in the current marketplace.

In the case of the WidgetMaker 5000 training application, broad adoption isn't important. Your market is defined for you: It will only be for trainees within your factory. Such an application likely wouldn't see any public release. Instead, it can be tailored toward a small group of individuals. In this case, you have the luxury of building the product for the hardware platform that it will perform best on, instead of having to potentially aim for the hardware you think most consumers have available. Being able to tailor your application for a certain device allows you to target that particular device's strengths and work around its weaknesses.

For applications that might require more public adoption focused on larger markets, you may find it necessary to build for multiple hardware executions or form factors. In these scenarios, you'll need to keep in mind that each device has its own strengths and weaknesses that you'll need to address.

What should the end-user experience be?

If you've gotten this far and you have yet to decide on a technological execution, this should help solidify your choice of direction. VR and AR share some technical similarities, but the end-user experience for both is vastly different.

Do you want to create a completely immersive environment or just augment an existing one? Do you require interaction with other users in the real world, or is this a solo experience? Do you need the highest possible graphic fidelity? Is this a sitting experience? A standing experience? Will a user need the ability to freely move around the environment? Should the user experience be portable? Easy to set up?

Returning again to the example WidgetMaker 5000 application, one requirement was the capability to interact with the training materials and with both the machine and other users in the real world. A portable experience is a must because users will need to bring it to the factory floor, as is the ability to move about freely around the machine. Trainees must also be able to utilize the training hands-free, potentially navigating with only their voices as they self-guide through the training while on the machine itself.

With all these features in mind, your technical execution becomes fairly clear. Although VR can virtually create a reasonable facsimile of your factory floor, you want your users directly on the real machine. Additionally, your WidgetMaker 5000 requires multiple users working on it together simultaneously. Again, a VR experience could likely include digital avatars to virtualize this experience, but in this instance, AR likely makes more sense. AR will allow for social interaction with users in the real world far more easily than VR. Additionally, AR will allow trainees to be interacting directly, hands-on with the machine itself.

In the WidgetMaker 5000 example, AR proved to be the execution that made the most sense. However, there are plenty of scenarios where VR's strengths make more sense (or where neither technology makes sense). Ultimately, the choice of technology for this project comes down to what features have the highest priority for the client.

REMEMBER

Make sure that you're properly evaluating all these items before deciding on an execution. Sometimes, a VR execution will be perfect. Other times, an AR execution makes more sense. And other times, neither is a good fit.

Choosing Virtual Reality

VR fully immerses users in the content, creating new experiences and environments, and more than any technology to date, encouraging users to have empathy for new people and situations. In this section, I walk you through its strengths and weaknesses in more detail.

Strengths

VR technology provides these benefits:

» **Complete immersion:** Due to the closed-off nature of current VR executions, users will be fully focused on the content of your application, undistracted by email, phone messages, or any other outside events. This complete immersion is perfect for apps that need a user's undivided attention, such as videos, storytelling, gaming, and educational applications.

» **Transporting the user:** VR can do just what its name implies — create a virtual environment that feels like reality to the end user. A user in an AR app is generally still aware of his current real-world surroundings, but a user in VR can be completely *unaware* of his surroundings. Sharing a small, one-bedroom apartment in New York with five friends? Strap on a VR headset and you can feel as if you live in a vast mansion. Flying on a transatlantic flight in cramped coach seating? Put on a VR headset and you'll feel like you're in your own empty movie theater, viewing content on a 70-foot screen.

» **Creating empathy:** VR can place users in situations they never would've imagined, including in the shoes of others. This ability to create a shared experience between users is unique to VR and one of its greatest strengths.

» **Technological maturation:** VR as a technology has been on the rise since the introduction of consumer-grade VR with the Oculus Rift DK1 in 2013. Many of the big names in tech, including Facebook, Google, Microsoft, and Samsung, have released one or more VR headsets and have plans to release more. AR interest has seen an uptick with the introduction of ARKit from Apple and ARCore from Google, but VR still leads in this category for consumer devices.

Weaknesses

As compelling as its benefits are, VR isn't a perfect platform on which to execute your project. Here are some of its drawbacks:

>> **Limited interaction with the outside world:** Users in VR are completely closed off from the rest of the world, which can be impractical for certain types of projects. It isn't uncommon for users in room-scale VR to need a fairly open space for their experience. Otherwise, they run the danger of knocking into other people or objects.

>> **Lack of strong social interaction:** The experiences offered by VR can be incredible, but they also can seem isolating. The environments VR can create feel so real that users expect the social interactions to be realistic, too. However, the technology for making social interactivity in VR seem real isn't quite there yet. The lack of eye contact and the inability to see a user's true facial expression in most social VR apps can leave the social experience of VR wallowing in the awkward uncanny valley between no social interaction and true personal connection.

Companies such as Facebook, Sansar, and Pluto are all working on their own visions of social interaction and personal connection in the future VR space, but it's still early days for this technology. Defining the social experience will be a big problem to solve in the next few years for both VR and AR.

Figure 6-1 shows a screen shot of users interacting via their virtual avatars in Facebook's social VR app, Facebook Spaces.

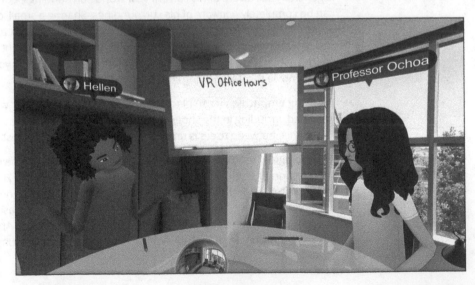

FIGURE 6-1:
Users' avatars interact in Facebook Spaces.

- » **Cost and hardware:** Some applications can be run both inside and outside a headset, such as YouTube's 360 videos. However, without the headset you've effectively removed the "reality" from VR and you're just looking at another 2D application. Regardless of the flavor of VR you choose, users need some sort of hardware to truly experience your application as VR. Low-cost hardware such as Google Cardboard is widely available, but it can't support high-performance VR applications. For higher-end VR experiences, the cost of the VR hardware (and the computer to run these experiences) can be enough of a barrier that even those with a strong interest in VR may be put off until the price comes down or, perhaps worse, experience a lower-end VR experience and think that's all VR has to offer.

- » **Not a frictionless experience:** In marketing terminology, a *frictionless* experience is one that doesn't require a consumer to go through any extra trouble to use. As it currently stands, VR technology is far from frictionless. Many VR experiences (especially on the higher end) require a specific location for your VR setup consisting of plenty of room to move about in real-world space and powerful external hardware for running VR. All this can lead to users being less likely to use their VR setup, if only due to the friction of having to set aside a time and place to get their VR fix. The second generation of headsets, featuring inside-out tracking and often fully self-contained, tether-less headsets, will hopefully take steps toward making the VR experience more frictionless.

- » **Mass market share:** Although VR is making strides to gain widespread consumer adoption, it hasn't achieved critical mass yet at the same level as the computer or the mobile phone. So far, VR headsets, especially high-end headsets, have still been mainly a plaything of early adopters. Facebook and Google both hope to improve this even further by releasing affordable, midrange second-generation headsets in 2018. However, if massive user adoption at the level of, say, mobile devices, is a requirement for your project or product, keep in mind that you probably won't get it with current VR execution.

Choosing Augmented Reality

AR's strengths dovetail with many of VR's weaknesses. The nature of AR and its access to the real world make it a perfect candidate for applications that require real-world interaction with other users or objects.

Apple CEO Tim Cook has claimed that he expects AR to be bigger than VR for that very reason. In an interview with ABC News in 2016, Cook said "Virtual reality sort of encloses and immerses the person into an experience that can be really cool, but probably has a lower commercial interest over time. Less people will be interested in that."

Whether Cook's bullish take on the commercial interest AR will prove correct remains to be seen, but his take on the different strengths of VR and AR is on the money.

Strengths

Here are some of the benefits that AR offers:

>> **Social and real-world interaction:** The ability to interact with people or objects in the real world is the core concept of AR. Augmenting the real world with digital artifacts expands on what the real world can do. And because AR doesn't close the user off from the rest of the world, it can more readily be used socially. When using an AR headset, glasses, or a mobile device, a user isn't closed off from the world, which allows for much smoother social interaction with those around you. After the release of the AR game Pokémon GO for Android and iOS, it wasn't uncommon to come across strangers in the real world exchanging notes on digital artifacts such as Pokémon and gym locations. This merging of the real and the virtual is precisely the area in which AR excels.

>> **Mostly frictionless:** Due in part to AR's openness to the real world, experiencing AR can be more frictionless to use than VR, especially the lower-end, mobile executions. Because current AR experiences don't close the user off from the real world, it can feel nearly as frictionless as opening an app on a mobile device, which is already familiar for millions of users. The higher-end experiences such as Meta 2 and HoloLens can require a bit more investment of a user's time and may require a specific location (because Meta 2 is tethered to a computer). Overall however, AR experiences seem to generate less friction for a user than most current VR experiences.

>> **Limited extra hardware required for mobile executions:** With the mobile versions of Google's ARCore and Apple's ARKit, millions of users are walking around with an AR-capable device in their pockets. The AR executions these technologies allow are fairly simple, but they open up a massive user base of potential consumers for your application.

Weaknesses

AR has its drawbacks in addition to its benefits. Here's a quick look at them:

» **Technological maturation:** Even with Google and Apple pushing AR capability to the forefront with their mobile releases, AR is still far behind VR in terms of technological maturity. This lack of technical maturity can reveal itself through a number of other deficiencies (for example, device access, lack of content, potential unknowns, and so on).

» **Mass market share:** Outside of mobile AR, the consumer market for AR devices is virtually nonexistent. Only a handful of companies currently are producing devices at close to consumer scale, and none of these devices is currently marketed toward consumers, only toward developers, businesses, and enterprise.

» **Device access:** AR has only a handful of companies competing in the low-, mid-, and high-end price ranges, with most of those devices still in beta or targeted toward enterprise and not consumers directly. Most users won't have access to an AR device (outside of mobile AR) for some time. For some projects, this may not be an issue. You may be able to control and provide access to hardware as the project requires. For a great many projects, however, this could be a nonstarter.

WARNING

Carefully consider device access for your next project. If you're planning on developing for AR and the mobile form factor works for you, great — you're all set! If the mobile form factor doesn't fit your project requirements, you'll be extremely limited in the market for which you can currently develop.

» **Lack of content:** AR is still in its very early stages. There is a noticeable lack of content, especially high-end content, for users to experience. This lack of content goes hand-in-hand with AR's technical maturation and device access. As AR matures technically and as content creators begin to get their hands on AR devices, more and better content will begin to roll out much as it has for VR. However, we have yet to reach that point. It will likely take a mass consumer release of an AR device to truly jumpstart the content creation race.

» **Limited immersion:** AR's strength can also be a weakness, especially AR within the mobile device form factor. The fundamental basis of AR is rooted in the ability to interact with the real world. That offers many benefits, but at the cost of potential interruptions to the users' experience. If your project will require any sort of fully realized artificial reality, or require a user to stay fully immersed within your reality without distraction, AR probably isn't the choice for you.

>> **The unknown:** The relative immaturity of AR comes at a price of the unknown. VR is still be in its infancy as a technology as well, but there is a generally agreed-upon road map pointing to where things seem to be headed. It's still possible for a startup to come along and shake up the VR industry with a new hardware/software, but the general direction VR is headed is seemingly established.

AR hasn't reached that state of predictability yet. Apple's ARKit and Google's ARCore, while not entirely unexpected for industry insiders, were surprises for the consumer market. Apple's AR Glasses are still an unknown, and Magic Leap's entry into the AR space is in early stages. These products or others could completely change the AR road map.

Currently, developing a project for AR requires embracing the unknown, and building your project accordingly. Some companies can align with these tenets, while others may be uncomfortable with the ever-changing landscape and be better off finding a different execution for their projects until the unknown becomes more, well, known.

Chapter **7**

Planning Your Virtual Reality Project

ongratulations! You've decided to take the plunge and create content for virtual reality (VR) consumption. Now, you may find yourself wondering where to start. It can be daunting to jump into a new technology without understanding everything that may go into planning that project.

This chapter explains the "getting started" phase of VR project development. Here, you find out what goes into planning a VR project, including defining the scope, target audience, hardware support, and timeline.

I also explain some VR design principles and best practices that have emerged from trial and error over thousands of applications of VR technology. Incorporating these principles and best practices will save you time, money, and countless headaches down the road.

Defining Your Virtual Reality Project

If you're at this point in your project planning, I assume you're confident that VR is appropriate for your project. I you aren't sure, turn back to Chapter 6 and work through the steps to determine whether your project is a good fit for VR in the first place. This may be the most important decision of all.

There are a number of standard project practices applicable to any project. These include steps such as clarifying goals, creating project specification documents, defining project budget, and defining project scope. I don't cover most of these subjects in depth in this chapter because their usage in a VR project is nothing out of the ordinary. However, there are some topics that, while applicable to both standard projects and VR, have unique ramifications with VR projects. Defining your timeline is one example — it's a general requirement for any project, but there are special considerations for VR projects.

Planning can be tricky. Each of these choices can affect and influence the others. Deciding how you envision your VR execution can determine the hardware you'll have to use. Determining the hardware to support can force your hand in defining your audience. And so on and so on.

TIP

Prioritize what's most important for your project and work from there. For example, if the level of user immersion is the most important component of your project, that likely means building to the best possible VR hardware specifications, which may end up limiting your market. If reaching the largest possible market is more important to you than final project execution, you may want to start with finding the hardware with the largest market share, and then work backward from there to determine how being limited to that hardware's capabilities will influence your project's level of immersion.

Determining your project execution

For VR, determining your *project execution* — how you'll complete the work to best meet your project's requirements — will require answering a number of questions. These questions will cover the goals of your project; your users; and the design and development of your application. Answering these questions is an important step. You often may find yourself with conflicting answers. Try to address all the following points; then prioritize which ones are most important to you. (Is it market penetration of headsets? Level of immersion in the headset? Support for a particular platform?)

REMEMBER

If you've reached this point in the book, I assume you've already worked through the steps in Chapter 6 to evaluate your project needs at a general level. If you have yet to do so, I encourage you to review those steps before proceeding.

Ask yourself the following questions to help determine your project execution:

>> **What is your vision for a successful project?** Your users' wants and needs should be the ultimate decision driver, of course, but establishing your own baseline can also be useful. What will it take for *you* to consider this a

successful project? Hitting certain sales numbers? Reaching installed user base numbers? Execution on a new or untested platform?

>> **What level of immersion and realism does your project require?** The level of immersion you require for your project can drive the type of headset you build for, the amount of development time, the development tools you may choose to utilize, and so on. A multi-user open-world real-time VR game with a high level of immersion and realism would likely require a large team of highly specialized designers and developers, a long project timeline, and the graphics processing capabilities of a high-end tethered VR headset. On the other hand, a business looking for a way to distribute 3D videos of their interiors for marketing purposes may set its timeline and requirements much lower.

Defining your audience

In order to define your audience, you need to consider a number of factors. Some of the factors are quite broad, such as who this application will help, how it will help them, and what other applications they may be using currently that accomplish a similar task. Other items to consider will be more targeted, such as whether you're developing for a tech-savvy audience that's comfortable exploring or a novice audience that will need a lot of guidance. You should also decide whether your experience will be targeted at the broadest audience possible who might be using a variety of hardware devices, or a small subset of known users using a specific device type.

The more targeted audience-based questions may help start to drive other application decisions. If, for example, you want to reach the largest number of users, you'll consult the latest sales numbers to define that market. Using current sales numbers would likely find you targeting the mobile VR marketplace (Samsung Gear VR, Google Daydream, and so forth), which in turn would drive you to create content for those platforms. If, instead, your target market were high-end gamers, you'd likely find yourself putting mobile VR aside and developing for desktop/gaming system devices such as Windows Mixed Reality, HTC Vive, and Oculus Rift.

Determining hardware support

There are plenty of VR options to choose from — from simple mobile-based VR viewers to full-scale VR gaming rigs with the highest resolution and realism available. You need to decide what VR hardware you want your application to support. This decision is intertwined with the others in this chapter. Here's an overview of your options:

>> **Low-powered mobile experiences:** If you target the lowest-powered mobile experiences, such as Google Cardboard, you'll be very restricted when it comes to the type of experience you can create. Most Cardboard experiences are little more than viewing experiences. You won't be able to offer users much interactivity, because you'll be hamstrung by the device's capabilities. Targeting the lowest-powered mobile experiences may also mean that your *test matrix* (the devices you need to check to make sure your application works on) could be very broad, because a user could be on any number of devices that support Google Cardboard.

On the upside, developing an experience targeting the lowest common denominator of headset often means that porting this same experience to higher-powered headsets will be a relatively easy task.

Good candidates for this level of hardware support are simple applications that are little more than 360 viewers with limited interactivity, or businesses looking to market themselves by supplying branded devices to an unknown hardware user base. For example, McDonald's in Sweden created what it dubbed "Happy Googles," Happy Meal boxes that could be turned into VR viewers similar to a Google Cardboard (see Figure 7-1). The experience ran off of the consumer's device, allowing McDonald's to create an engaging experience while providing little more than a standard Happy Meal box.

FIGURE 7-1: McDonald's Sweden instructional video for creating "Happy Googles."

Google Cardboard headsets are generally fragile, but they're also relatively low cost, making them a good choice for situations where damage concerns may exist. For example, middle schools and high schools looking to provide a

VR experience to students at a low cost may opt for inexpensive Google Cardboard headsets.

» **Mid-level mobile headsets:** Targeting a mid-level mobile headset (such as Google Daydream or Gear VR) offers decent market penetration, though only a smaller subset of Android devices can run on Google Daydream or Gear VR. This limits your potential audience, but unlike Google Cardboard, you have a baseline for the minimum level of performance. Only certain higher-powered mobile devices are compatible with Daydream and Gear VR. This smaller subset of devices also means that when testing your application, you'll likely have a smaller subset of devices to test against. Plus, experiences that run well on Daydream often can fairly easily be ported to Gear VR, and vice versa.

However, remember that mobile experiences still come at a performance cost. They don't come close to the level of immersion that can be offered by the higher-end externally powered devices. Current mobile executions don't offer physical movement (or room-scale movement) within VR (though the next generation of mobile VR devices seeks to cross that barrier). They also typically have lower refresh rates of the display, as well as a lower resolution than the high-end headsets.

» **High-level VR experiences:** The highest-level ("desktop") VR experiences can offer a far more immersive experience than the mobile-based VR headsets. Most of these high-level devices allow some sort of room-scale experience — that is, physical movement within the virtual environment. The level of realism offered can engage the user far more than less-expensive hardware options are capable of. The hardware you need to test against when creating your VR application is strictly defined, and that can help make testing and debugging simpler.

On the downside, the size of the high-end market is currently smaller than the mobile VR market, and development for these devices can be more complicated. The higher-end headsets can have more friction for users — meaning that, unlike mobile VR apps, they may require a user to set aside time and space to use. Porting a higher-level experience to lower-level ones can be much more difficult. A number of features that work for high-level experiences don't work at all on lower-level devices. Your entire app concept may need to be rethought, or it may literally be impossible to execute on lower-level devices.

Good use cases for this type of experience are high-end games, premium entertainment applications, and technical learning applications with a well-defined user base. Any applications that are looking at targeting the highest level of immersion for mass consumer devices belong here. Many games, entertainment applications, location-based solutions, or industry-specific executions where the hardware will be a known commodity build toward these high-end experiences.

TIP

Don't get too caught up in thinking that the best experiences have to be as high-powered as possible. The better performance offered by "desktop" VR is always a plus, but performance doesn't necessarily make for a great experience. There are millions of mobile apps in the Apple App Store and Google Play Store that are far more popular than they ever would have been if they were built to run only on more powerful desktop PCs. What's more, a number of mobile VR apps perform fairly processor-intensive work (such as live video streaming) without issue.

All that is to say you can create engaging experiences in both mobile and desktop VR. Make sure to evaluate your project based on project needs and feature requirements, and not by processor speed alone.

Defining your timeline

Defining a timeline is vital for any project, but VR development time can be difficult to estimate at this stage. With VR still in its infancy, a project with a long timeline will run parallel to advances in the VR industry. Consequently, the cutting-edge project you began developing nine months ago may no longer be so cutting-edge when it finally comes to market, thanks to the rapid advances taking place in the industry. Maybe a new headset has been released, making the older headsets you had been targeting appear dated. Maybe a new piece of haptic hardware has been released. Or maybe it's a piece of software that changes the way content in VR is being created.

Thankfully, this frenetic pace of development is becoming a bit more predictable for VR. Plenty of advances are happening almost daily, but many of them don't directly affect consumers or won't directly affect them for some time. Mass consumer devices take time to create, evaluate, and release to the public.

TIP

When estimating your project's timeline, consider how it will align with any upcoming hardware devices or software applications. You may need to support new devices that launch between project inception and completion, especially if the devices directly intersect your target market. For example, any VR project planning on launching in late 2018 should consider when the Oculus Santa Cruz (or any other HMDs) may be launching around the same time and how that should affect your project launch.

Fortunately, you'll likely have some advance notice before a major new product appears on the market. Companies developing hardware for large consumer bases typically announce a timeline of what they expect to launch in the near future. Many of the large headset manufacturers such as Oculus and HTC have announced what consumers can expect in the next 6 to 12 months. That doesn't tell the entirety of those companies' plans for VR in the future, but it can at least provide a general road map and timeline of where things are headed.

VR is still a fledgling industry. Out-of-the-blue releases still occasionally happen. If you plan on becoming part of an emerging industry such as VR, you may find a good deal of your job is simply keeping up with all the changes. It can be one of the most enjoyable parts of the job, but also one of the most frustrating. If you're hoping for an industry with more stability that requires less time exploring future trends, VR may not be for you — at least not until the dust settles a bit.

Exploring Design Principles in Virtual Reality

The term *design principles* refers to a set of ideas or beliefs that are held to be true across all projects of that type. Some examples of design principles within two-dimensional design include designing on a grid or creating a visual hierarchy of information to direct users to the most important information first. These principles, or agreed-upon standards, are created over many years, after much experimentation and trial and error. And although these principles can be broken, they should be broken only for good reason.

Because VR is such a new field, we're still in the process of discovering what its design principles are. Often, in order to find out what design principles work well, you have to find out what does *not* work well. Best practices and standards will emerge over time as the VR community grows and more mass consumer VR applications are produced. In the meantime, there are a number of generally agreed upon standards for VR, regardless of the platform for which you may be designing. I review them in the following sections.

Starting up

Upon initially entering an experience, users often need a moment to adjust to their new virtual surroundings. A simple opening scene where users can adjust to the environment and controls can be a good way to help them acclimate to your experience. Allow the user to acclimate themselves to your application and move into your main application experience only when they're ready.

Figure 7-2 shows how the game Job Simulator handles startup. Job Simulator's entry screen establishes a clean environment and asks the user to complete a simple task similar to the controls used within the game in order to start the game. This gives the user time to adjust to the game environment and get accustomed to the controls that she'll use in the game.

FIGURE 7-2:
The intro
screen for Job
Simulator game.

Focusing the user's attention

VR is much less linear than experiences within a traditional 2D screen. In VR, you must allow the user the freedom to look around and explore the environment. This freedom of exploration can make it difficult when you need to attract the user's attention to certain portions of your application. A director in a 2D movie can frame the user's vision exactly where he wants it. As the director within a 3D space, however, you have no idea if the user might want to face your main content or be focused on some other part of the scene. You cannot force a user to look a certain direction — forcing a users' view in VR is one of the quickest ways to trigger simulator sickness.

However, there are a number of ways to focus the user's attention where you want it. Subtle 3D audio cues can guide a user to the area where action is occurring. Lighting cues can be used as well. For example, you can draw the user's attention by brightening the parts that you want them to look at and darkening parts that you want to deemphasize. Another way is to reorient the content itself within the app to match the direction the user is facing.

In what is perhaps the easiest solution, some applications simply put messaging within their 3D environment instructing the user to turn around and face wherever they want the user's attention to be focused. This technique is also used in room-scale games in which a user may only have a limited number of sensors available to track his motion in the real world. It can be easy to get turned around in room-scale VR, and putting up a message can help a user re-orient himself in relation to the real-world sensors. Figure 7-3 shows this method in use in the game Robo Recall. The messaging is blunt, but it gets the point across for where the user should focus.

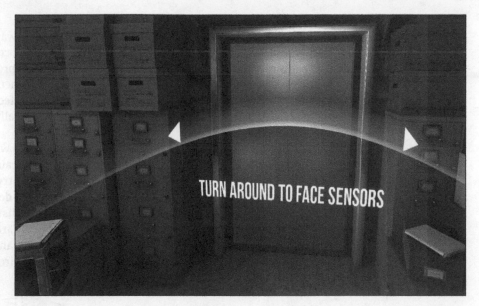

FIGURE 7-3: Robo Recall instructing a user to re-orient himself.

REMEMBER

Whichever way you choose to handle focusing the user's attention, realize that in VR, users must have freedom of choice. That freedom of choice can conflict with what you may want them to do. Finding ways to allow that freedom of choice while also focusing the user where you want him is a vital part of a well-designed VR experience.

Understanding the comfort zone

With traditional 2D design, user interface (UI) has been restricted to certain canvas sizes. Whether it's the size of the browser or the size of the monitor, something has always placed a limit on the dimensions in which your user interface could exist. VR removes those restrictions. Suddenly a 360-degree canvas is at your disposal to design with! UI can be anywhere and everywhere!

Before you start throwing interface elements 360 degrees around your users, there are a number of best practices to keep in mind for making your experience comfortable. If a user must rotate her head too much, strain to read interface text, or flail her arms about in an attempt to use your UI, it will most likely lead to a poor experience and cost you users.

Alex Chu of Samsung Research, in his presentation "VR Design: Transitioning from a 2D to a 3D Design Paradigm" (https://youtu.be/XjnHr_6WSqo), provides a number of measurements for the minimal, optimal, and maximum distance objects should appear away from a user. In the presentation, Chu discusses optimal distances for 3D object presentation. As objects get closer to your face, your eyes will begin to strain to focus on them. Around 0.5 meter away from the user and closer is typically the distance where this strain begins to occur; Oculus recommends a minimum distance of at least 0.75 meter in order to prevent this strain from occurring. Between that minimum distance and about 10 meters is where the strongest sense of stereoscopic depth perception occurs. This effect begins to fade between 10 and 20 meters, and after 20 meters, the effect basically disappears.

These limitations give you an area between 0.75 and 10 meters in which you should display your main content to the user. Content any closer will cause eye strain to your users, and any farther out will lose the 3D effect you're trying to achieve. These guidelines are illustrated in Figure 7-4, which is a top-down view of the user. Circle A represents the minimum comfortable viewing distance for users, 0.5 meter. You should avoid placing content within this space. Circle B represents the sweet spot where content should be placed: between 0.75 and 10 meters. At 20 meters, a user's stereoscopic depth perception disappears (circle C).

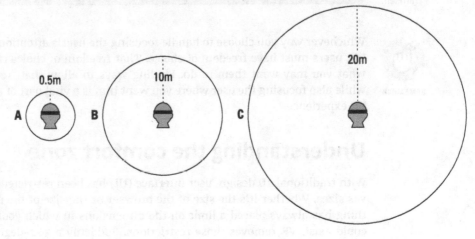

FIGURE 7-4:
Comfortable
viewing
distances
in VR.

TIP

As the resolution of VR headsets improves, the stereoscopic effect may be retained the farther you get from the user, past the 20 meters or so in which the effect disappears today. For now however, the 20-meter mark is still a good rule of thumb for content design.

Google VR Designer Mike Alger, in his "VR Interface Design Pre-Visualization Methods" presentation (https://youtu.be/id86HeV-Vb8), also discusses the range of motion users can comfortably rotate their heads horizontally and vertically. Chu and Alger both mention that the range users can comfortably rotate their heads horizontally is 30 degrees, with a maximum rotation of 55 degrees. Combined with the field of view (FOV) of the higher-end, tethered headsets (averaging around 100 degrees), this gives a user a range of around 80 degrees to each side for comfortable viewing of the main content, and around 105 degrees to each side for peripheral content. When displaying content to your users, focus on keeping your main content within the user's horizontal comfort zone of viewing.

Figure 7-5 displays these values in a top-down view. Circle A is an average horizontal FOV for a VR headset. Circle B represents the area a user can comfortably see when rotating his head (the FOV of the headset plus a comfortable rotation of 30 degrees to each side). Circle C represents the maximum rotation of a user's head (55 degrees to each side) combined with the FOV of a headset. For your applications, you should likely focus on keeping content within the comfortable viewing area as represented by circle B. As FOV of headsets improve, these values will change to allow further visibility to the side. However, it is worth noting that most headsets (with a few exceptions such as Pimax) seem to be unconcerned with greatly improving FOV in the upcoming second generation of devices. Regardless, you'll be able to use the same calculations to determine the comfortable viewing area yourself in the future.

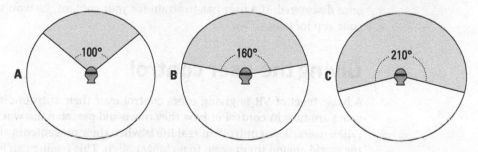

FIGURE 7-5: Horizontal comfort zone for head movement.

Similarly, there is a comfortable range of motion for users to rotate their heads vertically. The comfort zone here is around 20 degrees comfortably upward, with a maximum of 60 degrees upward, and downwards around 12 degrees comfortably and 40 degrees maximum.

Figure 7-6 displays the comfortable range of motion for vertical FOV. Most headsets don't publish their vertical FOV, only horizontal. We use 100 degrees as an average vertical FOV, as represented by circle A. The comfortable viewing zone is represented by circle B with the rotation combined with the headset FOV. A user can comfortably rotate her head upward 20 degrees and downward 12 degrees. Circle C represents the extremes, with a maximum vertical rotation upward of 60 degrees and a maximum rotation downward of 40 degrees.

TIP

Although horizontal head movements are a small annoyance, vertical head rotation can be extremely taxing to a user to hold for long periods of time. Vertical FOV of headsets is also not typically published, so it's approximated here. On some headsets, it may be even smaller. As a best practice, try to keep the user's vertical head rotation to a minimum for the most comfortable user experience.

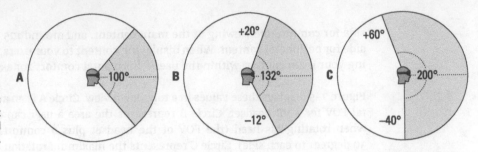

FIGURE 7-6:
Vertical comfort
zone for head
movement.

Using the preceding information, you can establish a set of guidelines for placing content relative to the user. You can place content wherever you like of course, but important content should stay within the areas where the horizontal, vertical, and viewing distance comfort zones converge. Content in areas outside of these zones is less likely to be seen. If you're creating content that is meant to be hidden, or only discoverable through deep exploration, areas outside of the comfort zone can be good areas to place that content. However, avoid keeping your content there once discovered. If a user has to strain for your content, he won't stick around in your app for long.

Giving the user control

A basic tenet of VR is giving users control over their surroundings. In real life, users are fully in control of how they move and perceive the world around them. When users "lose control" in real life is when their movements and perception of the world around them seem to no longer align. This feeling can be equated to the feeling of being inebriated, or what's commonly referred to as *simulator sickness* (discussed later in this chapter).

WARNING

Simulator sickness should be avoided at all costs — users hate it and it will drive them away from your product. You want to ensure your users always feels in control. Their movements should always be mirrored by movement within the virtual environment. Additionally, you should never wrest control away from the user. You don't want to move the user around without her actions triggering that movement. Also, don't rotate or reposition a user's view of the virtual environment. If a repositioning is needed, it is advisable to fading to black for a moment, then fade back up to your repositioned environment. Although it's not optimal, fading to black (triggered by a user's action of course) and back in can be a way to reposition the users environment without your user feeling as if she has relinquished control.

Understanding locomotion

Locomotion in VR has yet to be gracefully solved. One of the strengths of VR is the ability to create compelling environments that a user wants to explore. But it doesn't matter how compelling an environment is if a user can't move about to explore it.

If your experience is more than a static, seated experience, you need to enable users to move about your space. You can create a method for a user to move forward using a standard, non-VR method, such as a joystick, but this kind of motion is apt to produce nausea. It tends to trigger a feeling of acceleration, which in turn triggers simulator sickness, discussed later in this chapter.

TIP

When adding movement to your VR app, ask yourself how movement is enhancing the user's VR experience. Unnecessary movement can be disorienting to users. Focusing on what value movement adds to the experience can help strengthen your VR app.

Many applications find ways for users to be grounded on some sort of machine or platform, and then move the platform itself rather than the user. This can help alleviate some of the potential issues of simulator sickness, especially if the user remains seated.

For room-scale VR experiences, "teleportation" is one of the current standards for smoothly moving users large distances in virtual worlds. The user aims at the place they would like to move to, some sort of graphic appears to define the target destination, and then the user triggers the teleportation.

Figure 7-7 shows how a user in Vive's headset can teleport around the Vive home scene. Holding down the touchpad displays a graphic to the user defining where she'll teleport to if teleportation is triggered. A user can then choose to trigger the teleportation event, moving her to the new location, or cancel the teleportation event.

FIGURE 7-7:
HTC Vive's home scene teleportation visual.

Locomotion is very much an evolving best practice for VR, and one that is going to require plenty of exploration for what works best for your application. Application developers are implementing and improving upon this mechanic in a number of ways. Robo Recall, a game for Oculus Rift, enables the user to determine the direction he'll be facing when he arrives at his teleportation location, instead of just teleporting him straight to the location in whatever direction he's currently looking. Budget Cuts, a game by publisher Neat Corp, gives the user the ability to peek at his destination and how he'll be facing before he teleports, removing the confusion that can often occur when a user teleports to a new location.

And teleportation is not the only method of locomotion available. Many applications offer standard "walking" locomotion to users. *Smooth locomotion,* or sliding through virtual environments without jerky acceleration, can help retain some immersion of a standard method of movement with some of the potential "simulator sickness" triggers minimized.

Other solutions for locomotion within a limited space are also being explored. Saccade-driven redirected walking is a method of redirecting users away from real-world obstacles that allows users to traverse large virtual scenes in a small physical space. In saccade redirection, the virtual scene is rotated slightly in a way invisible to the user, causing the user to alter his walking slightly in response to the digital scene changes. For example, utilizing this method, a user may think he's walking in a straight line in the digital world, but in the physical world he's guided on a much more circular path.

TIP

Large-scale movement in VR is a mechanic that has yet to be completely solved. Teleportation is often used, but it's only one of many possible solutions for motion. If your application requires movement, review other applications and their methods of locomotion and see what you think makes sense. You may even be the one to come up with the new standard of motion for VR experiences!

Providing feedback

In the real world, a person's actions are usually met with some sort of feedback, visual or otherwise. Even with your eyes closed, touching a hot stove provides the tactile feedback of a burning sensation. Catch a thrown ball, and you feel the smack of the ball against your palm and the weight of the ball in your hand. Even something as simple as grasping a doorknob or tapping your finger on a computer key provides tactile feedback to your nervous system.

VR doesn't yet have a method for fully realizing tactile feedback (see Chapter 2), but you can still find ways to provide feedback to the user. If available on the VR device you're targeting, *haptic feedback* (via controller vibrations or similar) can help improve the user's immersive experience. Audio can also help notify the user of actions (when a user clicks a button, for example). Providing these audio and haptic cues alongside your visuals can help make your VR environments seem more immersive and help notify a user when actions have occurred.

Following the user's gaze

Knowing where a user's gaze is centered is a necessary part of VR interactions, especially in the current versions of head-mounted displays (HMDs) that don't provide eye tracking. Many VR applications rely on a user's gaze for selection. In order to utilize gaze, you may want to provide a visual aid, such as a *reticle* (see Chapter 2) to help a user target objects. Reticles are typically visually distinct from the rest of the environment in order to stand out, but small and unobtrusive enough to not draw the user's attention away from the rest of the application. Reticles should trigger some sort of indication to the user as to what elements are interactive within the environment.

Figure 7-8 shows a reticle being used for selection in PGA's PGA TOUR VR Live application. Without motion controllers, the reticle enables the user to see what interactive item her gaze should be triggering.

FIGURE 7-8:
A reticle in use in PGA Tour VR Live.

TIP

Depending on your particular VR implementation, you may also choose to display a reticle only when a user is close to objects with which she can interact. This allows a user's focus to be undisturbed by the extra visual information of a reticle when focused on things that she can't interact with at the moment.

Not every VR application needs a reticle. When using motion controllers to select or interact with objects outside of a user's reach, a reticle is typically discarded in favor of a laser pointer and cursor for selection. You could just display the cursor, but you're better off displaying a combination of a virtual model of the controller, a laser ray, and the cursor all together. Doing so helps users notice the motion controller and cursor, helps communicate the angle of the laser ray, and provides real-time feedback and an intuitive feel to the user about how the orientation of the motion controller can affect the input of the ray and cursor.

Figure 7-9 displays a motion controller and laser pointer in use in Google Daydream's home menu scene.

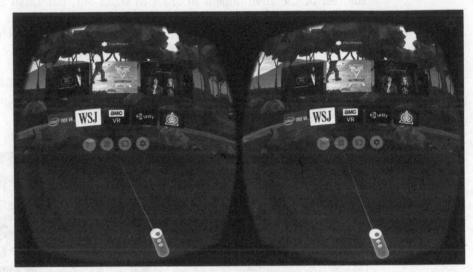

FIGURE 7-9:
A laser pointer in Google Daydream's home menu scene.

Avoiding simulator sickness

Discussed briefly in Chapter 2 as one of VR's biggest issues to overcome, *simulator sickness* is the feeling of nausea brought on by a mismatch between the user's physical and visual motion cues. At its simplest, your eyes may tell you that you're moving, but your body disagrees. Nothing will make a user leave your app more quickly than the feeling of simulator sickness.

There are a number of ways to avoid simulator sickness.

>> **Maintain application frame rate.** Sixty frames per second (fps) is generally considered the minimum frame rate in which VR applications should run in order to prevent simulator sickness in users. If your app is running at less than 60 fps, you need to find ways to get back to at least 60 fps. Maintaining this

frame rate is likely the most important tip to follow, even if it means cutting other portions of your application.

>> **Maintain continuous head tracking.** *Head tracking* in VR refers to the application continuously following the motion of your head, and having those movements reflect themselves within the virtual environment. Aligning your application's virtual world positioning with a user's real-world head movements is vital to avoiding simulator sickness. Even a slight pause while tracking a user's movements can induce motion sickness.

>> **Avoid acceleration.** In the real world, our bodies notice acceleration far more than we notice movement at a constant velocity. While you're traveling in a car going 65 mph on a highway, you may not feel any different than if you were sitting on a park bench. However, your body definitely feels the difference of the acceleration from zero to 65 mph.

Acceleration or deceleration in the real world provides a visual change as well as a sensation of motion to the end user. VR, however, provides only a visual update. This lack of sensation of motion in VR can trigger simulator sickness. Avoid accelerating or decelerating a user in VR. If movement within the space is required, try to keep users moving at a constant velocity.

>> **Avoid fixed-view items.** Any graphic that "fixes" itself to the user's view can trigger the feeling of nausea. In general, keep all objects in 3D while in VR instead of fixing any items to the user's 2D screen.

More best practices to consider

Here are a few more useful best practices for colors, sounds, and text usage, all of which can affect user experiences:

>> **Bright colors and environments:** Imagine the feeling of leaving a darkened theater and walking out into a bright sunny day. You find yourself shielding your eyes against the glare of the sun, squinting and waiting for your eyes to adjust. In VR, the same feeling can be triggered by quickly changing from any dark scene to a bright scene.

Immediate brightness changes from dark to light can annoy and disorient users, and unlike stepping out into bright sunlight, when in a headset a user has no way of shielding her eyes from the glare. Avoid harsh or quick changes between darker scenes to lighter scenes or items.

Extremely bright colors and scenes can be difficult to look at for an extended period of time and can cause eye fatigue for your users. Be sure to keep scene and item color palettes in mind when building out your experiences.

>> **Background audio:** VR applications should be immersive. In the real world, audio plays a huge part in helping you to determine your environment. From the bustling noises of a busy street to the white noise hum and background noises of an office environment, to the echoing silence of a dark cave, audio cues alone are often enough to describe an environment. Make sure to consider how not only event-based audio (such as audio triggers on user interaction), but also background audio will play a role in your experiences.

>> **Text input and output:** When in VR, users are surrounded with visual information from the environment. Adding large blocks of text to this environment can overload the user with input. Where possible, avoid using large blocks of small-font text. Short text excerpts rendered in large print are typically preferred.

Similarly, it can be difficult for a user in VR to input a large amount of text. As discussed in Chapter 2, text input in VR has yet to be completely solved. If text input is a requirement of your application, consider carefully how this can occur in the VR space.

Defining Your Social Experience

Another core issue to consider when developing for VR is how your experience may be used in social settings. The rise of personal computers and mobile devices led to unprecedented development of social experiences and ways to connect users either in the same room or across the globe. From playing games to networking for work to sharing our photos and videos, the options available for connecting with other users have spawned massive industries within the hardware and software worlds. VR has the capability to create entirely new methods of social interaction, but these interactions won't appear on their own.

VR as a standalone experience has the potential to feel very solitary. Due to the nature of VR headsets, most experiences close the user off from those in the room with them. The user's eyes are covered via the headset visuals, and the user often wears headphones as well, closing off external sound input. Without the ability to communicate with anyone in the physical world, most social interaction in VR needs to occur within the experience itself.

Experiences such as Altspace VR, Rec Room, or Pluto VR — social VR applications focused around meeting other users and hanging out and playing games in VR — are proving that social VR applications can be enjoyable experiences. And mixed media games such as Keep Talking and Nobody Explodes (a cooperative game wherein a single user with a headset communicates to a group of users in the same room without headsets) have shown that social interaction in VR can be thought of in outside-the-box ways.

Figure 7-10 captures gameplay of Keep Talking and Nobody Explodes VR. The user inside the headset is the only one who can see and disarm the bomb (right) but requires input from users outside the headset to do so.

FIGURE 7-10:
Keep Talking and
Nobody Explodes
VR gameplay.

When planning your own VR applications, put some thought into your social experience. Simply allowing multiple users in your experience often isn't enough to make something compelling. You shouldn't feel restrained by the norms of established social interaction. VR is a new tool that has the potential to create a whole new kind of social interaction. What could that mean to your application? What do your users gain by adding a social component to your experience? How will your application enable this social interaction?

Best practices for social experiences in VR are still being established. But much like Facebook for the web, whoever "solves" how VR may be used socially may change the norms of social interaction for years to come.

Chapter **8**

Planning Your Augmented Reality Project

Augmented reality (AR) has existed for some time, but the field is just now starting to be pushed forward at consumer scale. This is a great time to be entering the AR marketplace — it's wide open and in need of innovators! Nearly everyone is starting at square one. We're all on the learning curve together. However, it also means that there are few successful AR projects or applications to look to for best practices concerning how to approach building a successful AR app. But they are there. By analyzing some of the existing research around AR and various AR applications, a number of standards and best practices can be observed.

This chapter helps you plan your AR application and offers some best practices for developing your application. Use it as a set of guidelines, but don't be afraid to experiment on your own to find out what you think makes a great AR application. You may stumble across a new best practice for AR, or you may find that your method doesn't work at all, but don't be afraid of failure! In a field as new as AR, learning what does *not* work can be just as valuable as learning what does.

Defining Your Augmented Reality Project

WARNING

Before you begin planning your AR project, review the material in Chapter 6 to ensure that AR is an appropriate execution for your project. After covering the steps in Chapter 6, you may find that AR is not a good fit. If so, you'll have saved yourself a lot of wasted time and effort trying to fit a square peg into a round hole.

The steps for planning a successful AR project share many traits with traditional project planning, as well as some of the steps outlined in the Chapter 7. The following topics from Chapter 7 are also applicable to AR projects.

Determining hardware support

Determining what hardware or software to support is vital to any technology project, but AR presents some unique challenges. The field is very young, and options can be limited. Having limited options can actually be a benefit: Because only a handful of options are available, choosing what to support isn't that difficult. Of course, your project's execution will be limited by what the chosen platform can handle.

For AR projects intended for mass consumption, your choice will likely be limited to mobile AR solutions such as Apple's ARKit and Google's ARCore. Currently, AR headsets and glasses are mainly targeted for enterprise-level audiences.

Webcams

Webcam-based or video camera-based AR has been around for some time as a method of executing AR for mass consumption. As far back as 2009, *Esquire* released an AR-powered issue featuring AR and Robert Downey, Jr., intended for use with a reader's webcam. Holding the cover and certain pages of the magazine up to a webcam would reveal AR content on top of the page played back on a user's monitor, providing the consumer with additional audio and video.

Reviews of the experience were mixed. Although it was innovative at the time, the form factor of the experience was awkward. Having a properly configured webcam, downloading the specific AR software, and holding up the magazine in front of your computer while simultaneously trying to watch the results proved to be a lot of work and an awkward experience for what some viewed as minimal payoff. *Esquire*'s own editor-in-chief, David Granger, hand-waved their implementation of AR at that time as a bit of a "gimmick."

Tools do exist to produce AR content via consumer desktop hardware, but, as exemplified by *Esquire*'s AR issue, they aren't always the best experience for the consumer. If consumers have to configure a webcam, download files, and place markers to trigger AR holograms for a less-than-compelling experience, they quickly lose interest. So, if mass adoption is a requirement for your AR application, a mobile-device AR solution is likely appropriate.

ARToolKit is a powerful toolset for creating certain types of experiences on both desktop and mobile devices. It was created by Hirokazu Kato of Nara Institute of Science and Technology in 1999 and was often used to power early webcam-based AR experiences. It is now run as an open-source project after being purchased by DAQRI, an industrial AR company. ARToolKit can still be used on various platforms such as Windows, OS X, Android, and iOS.

A webcam-based AR experience can be compelling if it's an appropriate use for your audience. Figure 8-1 shows webcam-based AR at use in a LEGO store. A store customer can hold any LEGO box sets up to the LEGO Digital Box, which utilizes a webcam. A 3D model and animation of the LEGOs within the package is displayed via video screen on top of the box as if in the real world. Although it still can be a bit of an awkward experience having to hold the box up to the webcam, it's intended to be a short experience to generate buying interest. It's also a controlled environment where the hardware is known ahead of time, eliminating many variables that can cause problems with AR webcam experiences.

FIGURE 8-1:
Webcam AR at use at the Digital Box display in the LEGO store.

Mobile

The biggest strength of mobile AR executions is the prevalence of mobile devices. They also offer less friction for the user than most headsets, and the familiarity of the form factor can mean users need very little education about how to interact with the device.

However, mobile executions do come with drawbacks. Mobile devices are often underpowered compared to their desktop and headset counterparts. The larger device base means you're often creating an application targeting a number of different devices. You may have to test against a large number of devices to be sure of compatibility. As the AR-capable mobile device list grows, the sheer number of devices may make it necessary to test against only a sampling of devices instead of the entire list of potentially supported devices.

REMEMBER

The experience mobile devices offer exists as sort of a "training wheel" step to AR's ultimate form factor. Mobile AR offers a window into an augmented world, nowhere near the imagined future of AR glasses fully augmenting the world around us. Its form factor busies the users' hands and can force some awkward and tiring interactions with users holding devices out in front of them with one hand and awkwardly navigating with the other. The training wheels of mobile AR may sustain the mass consumer base for now, but expect a better-executed solution eventually.

Because of the awkwardness of navigation, strong use cases for mobile AR are mostly for experiences intended for brief consumption periods, or scenarios in which the user is allowed some time to rest in between interactions. Mobile AR is not yet a form factor that is suitable for using hours on end. Games such as Pokémon Go can be looked at as a good example of this. Rather than a full AR experience (requiring users to constantly hold their devices out in front of them and interact with an augmented environment), Pokémon Go uses AR to augment the main experience of the game itself only in small segments, allowing users to rest their arms in between holding the devices out in front of them for the AR experience.

Amazon's AR View also displays this in action — the AR portion of the experience is an enhancement to the main shopping application. Users shop as they normally would on a mobile device, entering the AR portion only when they want to view an item in their environment.

Headsets

If mass consumer adoption is not a requirement for your project, your choices for AR execution open up to allow AR headsets (as well as the aforementioned webcams). Wearable AR such as AR headsets, glasses, and goggles are likely the future of AR, so evaluating and building headset-based AR applications now can give companies a significant head start over their competitors. These devices also allow a much deeper level of interaction than other AR executions, and can uphold AR's promise of becoming the technology that helps us get things done.

However, the drawbacks of AR headsets can be significant for some projects. The mass consumer market is currently nonexistent, with no indication of when it will take off in popularity. There is also uncertainty about not only which device consumers will lean toward, but which sort of experiences as well, such as a device tethered to an external computer versus non-tethered devices. It could be that none of the currently available headsets wins out and the final form factor for consumer AR is radically different from what exists today.

That said, strong use cases for headset- or glasses-based applications do exist. These applications are typically built for enterprise consumption or with a specific market already in mind. Currently, you should find yourself designing for AR headsets only if you'll be directly defining the hardware and software for use in the experience.

REMEMBER

If you're defining the hardware, you need to understand the potential drawbacks of each available type of hardware before making a selection. Cost, tethered versus non-tethered, mobility of device, field-of-view (FOV) requirements, extra hardware requirements — these are all items you need to consider when choosing to build for AR headsets.

Defining your timeline

As with VR projects (see Chapter 7), you must carefully consider the length of the project timeline when building out an AR project. If you're planning a long-term AR project, advances in AR technology may force you to adjust your execution.

For example, if you were to decide upon a year-long AR engagement to build applications for the Microsoft HoloLens, recognize that in that year there may be significant software or hardware updates or releases that may change your project execution. Perhaps a new mixed-reality headset will be announced, or new software will change how you build your application. To help minimize such changes, I suggest shorter project timelines (if feasible) or breaking up your project into smaller sprints where industry updates can be addressed without the need to fully overhaul the project.

REMEMBER

Advances in AR hardware and software arrive fairly often, and can sometimes feel as if they come out of the blue even for those embedded in the industry. Don't let the possibility of these potential advances scare you away from AR projects! Advances are always welcome in the industry. Your project can take advantage of them, especially if you're keeping an eye on the industry, making adjustments to your project as you go. If you're creating an AR application, however, it's vital to keep up with industry updates and align your plans with upcoming innovations. Keeping up with the changes means you can adjust on the fly and stay ahead of the curve in your development efforts.

Exploring Design Principles in Augmented Reality

Design principles are a set of ideas or beliefs that are held to be true across all projects of that particular type. Design principles are typically created through years of trial and error within a field. The older a field of study is, the more likely a strong set of design principles has arisen around that field for what works well and what doesn't.

AR developers are still defining the design principles that will help guide the field forward. The field is still very young, so these best practices are not set in stone. That makes AR an exciting field to be working in! It's akin to the early Internet days, where no one was quite sure what would work well and what would fall on its face. Experimenting is encouraged, and you may even find yourself designing a way of navigating in AR that could become the standard that millions of people will use every day!

Eventually a strong set of standards will emerge for AR. In the meantime, a number of patterns are beginning to emerge around AR experiences that can guide your design process.

Starting up

For many users, AR experiences are still new territory. When using a standard computer application, videogame, or mobile app, many users can get by with minimal instruction due to their familiarity with similar applications. However, that is not the case for AR experiences. You can't simply drop users into your AR application with no context — this may be the very first AR experience they've ever used. Make sure to guide users with very clear and direct cues on how to use the application on initial startup. Consider holding back on opening up deeper functionality within your application until a user has exhibited some proficiency with the simpler parts of your application.

Many AR experiences evaluate the user's surroundings in order to map digital holograms in the real world. The camera on the AR device needs to see the environment and use this input to determine where AR holograms can appear. This orientation process can take some time, especially on mobile devices, and can often be facilitated by encouraging a user to explore his surroundings with his device.

In order for users to avoid wondering whether the app is frozen while this mapping occurs, be sure to show an indication that a process is taking place, and potentially invite the user to explore her surroundings or look for a surface to place the AR experience. Consider displaying an onscreen message to the user instructing her to look around her environment. Figure 8-2 displays a screenshot from the iOS game Stack AR, instructing a user to move her device around her environment.

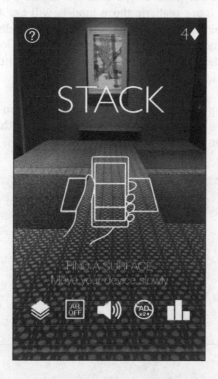

FIGURE 8-2:
Stack AR
instructing a user
to move camera
around the
environment.

TECHNICAL
STUFF

Most AR applications map the real world via a computational process called simultaneous localization and mapping (SLAM). This process refers to constructing and updating a map of an unknown environment, and tracking a user's location within that environment.

If your application requires a user to move about in the real world, think about introducing movement gradually. Users should be given time to adapt to the AR world you've established before they begin to move around. If motion is required, it can be a good idea to guide the user through it on the first occurrence via arrows or text callouts instructing him to move to certain areas or explore the holograms.

Similar to VR applications, it's important that AR applications run smoothly in order to maintain the immersion of augmented holograms existing within the real-world environment. Your application should maintain a consistent 60 frames per second (fps) frame rate. This means you need to make sure your application is optimized as much as possible. Graphics, animations, scripts, and 3D models all affect the potential frame rate of your application. For example, you should aim for the highest-quality 3D models you can create while keeping the polygon count of those models as low as possible.

3D models are made up of polygons. In general, the higher polygon count of a model, the smoother and more realistic those models will be. A lower polygon count typically means a "blockier" model that may look less realistic. Finding the balance between realistic models while keeping polygon counts low is an art form perfected by many game designers. The lower the polygon count of a model, the more performant that model will likely be.

Figure 8-3 shows an example of a 3D sphere with a high polygon count and a low polygon count. Note the difference in smoothness between the high-polygon model and the low-polygon model.

FIGURE 8-3:
High-poly versus
low-poly sphere
models.

Similarly, ensure that the textures (or images) used in your application are optimized. Large images can cause a performance hit on your application, so do what you can to ensure that image sizes are small and the images themselves have been optimized. AR software has to perform a number of calculations that can put stress on the processor. The better you can optimize your models, graphics, scripts, and animations, the better the frame rate you'll achieve.

Considering the environment

AR is all about merging the real world and the digital. Unfortunately, this can mean relinquishing control of the background environment in which your applications will be displayed. This is a far different experience than in VR, where you completely control every aspect of the environment. This lack of control over the environment can be a difficult problem to tackle, so it's vital to keep in mind issues that may arise over any unpredictable environments your application may be used in.

Lighting plays an important part in the AR experience. Because a user's environment essentially becomes the world your AR models will inhabit, it's important that they react accordingly. For most AR experiences, a moderately lit environment will typically perform best. A very bright room such as direct sunlight can make tracking difficult and wash out the display on some AR devices. A very dark room can also make AR tracking difficult while potentially eliminating some of the contrast of headset-based AR displays. Many of the current AR headsets (for example, Meta 2 and HoloLens) use projections for display, so they won't completely obscure physical objects; instead, the digital holograms appear as semi-transparent on top of them.

AR is all about digital holograms existing in the environment with the user. As such, most AR usage is predicated on the user being able to move about their physical space. However, your applications could be used in real-world spaces where a user may not have the ability to move around. Consider how your application is intended to be used, and ensure that you've taken the potential mobility issues of your users into account. Think about keeping all major interactions for your application within arm's reach of your users, and plan how to handle situations requiring interaction with a hologram out of the user's reach.

In the real world, objects provide us with depth cues to determine just where an object is in 3D space in relation to ourselves. AR objects are little more than graphics either projected in front of the real world or being displayed on top of a video feed of the real world. As such, you need to create your own depth cues for these graphics to assist users in knowing where these holograms are meant to exist in space. Consider how to visually make your holograms appear to exist in the real-world 3D space with occlusion, lighting, and shadow.

TECHNICAL STUFF

Occlusion in computer graphics typically refers to objects that appear either partially or completely behind other graphics closer to the user in 3D space. Occlusion can help a user determine where items are in 3D space in relation to one another.

You can see an example of occlusion (foreground cubes partially blocking the visibility of the background cubes), lighting, and shadow all at play in Figure 8-4. The depth cues of occlusion, lighting, and shadow all play a part in giving the user a sense of where the holograms "exist" in space, as well as making the holographic illusion feel more real, as if the cubes actually exist in the real world, and not just the virtual.

FIGURE 8-4:
3D holographic
cubes within the
real world.

Understanding comfort zones

Understanding users' interaction within their comfort zones is important, especially for AR applications that may be more focused on getting work done. You also need to understand the differences between comfort zones for interaction with a head-mounted AR device versus comfort zones for interaction with AR on a mobile device.

Head-mounted AR experiences are fairly similar to that of VR, with a few exceptions. As discussed in Chapter 7, you need to minimize how much users will be required to move their heads for any experiences longer than a few minutes. Though their work was focused on VR, Google VR Designer Mike Alger and Alex Chu of Samsung Research claim that users' comfort level when rotating their heads horizontally is 30 degrees to each side, with a maximum rotation of 55 degrees. For vertical motion, rotation of 20 degrees upward is comfortable, with a maximum rotation upward of 60 degrees. Rotation downward is around 12 degrees comfortably with a maximum of 40 degrees.

When defining your comfort zones for head-mounted AR, it's also important to consider how your application will be used. Will it require users' direct interaction, such as with hand tracking and gestures, or just point and click via controller or touchpad? If it will require direct interaction, consider how that can be used comfortably, especially if the application is intended for extended use. As more and more AR applications are utility based, this consideration will become more important.

TECHNICAL STUFF

A report on office ergonomics by Dennis Ankrum (https://humanics-es.com/setting.htm) provides a good guide for seated AR experiences requiring user interaction, especially AR applications intended to be used in conjunction with (or as a replacement to) traditional computer usage. Ankrum lists the correct eye-to-screen distance for most users as 25 inches from the eyes, preferably more, and optimal placement for screens as 15 to 25 degrees below the horizontal plane of a user's eye, resulting in a small "comfort zone" for seated AR experiences.

Meta has completed similar studies and achieved similar results with its headset for both standing and seated experiences. There is an "ideal content area" that exists between the intersection of where a user's hands will be detected by the headset, the FOV of the headset itself, and the comfortable viewing angle for a user's line of sight. Each headset is slightly different, but in general the ergonomics of a comfortable AR headset experience hold true across most platforms.

Figure 8-5 shows the best area for content display within the FOV of the Meta 2 headset. The tracking technology utilized for Meta 2's hand tracking has a detection area of 68 degrees, optimized at a distance of 0.35 meter and 0.55 meter from the user. Combined with the 40 degree vertical FOV of the headset, an ideal content area can be established at the intersection of what is comfortable for the user to reach and see.

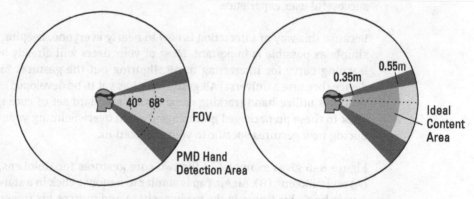

FIGURE 8-5: Ideal content areas for standing and seated Meta 2 experiences.

This comfort zone for interaction is not the same for every AR headset, but defining these zones will be similar for any current or future headsets. Carefully consider the amount of user movement and interaction that your application requires and what the comfort zones of your hardware may be. Take care to minimize the amount of neck rotation or unnecessary user motion. The first time a user has to reach up to "turn on" a virtual light bulb in your AR experience may be novel. If a user has to perform this action multiple times, it'll quickly become tedious.

TIP

Mobile device comfort zones are very different from that of head-mounted AR devices. In a mobile AR experience, a user is forced to hold his device a certain distance in front of his eyes and angle his arm or his head to get a view into the augmented environment within the device. Holding a device in this manner can be extremely taxing after a period of time, so try to find a way to minimize the user's discomfort. If your application requires a large amount of user motion or long periods in which a user must hold his device out in front of him, find ways to provide rest periods to allow the user to rest his arms for a bit before continuing.

Interacting with objects

Most VR interaction takes place via a motion controller, but most headset-based AR devices utilize a combination of gaze and hand tracking for interaction. Often, AR headsets use gaze-based navigation to track where a user is looking to target items within the environment. When an item is targeted, a user will often interact with that item via hand gestures.

As such, you need to design your experience to keep the user's hands within the headset's area of recognition and work with each headset's specific set of gestures. Educating the user about the area of recognition for gestures — and notifying users when their gestures are near the boundaries — can help create a more successful user experience.

Because this way of interaction is new to nearly everyone, keeping interactions as simple as possible is important. Most of your users will already be undergoing a learning curve for interacting in AR, figuring out the gestures for their specific device (because a universal AR gesture set has yet to be developed). Most AR headsets that utilize hand tracking come with a standard set of core gestures. Try to stick to these prepackaged gestures and avoid overwhelming your users by introducing new gestures specific to your application.

Figure 8-6 gives examples of the two core gestures for HoloLens, the "Air Tap" (A) and "Bloom" (B). An Air Tap is similar to a mouse click in a standard 2D screen. A user holds his finger in the ready position and presses his finger down to select or click the item targeted via user gaze. The "Bloom" gesture is a universal gesture to send a user to the Start menu. A user holds his fingertips together and then opens his hand.

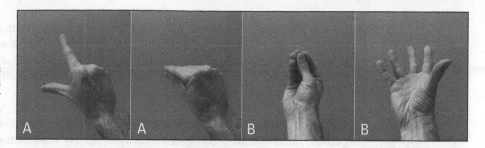

FIGURE 8-6:
Microsoft's
example of a user
performing an
"Air Tap" (A) and a
"Bloom" (B).

Grabbing an object in the real world gives a user feedback such as the feel of the object, the weight of the object in his hand, and so on. Hand gestures made to select virtual holograms will provide the user with none of this standard tactile feedback. So it's important to notify the user about the state of digital holograms in the environment in different ways.

Provide the user cues as to the state of an object or the environment, especially as the user tries to place or interact with digital holograms. For example, if your user is supposed to place a digital hologram in 3D space, providing a visual indicator can help communicate to her where the object will be placed. If the user can interact with an object in your scene, you may want to visually indicate that on the object, potentially using proximity to alert the user that she's approaching an object she can interact with. If your user is trying to select one object among many, highlight the item she currently has selected and provide audio cues for her actions.

Figure 8-7 shows how the Meta 2 chooses to display this feedback to the user. A circle with a ring appears on the back of a user's hand as he approaches an interactive object (A). As the user's hand closes to a fist, the ring becomes smaller (B) and draws closer to the center circle. A ring touching the circle indicates a successful grab (C). A user's hand moving near to the edge of the sensor is also detected and flagged via a red indicator and warning message (D).

FIGURE 8-7:
A screen capture
of in-headset
view of a Meta 2
drag interaction.

Mobile device interaction

Many of the design principles for AR apply to both headsets and mobile experiences. However, there is a considerable difference between the interactive functionality of AR headsets and mobile AR experiences. Because of the form factor differences between AR headsets and AR mobile devices, interaction requires some different rules.

Keeping interactions simple and providing feedback when placing or interacting with an object are rules that apply to both headset and mobile AR experiences. But most interaction for users on mobile devices will take place through gestures on the touchscreen of the device instead of users directly manipulating 3D objects or using hand gestures in 3D space.

A number of libraries, such as ManoMotion (www.manomotion.com), can provide 3D gesture hand tracking and gesture recognition for controlling holograms in mobile AR experiences. These libraries may be worth exploring depending on the requirements of your app. Just remember that your user will likely be holding the device in one hand while experiencing your app, potentially making it awkward to try to also insert her other hand in front of a back-facing camera.

Your users likely already understand mobile device gestures such as single-finger taps, drags, two-finger pinching and rotating, and so on. However, most users understand these interactions in relation to the two-dimensional world of the screen instead of the three dimensions of the real world. After a hologram is placed in space, consider allowing movement of that hologram in only two dimensions, essentially allowing it to only slide across the surface upon which it was placed. Similarly, consider limiting the object rotation to a single axis. Allowing movement or rotation on all three axes can quickly become very confusing to the end user and result in unintended consequences or placement of the holograms.

In Figure 8-8, a cube has been placed on a flat surface. Instead of allowing a user to move the object up and down off the plane (along the y-axis), consider locking that movement to only the x- and z-axes. Similarly, if you're rotating an object, consider allowing rotation only around the y-axis. Locking these movements prevents your user from inadvertently shifting objects in unpredictable ways. You may also want to create a method to "undo" any unintentional movement of your holograms, as placing these holograms in real-world space can be challenging for your users to get right.

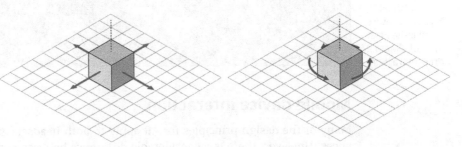

FIGURE 8-8:
Locking motion and rotation of AR holograms in space.

Most mobile devices support a "pinch" interaction with the screen to either zoom in on an area or scale an object. Because a user is in a fixed point in space in both the real world and the hologram world, you probably won't want to utilize this gesture for zooming in AR.

Similarly, consider eliminating a user's ability to scale an object in AR. A two-fingered pinch gesture for scale is a standard interaction for mobile users. In AR, this scale gesture often doesn't make sense. AR hologram 3D models are often a set size. The visual appearance of the size of the 3D model is influenced by the distance from the AR device. A user scaling an object in place to make the object look closer to the camera is really just making the object larger in place, often not what the user intended. Pinch-to-scale may still be used in AR, but its usage should be thoughtfully considered.

Voice interaction

Some AR devices also support voice interaction capabilities. Although the interaction for most AR headsets is primarily gaze and gestures, for those headsets with voice capabilities you need to consider how to utilize all methods of interaction and how to make them work well together. Voice controls can be a very convenient way to control your application. As processing power grows exponentially, expect voice control to be introduced and refined further on AR headsets.

Here are some things to keep in mind as you develop voice commands for AR devices that support this feature:

>> **Use simple commands.** Keeping your commands simple will help avoid potential issues of users speaking with different dialects or accents. It also minimizes the learning curve of your application. For example, "Read more" is likely a better choice than "Provide further information about selected item."

>> **Ensure that voice commands can be undone.** Voice interactions can sometimes be triggered inadvertently by capturing audio of others nearby. Make sure that any voice command can be undone if an accidental interaction is triggered.

>> **Eliminate similar-sounding interactions.** In order to prevent your user from triggering incorrect actions, eliminate any spoken commands that may sound similar but perform different actions. For example, if "Read more" performs a particular action in your application (such as revealing more text), it should always perform the same interaction throughout your application. Similar-sounding commands should also be avoided. For example, "Open reference" and "Open preferences" are far too likely to be mistaken for each other.

>> **Avoid system commands.** Make sure your program doesn't override voice commands already reserved by the system. If a command such as "home screen" is reserved by the AR device, don't reprogram that command to perform different functionality within your application.

>> **Provide feedback.** Voice interactions should provide the same level of feedback cues to a user that standard interaction methods do. If a user is utilizing voice commands, provide feedback that your application heard and understood the command. One method of doing so would be to provide onscreen text of what commands the system interpreted from the user. This will provide the user with feedback as to how the system is understanding his commands and allow him to adjust his commands if needed.

Exploring user interface patterns

Best practices for AR user interface design are still being defined. There are not many defined user experience (UX) patterns that AR designers can fall back on as best practices for what a user will expect when entering an augmented experience. Plus, AR is a totally new form factor, different from the 2D screens people have become accustomed to. AR will enable people to totally rethink the way we handle user interface (UI) design.

The 2D world of the computer consists of flat layouts with multiple 2D windows and menus. AR enables developers to utilize 3D space. When designing your AR UI, consider creating a spatial interface and arranging your UI tools and content around the user in 3D, instead of the windowed interface that computer screens currently confine us to. Consider allowing the user to use 3D space as an organizational tool for her items, as opposed to hiding or nesting content in folders or directories — a practice common in current 2D UIs. AR has ways to gracefully avoid hiding content.

Instead of hiding menus inside other objects, use the physical environment available to you to organize your setup. Hidden menus in 2D screens are usually created due to space constraints or a designer feeling that the amount of content would be overwhelming for a user to consume. For augmented experiences in cases of what you may consider an overwhelming amount of information, considering organizing items in groups in 3D space.

TIP

Instead of nesting content within menus, explore the possibility of miniaturizing content to optimize the space around your user. Content that may normally take up a large amount of space could be made small until a user has expressed a desire to interact with it.

That is not to say that you can always avoid hidden or nested structures. Both will likely always exist in UX designs for AR. If you do find the need to nest content, try to keep the levels of nesting to a minimum.

In most traditional 2D UIs, nested content is a given. On a traditional computer, users are fully accustomed to having to click into four or five different nested directories in order to locate a file. However, deep nesting of content can be very confusing to end users, especially in the 3D environment of AR. A user having to navigate in 3D space through multiple nested items will likely quickly grow frustrated with the experience. Shallow nesting and making items easily accessible within the spatial environment should enable users to retrieve content quickly.

WARNING

Limit expandable and hidden menus as much as possible in the AR space. These patterns may have worked well in the 2D screens of the past, but they aren't necessarily relevant in the 3D world that AR is trying to emulate. Expandable/hidden menus can introduce a level of complexity that you should avoid, if possible.

The windowed 2D world of current computing UIs has accustomed us to iconography and abstract 2D shapes that represent real-world tools. These icons also can often hide further functionality, such as expandable or hidden menus. However, the world of AR is full of new patterns for users to learn. Try to avoid creating a new system of 2D icons for your AR experiences. These can force users to have to guess and learn a system you've created that may not have relevance to them.

TIP

If a tool is intended to be used within the 3D space of the experience, replace abstract icons or buttons with 3D objects in space that give the user a sense of the tool's purpose. Look to real-world environments such as drafting desks or art studios for inspiration. Such real-world workspaces can provide examples of how real 3D objects are organized in a physical environment, which is generally what your UI in AR will try to emulate.

Finally, enable your user to personalize and organize her own spaces in a way she finds comfortable, in the same way she may organize her physical desktops or work areas at home or work. This will increase the likelihood that she'll be comfortable using the system you've created.

Understanding text

Carefully consider the legibility length of text when creating your AR application, and proofread it during testing on as many hardware platforms and as many environmental conditions as possible. You likely won't know what type of environment your application will be running in. A very dark area at night? An overly bright room at midday? To make sure text can be seen, consider placing it on contrasting-colored background.

Figure 8-9 shows an example of potentially poor legibility on top of a sub-optimal environment (left), and how that legibility can be resolved for unknown environments via a text background (right).

Photo by Jeremy Bishop on Unsplash (https://unsplash.com/photos/MhHbkyb35kw)

The text size and typeface (font) can also affect text legibility. In general, you should opt for shorter headlines or shorter blocks of text whenever possible. However, many AR applications are utility based, and sometimes involve consuming large blocks of text, so ultimately designers will have to find a way to make long-form text documents manageable in AR. If long document consumption is required for your application, make sure that the font size is large enough that the user can read it comfortably. (Meta recommends a minimum font size of at least 1cm in height when the text is 0.5 meter from the user's eye.) Avoid overly complicated calligraphic fonts. Instead, stick with utilizing simple serif or sans-serif fonts for these large text blocks. In addition, narrower columns of text are preferable to wider columns.

TECHNICAL STUFF

Rapid serial visual presentation (RSVP) speed reading is a method of showing a document to a user a single word at a time. This could prove to be a good way of consuming large blocks of text in AR, because it allows a single word to be larger and more recognizable, instead of forcing your application to account for displaying these large blocks of text.

For any informational or instructional text display, try to favor conversational terms that most users would understand over more technical terms that may confuse a user. "Unable to find a surface to place your object. Try moving your phone around slowly" is preferable to "Plane detection failed. Please detect plane."

START SMALL

If this is your first foray into building an AR application, consider starting as small as possible. Instead of biting off a full-blown app, think about developing a small piece of the app and treating that as if it were the full application. If you're building out a full-blown AR shopping experience complete with user profiles, clothes selection, online store purchases, and so on, break off a small piece of that application to build out.

For example, break off a simple piece such as the user login screen to loosely wireframe, design, develop, and test. This can help quickly bring to light what assumptions you've made concerning AR that may or may not work when the application is consumed in a headset. After a few simple pieces of your app are built out, you'll be much more confident in moving forward developing your larger final product.

Testing, testing, 1, 2, 3

AR applications are still defining what make an interaction good or bad. So, you'll often need to work from your own assumptions, and then test those assumptions as frequently as possible. Testing with multiple audiences will help reveal what's working well and what you may need to go back to the drawing board with. When testing your application, give your test users only the same amount of information a standard user of your application would receive. Letting your testers try to use the app without assistance will help prevent you from inadvertently "guiding" them through your application and will result in more accurate test results.

Defining Your Social Experience

Social interaction in AR is one area where VR and AR differ fundamentally. Directly out of the box, VR has the potential to be a solitary experience. Without careful planning for how social interaction can be introduced to your VR app, you could leave your users feeling very lonely.

AR experiences are different. Unlike VR, users experiencing AR either via headset or other form factor aren't blocked off from the rest of the physical world. They can still see, talk to, and interact with those around them. However, you still need to put the same amount of thought and care into how your AR application will be used socially. Consider what your social experience within AR means. Although the user is physically present in the room, a user with AR hardware won't have the same experience as someone without AR hardware. Even with matching hardware, if you haven't built social connection into your app, users won't be able to share the experience.

Developers of the Mira Prism AR headset have come up with an interesting solution for what these new types of AR experiences can mean for users of their hardware. The Prism allows for collaboration between users within the headset, but it also allows users without a headset to join in the AR experience in real time in Spectator Mode on a mobile device.

Spectator Mode allows users without a headset to join the experience of users with headsets in real time, seeing the same things a user with a headset sees. It also allows for quickly capturing photos or videos of the AR experience for quickly sharing via social media.

Spectator Mode is a small but clever step in extending AR from an experience that may otherwise fall into the same solitary trap that VR experiences can become. As you plan out your AR applications, be sure to consider how you can introduce social interaction between users both inside and outside your application.

Chapter **9**

Creating Content for Virtual and Augmented Reality

This chapter explores a broad range of options for creating virtual reality (VR) and augmented reality (AR) applications. These options include user experience (UX) software, design software, media asset websites, and programming tools. I mention a few of the available methods for each. I also provide a brief summary of some of their benefits and drawbacks to help you evaluate which may be right for you as you begin your VR/AR creation journey.

Although this chapter covers a range of options for creating VR or AR applications, it's not an exhaustive list of all pathways. There are hundreds of different ways to create these experiences, with new methods being developed all the time. Consider each section of this chapter a collection of ideas and possibilities, and be sure to evaluate any additional methods you may discover outside this book alongside the items covered here.

This chapter is a high level overview for anyone interested in learning about some of the types of roles and applications that are involved in creating VR/AR applications. Any one of these roles (UX, designer, videographer, developer) can take years of study to master. Consider the items covered within this chapter tips for learning just what goes into creating content for VR/AR projects.

TIP

Some of the options I cover in this chapter may be VR or AR specific, but many can be utilized for both VR and AR creation. If a tool is only appropriate for one or the other, I make that clear.

Assessing Design Software

Chapters 7 and 8 cover some of the rules that can help define a good UX in VR or AR, respectively. When you understand some of the general rules and principles that create a good UX, the next step is to begin to design your own application's UX.

User experience design software

Before jumping straight into designing the visuals of your final application assets, roughly sketch out how you believe your interface should lay out in the virtual world. This is often called the "UX design stage" or "wireframing stage."

There are a number of different options for wireframing out your experience, from low-fidelity options such as paper prototyping, to standard 2D tools you may already be familiar with, to full-blown applications dedicated solely to building complex VR or AR prototypes.

REMEMBER

It can seem daunting to enter into the world of UX in 3D, especially because most of our experience comes from 2D screens. Suddenly instead of being confined to a small screen, the entire world is opened up for you to place your interface elements. However, when focusing on the interface aspects of your design, remember that the "usable area" is often much smaller than the total area of the 360-degree environment. The user interface (UI) should mostly (but not always) reside somewhere within the user's "comfort zone," as defined in Chapters 7 and 8.

In the following sections, I take a look at some of the options available for creating mockups, wireframes, and prototypes. You can choose the method that best fits into your workflow, but it's important to prioritize this step in the process. You can revise and tweak decisions about interaction and functionality at this stage much more quickly than you can at later stages. The extra time you spend upfront making these decisions will save you even more time in the long run.

Paper prototyping

This method isn't software, but it's a method many UX designers use, so I'm including it here for your consideration. *Paper prototyping* is a system of creating hand-drawn UIs in order for them to be rapidly designed and tested. It's a great way to quickly get ideas down on paper and communicate these ideas between stakeholders. The system works especially well when you can upload images of your paper prototype to the device it will run on to have a look at it there. For example, you might display a paper prototype directly on a mobile device when designing a mobile interface, or within a web browser when designing a web interface. When designing an AR application, you can place physical objects or people within your real-world space as you might expect to see them through your device in the application, giving you a loose approximation of how the AR app will feel when placing digital holograms within the real world.

Although paper prototyping can give a general idea of how things may feel when in a VR or AR environment, it can fall short of delivering how the interface will feel inside a 3D environment or in 3D real-world space. Paper prototyping is typically best utilized for quickly mocking up ideas.

Traditional user experience applications

A number of tools are available for creating 2D wireframes and prototypes, such as Adobe XD or Sketch. You can use these tools to rapidly create wireframes and prototypes of your VR application. However, these tools on their own can leave a bit to be desired for prototyping VR and AR. Their purpose is translate 2D designs to a 2D screen. The flat designs they produce may not enable you to get a feel for the application flow in a virtual environment. Figure 9-1 displays Adobe XD being used for wireframing a standard 2D web page.

Through various plugins and workarounds, you can create simple experiences with these tools that can be viewed in virtual environments. The Sketch-to-VR plugin, for example, enables you to take a standard Sketch file and view it in a VR environment via WebVR. Although it's not an optimal experience, it will at least get you one step closer to what a user may actually experience in VR.

With the rise in popularity of VR and AR, it wouldn't be surprising to see these tools adjust to include the ability to more easily prototype VR/AR/MR experiences in the near future.

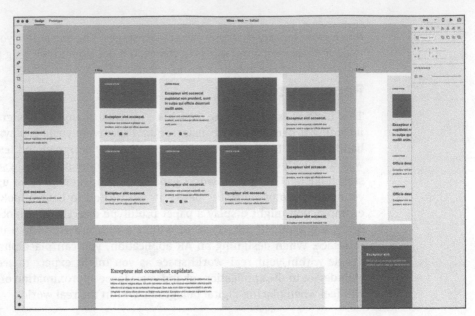

FIGURE 9-1:
Adobe XD
being used for
wireframing.

Virtual reality prototyping tools

The traditional 2D methods may work to rapidly prototype UIs, but there is no substitute for viewing prototypes within a 3D environment. 2D tools were meant for 2D applications. To truly visualize the experience you're attempting to create, you need a tool that enables you to quickly create a VR environment or place objects within an AR environment.

Tools are emerging to assist in creating rapid virtual environmental prototypes. Tools such as StoryBoard VR, Sketchbox, and Moment were all designed with VR and AR in mind, taking advantage of the strengths and working around the weaknesses of both.

Figure 9-2 shows a screen shot of Sketchbox's promotional video, in which a user within Sketchbox is creating a UI mockup in VR.

These storyboard and prototyping applications are designed specifically for creating VR or AR interfaces or storyboards while inside a VR headset. Moving beyond creating a loose representation of the VR or AR environment on a 2D screen, these tools enable you to create the VR or AR environment as a user will experience it in 3D space. You can quickly iterate on the general look and feel of your application, the placement of objects in 3D space, the sizing of items relative to one another, and so on. Some of the applications also enable you to create a step-by-step storyboard of how an animation or series of events should play out. This capability makes it possible to rapidly iterate designs and animations before taking the time to fully design and develop the ideas, saving you time in the long run.

Most of these tools are specific to VR but some, such as Moment, include the ability to prototype AR experiences as well. Moment enables users to mark certain objects as "AR objects" that, once marked, can be viewed only when utilizing a virtual mobile device in the VR environment.

Figure 9-3 displays a user prototyping AR elements within the VR Moment application. Raising an "AR device" in VR reveals models or assets marked for AR display only, allowing you to rapidly prototype AR experiences within VR.

FIGURE 9-3:
Moment being
used to rapidly
prototype AR
experiences.

Courtesy of Moment

TIP

The best way to get a feel for what a UX will be like is to choose a tool that enables you to view your interface designs as a user will view them, whether within a headset or on a mobile device. And there are plenty of options available for doing so. Try experimenting with several tools to find the ones that best suit your workflow.

TIP

Each hardware device has a different set of strengths and weaknesses. When prototyping, keep in mind the capability of the hardware you're designing for. Your room-scale UX design may plan for users moving around to reach various interaction points in your experience. Requiring the same movement in a seated-experience headset such as Google Cardboard would be a design failure.

BRAVE NEW UX WORLDS

Michael Markman is the CEO of Moment Labs. He's on the cutting edge of defining what it means to be a UX designer in the new worlds of VR and AR. Originally working as a 2D UX designer, Mr. Markman explored utilizing traditional UX techniques to try to get his ideas across to other designers and developers via Sketch or other prototyping tools. After sketching out an idea or acting it out for developers, he would often find that, once rendered in a VR headset, the results didn't align with the idea he was trying to get across. "Utilizing general discussion got us to a certain spot, but upon seeing the first prototype, we would realize, 'Oh, that's not what I was describing,'" Mr. Markman said.

This revelation led Mr. Markman and his co-founders to decide to create Moment, a rapid prototyping tool focused on creating prototypes for VR and AR. According to Mr. Markman:

> Within VR, it is important to determine what a scene feels like. What does it feel like to be within a darker space or a lighter space? What does it feel like to be in a small room? In a large room? Standing in a void? All these things that you cannot accurately portray with traditional methods, but are an integral part of VR. We did not care just about the UI, but about prototyping the entire space.

> One of the things we see now in VR and AR, partially due to the limitations of our tools, is a lot of 2D UI designs. Direct translation from 2D web design and mobile just being dropped into VR. Sometimes that may be the right decision, but you often end up with poor ergonomics and miss out on taking advantage of what's unique about VR.

> There was no great tool for prototyping 3D UI for VR/AR. We think we have a good solution for that space. There are many apps that are designed beautifully but have little things that do not translate well to VR or AR, or some things that may not have been planned fully for VR or AR. We think we can help those apps focus on what they do well.

> As the industry grows, we will start seeing a set of universal practices and principles in VR and AR. It just takes time, and we are excited to be helping define those principles in the early stages.

> Moment is currently in beta and will see a wide release in 2018.

However you choose to do it, finding a way to rapidly prototype your VR and AR apps is an important step and can be the difference between an app that is frustrating to use and an app that is truly great.

TIP

An emerging field for VR/AR will be the field of accessibility. The onus will be on content creators to ensure that VR/AR does not follow the historical path of the web concerning accessibility for its end users. In the early days of the web, accessibility for differently abled users was often an afterthought. As we begin to define the VR/AR space, accessibility for differently abled users can be front and center in our minds.

Traditional design tools

A number of popular 3D computer graphic programs are currently on the market. None of these tools was built specifically with content development for VR or AR in mind, but nearly all of them transition fairly seamlessly to that task. These graphics programs were created to build out 3D graphics out of the box, so utilizing them to create 3D graphics for VR or AR experiences is a natural step.

3ds Max, Cinema 4D, Maya, and Modo are all examples of full-featured, diverse 3D graphic applications you can use to create 3D graphics and models. You can then export these models to a format that your development environment can understand as part of your 3D workflow. Depending on your needs, this could mean importing single models for your environments, importing entire scenes created in these 3D packages, or even rendering and importing 360-degree imagery to be brought into your development environment as a texture alone.

TECHNICAL STUFF

360-degree photos are often utilized for VR experiences. When discussing 360-degree photos, you may hear terms such as *equirectangular projection* or *cubemap*. These terms refer to various ways of how an image may be projected for display in 360 degrees. A *cubemap image* is an image that consists of six square image faces that represent a view from one of six perspectives: up, down, left, right, forward, or backward. An *equirectangular image* is an image consisting of one single image face containing the entire 360-degree image, causing more distortion the closer you get to the poles (top and bottom) of the image. And more projection types are always being defined. Google recently announced "equi-angular" images, which seek to solve some of the shortcomings of equirectangular or cubemap images (https://blog.google/products/google-vr/bringing-pixels-front-and-center-vr-video/).

When you're viewing an equirectangular or cubemap image in 2D, you may notice that it looks a bit odd. Equirectangular images seem stretched at the top and bottom, while cubemaps appear divided into six square images. In VR environments, these images are "projected" onto 3D models (equirectangular images onto a sphere, cubemaps onto a cube) where they appear as normal 360-degree environments to a user within that environment. Figure 9-4 illustrates the differences between an equirectangular image on the left and a cubemap image on the right. While they may appear strange as 2D images, when projected onto the inside sphere or cube, respectively, these images appear "correct" to a user whose view is positioned within the sphere or cube.

FIGURE 9-4:
Examples of
equirectangular
and cubemap
images.

Each of these applications has a different set of strengths worth keeping in mind as you evaluate your options for creating graphics for your VR/AR application. For example, modeling in 3ds Max is incredibly robust, whereas animation in Maya and Cinema are considered very powerful and fast. Evaluate how you'll be utilizing each package, and find the platform that best fits the direction of your asset creation.

Figure 9-5 shows Modo in use. Every 3D tool is different, but the basics are very similar. Figure 9-6 shows a different modeling tools interface, Blender, for comparison.

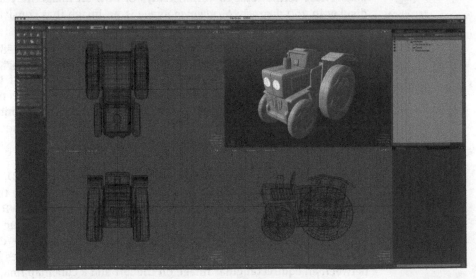

FIGURE 9-5:
Modo's UI for
3D modeling.

WARNING

If you're interested in diving into the world of 3D modeling for VR, be advised that the waters can be very deep! Don't be discouraged if it takes a bit of time to learn 3D modeling, even if you're a power user in other programs. The transition from the 2D world of the screen to a 3D world can be difficult for even the most experienced 2D graphics artists. In 2D work, you need to visualize only the side facing the user. In 3D for VR/AR, you have to concentrate on all sides of an object, because any side may end up being presented to the user. Keep working at it! 3D is everywhere in today's world. Those skill sets are in high demand, and the demand will only grow as VR and AR grow as well.

WARNING

There can be drawbacks to some of the higher-powered 3D modeling programs. 3D modeling software is processor-intensive work — many of the programs require a fairly powerful computer to run. Many of these programs can also be expensive to purchase and keep up to date. Most of them have trial periods (typically 30 days) in which you may download and try them out to see if they're right for you. Often, however, 30 days is hardly enough to even scratch the surface of what these programs can do.

If you're just beginning to learn 3D modeling, almost any 3D program can teach you the basics. Most of these programs share similar traits or terminology, so learning the basics from one program can carry over skills to other programs. Some of the programs carry "student," "light," or "indie" versions, which are either full or slightly scaled-back versions of their software that can be purchased or subscribed to for a much lower price than the full versions.

If none of these options is available to you, there are also free versions of 3D software available. In-browser solutions such as Sketchup Free can be used to create and export models to VR or AR. A more full-featured solution for users looking to kick the tires of a professional modeling package without the associated cost of a high-end 3D modeling package is Blender. Blender is a free and open-source 3D modeling suite. It's cross-platform and tailored to run well even on older, less-powerful computers. The Blender community is large and diverse, and there are many tutorials available for learning Blender — from the Blender site itself, to YouTube, to *Blender For Dummies* (Wiley). For those just starting out in 3D modeling, Blender is a great way to test the waters and start your journey.

Figure 9-6 shows a screenshot of Blender's interface for 3D modeling. Note the similarities and differences between Blender and the Modo UI shown in Figure 9-5.

After you've established a baseline of skills for 3D modeling, you can decide if you'd like to move on to one of the other modeling tools. If you plan on working in the industry at a studio or agency, research what toolset those studios are typically using. Blender is a great tool for learning 3D modeling, but many studios have a preference for working with one of the higher-powered tools such as Maya or 3ds Max and often have a workflow tailored to a particular toolset.

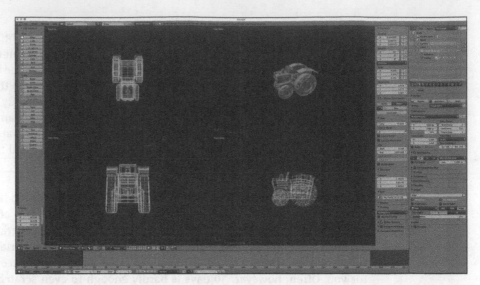

FIGURE 9-6:
Blender's UI.

VR/AR-based design tools

The 3D programs mentioned in the preceding section were mainly created before VR/AR's recent rise to prominence. With the ascent of VR and AR, these tools have begun adapting to these new workflows. 3ds Max Interactive, for example, is a VR engine that extends 3ds Max to help non-developers quickly create mobile, PC, and room-scale VR experiences.

However, there has also been a rise in new tools specifically catered to designing in VR. Tools such as Google Blocks and Oculus Medium are prime examples of tools built specifically for creating and sharing 3D models within a VR environment. These programs are vastly different from the traditional 3D modeling applications previously discussed, in that they focus specifically on VR models. These applications require specific hardware (HTC Vive or Oculus Rift for Google Blocks, Oculus Rift for Oculus Medium), and utilize the motion controllers of these hardware devices to sculpt and create 3D models in a virtual world. You can then export the models for use in a traditional 3D modeling engine or directly to your VR or AR development environment.

Blocks currently feels a bit less full-featured than Medium; however, the simplicity of Blocks makes it much easier for new users to pick up quickly. You may find yourself utilizing a tool like Blocks for quickly prototyping 3D objects to modify in other 3D applications. You'll likely experience a steeper learning curve before you feel comfortable working in Medium; however, you'll be able to take your models a long way inside Medium without the need for other tools.

Figure 9-7 shows the tools and palettes available for a user within the Google Blocks VR interface. The 3D well model shown is by Don Carson and is available on Google Poly (https://poly.google.com), Google's shop for 3D artifacts created in their tools such as Blocks or Tilt Brush.

FIGURE 9-7: Google Blocks VR interface.

These applications offer an entirely new way of thinking about and creating 3D models. Like many things in the VR and AR world, it's still early days for these applications, and best practices and ideas are still emerging. Working in VR for 3D modeling could quickly become the de facto standard for creating 3D assets, especially 3D assets that will be utilized in VR or AR setups. Before VR, designers and artists had to acclimate themselves to creating 3D assets in the 2D world of a computer screen. With the rise of VR and AR, the ability to see your 3D assets fully realized in a 3D setting while working on them is a game changer.

Ready-made models

Premade models are used throughout all industries, from game development to architectural renderings to featured films. Even with a full 3D staff on hand, you can often save time by utilizing a model from one of these resources as a starting point. Like the real world, VR environments often need to be populated with "stuff"; otherwise, they can feel bleak and empty. Many studios use models from sites such as these to populate background items within their environments while concentrating their graphics team on building out the models, which may be the main focus of their application.

In these instances, sites such as CGTrader (www.cgtrader.com) or TurboSquid (www.turbosquid.com) can be very useful. These sites offer high-quality 3D models that range from simple one-off models to highly detailed environments and everything in between. If you have a need for a model, there is likely a model available on one of these sites that covers your need, or can at least get you started.

WARNING

Almost anyone of any skill level can sell models on these sites, which makes for a very large marketplace. It also leads to a large variance in quality and price of the assets. So, buyer beware: Make sure you understand exactly what you're getting before you download. Even if you have no interest in 3D modeling yourself, you need to know what to look for when downloading assets for your application. You need to understand things such as polygon counts, 3D file types, and texturing to ensure that the assets you're downloading will work for your application.

Google Poly (https://poly.google.com) has emerged as an interesting choice for free models. With Tilt Brush and Google Blocks, Google took steps to make the creation of 3D artifacts easier. Google has added to that with Poly, a one-stop shop for users looking for 3D objects or scenes created by users using Tilt Brush and Blocks. Because many of the models in Poly are generated from Blocks, the models generally are simple and low polygon, which may not work stylistically for every scenario. However, they can be a great way to quickly populate VR or AR scenes with 3D objects, and the low-poly models can help ensure that your VR or AR experiences' performance won't be slowed by more resource-intensive high-polygon models. Figure 9-8 shows the process of searching for and viewing 3D objects at the Google Poly site.

FIGURE 9-8:
The Google Poly interface for searching and browsing models.

Capturing Real Life

There are many instances where, instead of creating computer-generated graphics for your virtual worlds, you may want to bring in content from the real world. This could be for any number of reasons. Perhaps you want to enable the user to explore a real place or person, so you want to use actual still images or video. Perhaps you're a photographer or videographer and you want to know how to bring your images or video into VR or AR. Or perhaps you just think you'll be able to create content for your vision more quickly through real-world objects.

Up until very recently, the consumer-grade options available for capturing 360-degree content were limited, forcing most of the early VR and AR experiments to utilize computer-generated imagery alone. Today, however, a number of options are available for capturing real life and translating those captures into virtual worlds.

Video-capture options

The options available for capturing 360-degree video have grown from few to many in a short span of a few years. The upsurge of interest in VR and AR has also triggered the same sort of interest uptick in 360-degree capture devices. Just a few years ago, the cost of 360-degree video-capture devices put them far out of reach of most consumers, and the quality of captured images often left much to be desired. As the industry has matured, however, we're beginning to see a number of options available at the consumer level where price and quality are beginning to align with users' expectations.

Video-capture options typically fall into one of two categories: a lower-end, mass-consumer-friendly model, or a higher-end model targeted more toward professional users. When evaluating these options, make sure that the quality of the output aligns with your expectation for your experience.

Mass-consumer models

The mass-consumer models for capturing VR video include cameras such as the Samsung Gear 360, the VIRB 360, the Ricoh Theta V, and the GoPro Fusion 360. Most of the cameras in this space are relatively small in size and have few on-camera controls. You must pair them with an external device such as your cell-phone and use a mobile app for control.

These cameras often utilize multiple lenses to capture a full 360-degree environment and create multiple videos or still image files that may need to be stitched together to create a single 360-degree environment. Most consumer models have the ability to stitch these videos together automatically. Cameras that can stitch their footage together automatically will output a single file, ready for 360-degree playback. Cameras that cannot automatically stitch together their footage will output multiple files, and you must use specialized software to stitch the footage together yourself. Doing so can be time consuming, but it can also result in a more seamless stitch, because you have finer-grain control over the final output.

You can often notice the evidence of stitched footage, especially in footage from lower-quality consumer cameras. For example, you may see seams in the video where the environment doesn't quite align with where it should. This was especially noticeable in very early consumer 360-degree cameras — less so today through better image-stitching software. It's still worth paying attention to as you look to compare consumer video-capture models, though. A low-quality stitch with noticeable stitching lines can pull users out of your experience.

REMEMBER

The price of consumer 360-degree camera models can vary wildly, from less than a hundred dollars to thousands of dollars. Typically, you get what you pay for, but not always. When evaluating these cameras, pay attention to things such as the resolution, the *frame rate* (the frames per second the camera can capture), and how well the stitching seems to function. Try to review footage captured by the camera you're looking to purchase, both in 2D 360 mode (as you may see on YouTube on your computer), and in the VR headset you may be looking to target with your output video. Often, the quality of the stitched image output and the final resolution will be the determining factors in what can make or break a 360-degree camera.

Figure 9-9 shows the Samsung Gear 360 camera, popular for its portability and ability to quickly shoot 360-degree still images and video.

FIGURE 9-9:
The Samsung Gear 360 camera.

Professional camera models

When capturing for VR, especially if capturing for a client, you may find that consumer 360-degree video cameras don't offer the level of professional output your project requires. Many of the consumer cameras deliver impressive output for their price point, but they can't compare to some of the higher-end models in terms of features and quality.

Options such as the GoPro Omni, Google Jump, Insta360 Pro, the Vuze+, and Nokia OZO+ offer more features and a much higher-end experience than any of the mass-consumer models. Many offer 360-degree live broadcasts and ultra-high resolution, as well as the ability to capture both still images and stereoscopic imagery in 360 degrees. Most mass-consumer cameras provide only monoscopic 360-degree images, which lack the sense of depth that stereoscopic imagery provides.

TECHNICAL STUFF

Stereoscopic imagery is the process in which two images are taken at slightly different placement; when they're viewed at the same time through each eye, they create the illusion of depth. This mimics what the human eyes do automatically, resulting in very realistic 3D imaging. Your eyes are separated on your face and provide different images of the world around you that your brain interprets as depth. A simple way to visualize this is to hold one finger up in front of your face at arm's length. Align it with an object in the distance with your left eye closed and your right eye open. Keeping your arm still, open your left eye and close your right eye. This shift in placement illustrates the slightly different image each eye is feeding to your brain.

Stereoscopic imagery can be an important piece in making a virtual environment feel more "real." Standard 360-degree monoscopic video, as shot by most consumer-grade cameras, is typically a single equirectangular video displayed on the inside of a sphere. A virtual camera is then added to the center of the sphere, so everywhere a user turns his head he has the appearance of being within the virtual environment. However, because both eyes are seeing the exact same image, any sense of depth is lost. By capturing stereoscopic images and displaying a different image for each eye, you can simulate that sense of depth back into the images you're displaying.

WARNING

Be wary, shooting in stereoscopic can come at a cost. Due to various factors (device performance, network speed, and so on), you can often only send a certain amount of video data to some devices, especially mobile VR headsets. This means that stereoscopic video content is often stacked on top of one another in the video signal or sent side-by-side. This means you're often limiting the resolution of the video you're sending to the user to half the width or height of what you might be able to send if you were using monoscopic video. It also can make video stitching much more difficult to get right, which can be uncomfortable to the end user.

Additionally, the stereoscopic effect works well only at certain distances. Being too close to the subject can result in awkward stitching. Being too far away can mute the effect of stereoscopic imagery in the first place.

Stereoscopy can be amazing, but it's not the best choice for every application. Monoscopic video tends to have more hardware solutions available to shoot with at a lower price point, and it can often push across higher-resolution video files to lower-end devices. It can be a good choice if your user base has lower-end headsets or doesn't expect the highest-end immersion experience. Stereoscopic video is typically more expensive to do well, and it can be difficult to push across higher-resolution video to lower-end devices. On the upside, it can result in more realistic visuals. Stereoscopic video is appropriate for professional scenarios targeting a highly sophisticated user base for whom the most realistically captured scenes are needed.

Still-image capture options

Many of the options for video capture described earlier in this chapter enable you to take both still images and video. On the consumer side, the Samsung Gear 360, the VIRB 360, the GoPro Fusion, and the Ricoh Theta V all have options to shoot either 360-degree video or still images. Other options are available for capturing still images, too, including some options that may enable you to use hardware you already have access to.

Mobile applications

If you want to capture a 360-degree still image of a scene and you don't have access to any other hardware, you can use your smartphone or other mobile device to create a quick-and-dirty 360-degree equirectangular photosphere. On some mobile devices, this mode exists already, though many users may not be aware of this capability. On the Google Pixel, for example, there is "Photo Sphere" mode that enables you to rotate your camera around you while it captures and stitches together the scene.

For users who don't have this ability built into their devices, a number of apps exist that offer similar functionality. Apps such as Occupital's 360 Panorama for iOS or Google Camera for both iOS and Android both enable you to move your phone around a scene while they capture and stitch the various parts of the scene together.

These applications do all the heavy lifting for you, guiding you through the photo taking and stitching process in a method similar to the way you may capture a panoramic image, all without the need for extra hardware.

Photosphere software is impressive in its ability to inexpensively create 360-degree photos on the fly, but the results aren't professional quality. The photospheres these apps produce are typically low resolution and have noticeable stitching lines, especially if you're shooting without a tripod or in conditions with varying lighting conditions. An indoor scene with a window in the shot can result in a very overexposed area in one part of your 360-degree image and very dark spots in others. These solutions are best used in non-professional settings, or to create a quick mock-up for something you plan to re-shoot later.

Figure 9-10 displays Google's Photo application in use in *Photo Sphere* mode. By guiding your movement around your environment, Google takes multiple photos and stiches them together to create a usable 360-degree format such as an equirectangular image.

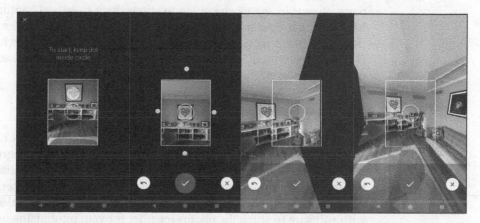

FIGURE 9-10:
Google's Photo
application in
Photo Sphere
mode.

Standard cameras

You can create photospheres with a relatively small and inexpensive standard camera setup. A camera body along with a separate fisheye lens capable of capturing a 180-degree field of view (FOV), a tripod, and a lens ring camera mount are enough to enable you to capture extremely high-quality 360-degree photospheres. Although these photos can have much higher resolution and higher quality than those captured via mobile phone camera applications, the photo-capturing process is not as automated and requires more work on your end for the best result.

The camera is mounted vertically, with the fisheye lens enabling you to capture four photos in 90-degree increments. These photos can then be stitched together to create the full 360-degree photosphere. The lens ring mount enables the camera lens to act as the focal point of the rotation (in contrast to a standard camera mount, which would rotate the camera body as the focal point and throw off how the photos would be stitched together).

The photo stitching process is not nearly as automated as with the mobile apps. You need to process your photos using a tool such as Adobe Lightroom and then utilize specialized stitching software such as PTGui Pro or Kolor Autopano to stitch the resulting photos together into an equirectangular photosphere.

The process is more laborious than with the mobile app photosphere software, but the results you can achieve utilizing this method are very high quality. It's a tried-and-true method for capturing high-quality photosphere imagery, and it can be used for many professional applications.

WARNING

Using any method that does not take all 360 degrees of a photo at once requires a static scene, because multiple photos will be stitched together to create the final photosphere. For example, if people are walking around in the background of your shot, you may find yourself with multiple images of the same person in different parts of your image when you go to stitch them together! Capturing images via hardware that does not shoot the full 360 degrees at once works best for scenes that will remain motionless and can be controlled, such as the inside of a store (without customers). Many Google Business View photos are taken with standard cameras during off hours for this reason.

360-degree professional cameras

In recent years a number of higher-priced still image cameras have cropped up that are designed specifically to take high-resolution 360-degree still images. Most of these cameras eliminate the drawbacks of traditional photography (having to turn the camera manually 90 degrees, trigger the shutter, and so on) by automating the processes of rotation and picture taking. Many also come bundled with software to stitch the photos together for you, minimizing or removing that laborious step for most users.

Two popular cameras in this category are the NCTech iris360 Pro and the Matterport Pro line. These cameras have seen heavy use in the real estate industry for 360-degree imagery, and many of their features have been developed around solving the sorts of problems arising from the creation of virtual walkthroughs of buildings. NCTech recently announced plans to move production from the iris360 Pro to the iSTAR pulsar, which it lists as the world's most powerful fully automated Google Street View–ready camera. It has the capability to output the standard imagery used for Google Street View or Google Business View 360 photos.

These cameras all come with a variety of features and benefits. Many of them come with software that can not only capture and stitch your photographs as needed, but also host your experiences online, potentially eliminating the need to create standalone applications to host or view your imagery.

These high-end 360-degree cameras are feature-rich and can eliminate some of the manual labor and technical skill needed to create 360-degree photos from a standard camera. Such a camera can be a good investment if you intend on making 360-degree photography a large part of your work going forward. However, they come at a cost, and the feature sets can vary wildly between brands and models. Be sure to evaluate the available choices carefully, and be prepared to invest both time and money to get the best photos out of these cameras.

Figure 9-11 shows the compact iSTAR pulsar being used to capture 360-degree images as it would be used for Google Street View.

FIGURE 9-11:
The iStar pulsar.

Courtesy of NCTech

Audio options

Audio is often treated as a second-class citizen in VR and AR experiences — and unfairly so! Poorly executed audio within VR can make or break your experience in the exact same way poorly executed visuals can. Building a full virtual environment requires stimulating *all* the senses, and VR currently best simulates the visual and auditory experience. (Perhaps thankfully, it isn't quite there yet with taste and smell.) Focusing on the aural experience as much as you focus on the visuals in VR and AR can take your experience from good to great.

Audio is important in AR, but in a more subtle way than in VR. VR projects need to fully simulate the audio of the virtual environment. AR needs to take into account the fact that the user is already in a real-world environment and is experiencing your digital holograms as pieces of that environment. Rarely will you find yourself supplying a full-blown environmental audio experience in AR as you would with VR. Instead of spatial audio, you'll most frequently use interface audio cues and audio for directing the attention of your users in AR applications.

There are three main types of audio used in VR and AR projects: voiceover, sound effects, and background audio. Not every project will require all three, but it's very common for at least two to be present.

Voiceover

Many VR and AR applications can benefit from the strategic use of voiceover. Long-form text can be cumbersome to read in both VR and AR, and it can over-whelm users who are already concentrating on the environment or holograms around them. Voiceover can convey information while avoiding long-form text and its associated problems.

Creating voiceover audio isn't difficult and doesn't necessarily require high-cost specialized equipment. Microphones such as the Zoom H2n can act as a field recorder, capturing both background audio and foreground voice. The Zoom H2n even has a built-in "spatial audio" mode, which creates an audio file containing omnichannel, left and right channel, and front and back channel tracks. This spatial audio file can then be combined with 360-degree videos right out of the box to provide a full 360 degrees of sound.

Capturing voiceover on your own is not particularly difficult, but there is a lot to be said for utilizing professional talent. There are any number of studios available to do so for you, though you may also consider using a site such as Fiverr (www.fiverr.com) to contact voice and audio freelance talent directly for your custom recordings.

WARNING

You can often save money going this route, but the talent level of freelancers on sites like these can vary wildly, so be sure that you're confident in the talent you hire.

Sound effects

Almost every VR or AR project will require sound effects. For example, it's common to use interface sounds to alert users that something is interactive or that something is happening. Sound can also be triggered by in-environment interactions, such as a user opening a door or breaking a window. If executed without audio or, perhaps even worse, audio that feels incorrect, these interactions can feel "false" in VR or AR. Nearly every project will benefit from some well-placed sound effects.

If you already have a license with an application suite such as Adobe Creative Cloud, you may already have a package of sound effects available to use. Audio-specific applications such as Adobe Audition often have a large variety of royalty-free sound effects available. These range from the standard Foley sound effects (everyday sound effects such as the creaking of a door, echoing footsteps, or wind in the trees), to cartoon beeps and buzzes, high-tech squeals, or the roar of a large crowd.

There are also a number of downloadable collections of sound effects packages. You can find these collections via your preferred music download service such as iTunes or Amazon, by searching for *royalty free sound effects* or similar terminology. You may not find what you need in grab-bag selections of sound effects such as these, but they're worth exploring, because you may be able to get a lot sounds at a low cost.

If you're unable to find what you need in these broad audio selections, there are a number of sites that cater to one-off sound effect downloads or even custom sound effect creation. Sites such as Pro Sound Effects (http://prosoundeffects.com) or Pond5 (http://pond5.com) enable you to search for and download specific audio sound effects or voiceovers, or even license their entire sound effects library for a price. This option is typically for more advanced sound designers, but it's something to consider, depending on the depth of your sound-effects needs.

WARNING

When choosing a collection, be sure to look at the licensing rights of the collection and make sure the sounds are royalty-free. *Royalty-free* means you don't have to pay a licensing fee for each usage of the sound effect in your application.

Background audio

It's very rare for a real-world scenario to have no background audio whatsoever, even in environments you may picture as nearly silent. In a quiet office building, there are often white-noise sounds and other sounds that users would immediately associate with being in an office — the soft patting of keyboard keys being depressed, a phone ringing off in the distance, the hum of fluorescent lighting. A "silent" forest at night may include the sound of wind through leaves, crickets gently chirping, and soft footsteps on leaves. In a massive quiet room such as an empty cathedral, a user moving about would likely expect to hear her footsteps echoing off the cathedral walls. When developing your application, be sure to consider what sort of real-world background audio the user may expect to hear in the digital location you're providing and try to evoke the same sort of atmosphere through your background audio selection.

WARNING

Background sounds may seem secondary to your application or game, but they set the scene for the user. Poorly implemented audio can prevent users from fully immersing themselves in your application.

Background audio and sound effects also help orient users to the environment, without requiring them to be looking everywhere all the time. Imagine a survival game where your user is constantly being hounded by a zombie horde. If a zombie is approaching your user from behind, you would want the user to be alerted to its presence via growling, footsteps, and so on, and for those sounds to appear to originate behind the user. This not only makes the experience more intense, but also makes it feel more *real*, the ultimate goal.

Background audio in AR experiences should be evaluated slightly differently. Because AR experiences already exist "in the real world," there is less of an imperative to establish an environment. For AR experiences, focus more on sound effects and spatial audio to pull users into your experience and make the digital holograms feel more integrated into the physical world.

Spatial audio

After your audio is captured — whether through voiceovers, background audio, or sound effects — you need to consider how it will be used within your application. Audio in VR or AR experiences should almost always be spatialized in 3D. The virtual sound sources should feel as if they're coming from a given point in a virtual environment. An audio source on a car in a VR environment should change as it drives closer to a user or as it moves farther away. Audio being played from a digital hologram in AR space should feel as if it's coming from the object's positioning in space. Distributing your sound effects throughout your virtual environments as spatial audio sound sources help to create a realistic audio experience for your VR or AR user.

Development platforms such as Unity and Unreal make it easy to create spatial audio for VR/AR within their own applications. Facebook offers a software suite named Facebook Spatial Workstation, which assists in designing spatial audio in 360-degree video and cinematic VR. Google has also launched Resonance Audio, a multi-platform, open-source spatial audio software development kit; Resonance Audio works across a number of development and consumption environments.

 REMEMBER Audio should be a first-class citizen in your planning, not an afterthought. Consider how audio will play a part in your application upfront, while you're storyboarding the visuals. A combination of sound effects, voiceover, spatial audio, and background audio goes a long way toward getting your users immersed in your virtual worlds.

Assessing Development Software

After you've created or captured your visual and audio assets, you need a way to share them with the world. Luckily, options abound for creating VR and AR experiences. From simple one-click solutions to full-blown gaming engines, there are myriad ways to release your content to the public. The ideal development software depends on what your application needs to accomplish and the audience it needs to reach.

REMEMBER

Many VR or AR hardware devices can only be developed for by using a specific combination of hardware and/or software. For example, a Mac is required for ARKit development. Ensure that before diving into a specific development platform you are aware of the platform's output capabilities, especially if you're targeting a specific VR/AR device.

Game development engines

Using a game development engine to build VR or AR applications can give you a lot of flexibility compared with other options that allow you to develop for only a specific piece of hardware. For example, learning XCode and the ARKit development platform would enable you to develop only iOS ARKit applications, whereas using a game engine enables you to output to ARKit, ARCore, HoloLens, VR devices, and so on. It may take a while to learn the game development engine software, but you'll be able to put that knowledge to work across a broad range of projects and platforms.

Unity and Unreal Engine are two of the most popular game engines available to the general public. They've been used to create everything from simple mobile games, to desktop software, to extremely high-end gaming titles and everything in between. What's more, they're both well supported and frequently updated, and both integrate the latest in VR and AR development into their workflows. Which engine you decide to pursue will ultimately be up to the specifics of your project, but both engines can output to many different devices or experiences, providing great flexibility and versatility.

Here's a comparison of Unity and Unreal Engine:

>> Both engines offer development on PC or Mac.

>> Both support almost all flavors of VR development and VR hardware.

>> Both support developing AR experiences with ARKit and ARCore plugins.

>> Unity supports a broad platform base. Unreal does as well, but it focuses more on PC and console experiences.

>> Unity offers extensive software development kit (SDK) support for AR hardware (HoloLens, Meta2, Mira Prism). Unreal does not offer the same level of support for these devices just yet.

>> Unity mainly focuses around coding in C#, while Unreal Engine is coded in C++.

TECHNICAL STUFF

The flexibility to output to many different platforms can come at a price. Game engines such as Unity and Unreal are downstream from the platforms they can develop for, meaning they may be slightly behind in integrating features as they're released for certain platforms. If Apple releases an update to ARKit, it will be available to ARKit developers immediately, whereas developers on the game engine may need to wait for the development team to integrate it into the game engine before they can utilize it. Additionally, the flexibility offered can come at a performance or architecture cost. Gaming engines will typically enable users to write in one programming language (for example, C++ or C#) and compile that code down to the machine code needed for the device to which they're exporting. This can sometimes result in suboptimal code or remove a developer's understanding of what her compiled code is actually doing. The flexibility benefits nearly always outweigh the costs, but it's worth keeping some of these potential drawbacks in mind as you begin your VR and AR explorations.

Figure 9-12 shows a screen shot of the Unity interface. The interface of these engines are fairly similar, typically consisting of Scene/Game windows to display your game's visual design and actual gameplay for testing, Project and Hierarchy windows to display your project's assets and items within the scene, and an Inspector window to list a selected item's attributes.

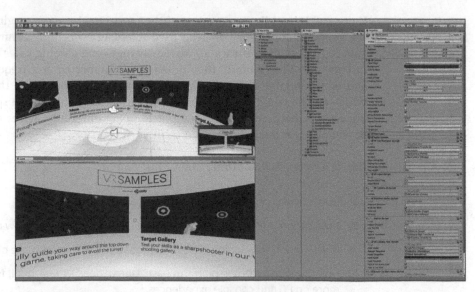

FIGURE 9-12: The Unity interface.

Unity and Unreal offer sliding payment scales, which can be perfect for beginners just learning the software. If you have trouble creating assets or get stuck on certain development assets, both offer free and paid assets through their asset stores that make it easy to quickly spin up projects. For VR development, both Unity and Unreal have gone so far as to create in-VR version of their development tools, where users can enter VR and build out scenes as they would in the standard editor.

Figure 9-13 shows a screenshot of Unreal's example of a user working in VR mode. The left side of the image shows what the user sees while in VR, while the right side shows the user in the Vive hardware.

FIGURE 9-13:
The Unreal
Engine in
VR mode.

For developing AR experiences, both support ARKit and ARCore experiences, but Unity has been the better choice for developing for AR headsets such as the HoloLens, the Meta2, or the Mira Prism. As these devices grow in popularity or other hardware is introduced, expect this to level out between these engines over time. If you're looking to create headset AR experiences for these specific headsets in the near future, however, Unity may be the better choice for you.

Both Unity and Unreal are fantastic tools to learn, and the skills it takes to use them will only become more desirable as VR and AR grow in popularity. If you're serious about becoming a developer for VR or AR experiences, learning one of these platforms is a great way to go.

UNITY AND THE HoloLens

Zeke Lasater is a senior interactive developer with experience building everything from web applications to mobile games and VR and AR experiences. Microsoft invited him to take part in the agency readiness program for the HoloLens, which brought in users to test Microsoft's new hardware and the software tools used to create AR experiences before initial release. He had the following to say regarding his development work with Unity and the HoloLens:

> When first developing for the HoloLens, there was a general learning curve for the HoloLens platform and understanding the capabilities of the HoloLens. On the plus side, the team already knew Unity well, which allowed us to spin into development for the device quickly.
>
> As we began to understand the device capabilities, I found we were able to iterate much quicker within Unity and Visual Studio. Unity's ability to visualize the 3D environment within the editor helped, though in the beginning we were pushing builds to the device at a high frequency to visualize how things would feel in headset. Once we felt we knew the device's strengths, we were able to imagine features within the headset far quicker and would need to send builds to the device less and less. The HoloLens emulator within Visual Studio also helped eliminate the time we spent pushing to device. And thankfully both Unity and Microsoft have made strides in improving the development workflow for creating AR experiences since then to be as painless as possible.
>
> You have to think very differently when designing and building for AR experiences, and especially for the HoloLens. Removing the 2D screen that we have become so familiar with developing for is a huge change. You take for granted how much thought and time has been put into the user experience of 2D screens to get it to where our usage of them seems second nature. It can feel unnatural to anyone jumping into a full AR headset experience. You need to reduce controls to their simplest form possible and really think about the easiest way you can help users accomplish their tasks.
>
> Networking HoloLens devices together to have a shared experience is where the hardware really stepped into its own. This is where HoloLens and AR in general will really start to shine — the potential of a social experience. Combine the already great tracking, spatial sound, and a shared social experience with an improved field of view will be a huge step forward for AR in the next version of the HoloLens.

TIP

Unity and Unreal are also not the only choices available when you begin evaluating game engines, and even after making a choice between the two it's worth re-evaluating other game engines from time to time. A recent entry to the game engine market is Amazon's Lumberyard. Although Amazon is not thought of as a game engine developer, it purchased an existing game engine, CryEngine, from which to build Lumberyard. Lumberyard is an interesting competitor to Unity and Unreal, and it offers many similarities to those two engines. Unfortunately, Lumberyard is currently only built for the PC. (Sorry, Mac users.) And although Lumberyard offers fairly extensive support for VR, it doesn't currently support AR directly. Regardless, with Amazon's broad reach and extensive background of catering to developers, if you're interested in game development engines, Lumberyard is a choice to keep an eye on.

Figure 9-14 shows the Amazon Lumberyard interface. Although it uses different terminology, the basic options it offers developers are similar to other game development engines such as Unity and Unreal.

FIGURE 9-14:
The Amazon Lumberyard engine interface.

Mobile augmented reality development

Many development environments offer the ability to export to mobile AR devices, but you can also develop mobile AR applications directly using the SDKs created for developing Apple and Android mobile applications.

You can create iOS ARKit applications by directly accessing the ARKit SDK through XCode (the development environment) and Swift (the coding language) for building iOS applications. For building out ARCore–based Android experiences, you can use Android Studio and the Java coding language.

Whether developing within the Android or iOS ecosystem directly makes sense for your AR application will depend on a number of questions: Do you know either coding ecosystem already? Are you certain that you'll only ever want to work within either the Android ecosystem or Apple ecosystem?

For some, especially those with prior knowledge of either XCode/Swift or Android Studio/Java, the ability to interact directly with the AR SDKs for a particular environment may make sense. However, if you aren't sure about where your AR development may take you in the future, the flexibility to distribute other options (such as the game engines Unity or Unreal) to many ecosystems may make more sense.

WebVR

Desktop applications have long been the go-to method for creating and developing for 3D experiences such as VR and AR. 3D design and development have always been resource-intensive processes, requiring power that only desktop applications could provide. However, the rise in popularity of VR and AR, combined with the rise in computing performance, have led to the development of a number of browser-based tools that can be used for VR and AR development.

Most of these VR experiences for the web are powered by WebVR. WebVR is a JavaScript application programming interface (API) that enables you to create immersive 3D experiences within your browser. WebVR is supported across a number of web browsers; you can find specific information on which browsers are currently supported at https://webvr.rocks.

TECHNICAL STUFF

The WebVR API is powered by WebGL, a JavaScript API for rendering 2D and 3D graphics without the use of a plugin. An API is a set of rules and definitions put in place for creating software. WebGL is based on OpenGL, a powerful cross-platform API built for embedded systems like smartphones and videogame consoles. Because it's based on OpenGL, the WebGL API can provide an extremely powerful way to render content through a browser.

Unlike most VR applications, within WebVR there is no need for a special setup. To experience WebVR, you simply click a link and you're taken to the VR experience, much as you would be with any web page. In this way, WebVR can potentially help eliminate much of the friction that has come along with traditional VR applications, enabling users to get into and out of experiences immediately. Plus, in many instances, a WebVR experience can run directly in your browser without the need for a headset. Many people may not consider VR experiences taking place on a 2D screen to be "true" VR. However, the market size of users without a VR headset but with a WebVR-enabled browser is enormous. The ability to send potential users your experience over the web and let them view it in their browsers without the need for a headset can be a big plus and can extend the potential market of your application.

WebVR does have drawbacks. Web browser support is not fully implemented in every browser, and the browsers that do support it often support it only for certain headsets. (For example, Microsoft's Edge browser offers support for Windows Mixed Reality headsets, but not Vive or Rift, Mozilla's Firefox browser offers support for Vive and Rift, but not Windows Mixed Reality, and so on.) Web browsers were also not originally built with the intention of running intense graphic applications such as WebVR. Browsers have made great strides in terms of performance, but it's unlikely that a WebVR experience that must run inside a browser will be able to compete with the performance offered by a native application.

As is the case with AR standalone applications, AR on the web lags a bit behind VR — and with good reason. WebVR is a powerful tool, but it can suffer from performance issues on underpowered machines. AR applications can often be more demanding than VR experiences. Not only do they have to potentially render the same amount of 3D content as a VR experience, but they also have to track your surrounding environment and make calculations about how your content should appear. In addition, mobile-AR experiences must render video input of your environment to overlay other graphics on top of.

However, advances are being made in this space as well. Google has released experimental versions of mobile AR browsers for both newer Android and iOS devices. Expect AR experiences on the web to begin slowly building traction within the next few years, especially if WebVR is able to gain a solid foothold among users.

Figure 9-15 shows a WebVR experience being used to draw a shape in 3D space in a web-enabled browser.

There are a few options for developing WebVR content, but they generally fall into three categories: accessing the WebVR API directly, coding frameworks built on top of WebVR, and using online development environments. In the following sections, I look at each of these approaches.

Accessing the WebVR application programming interface

If you're interested in diving directly into the source that powers VR experiences on the web, exploring the source code for WebVR and WebGL may be for you. You can find the specification draft for WebVR hosted on Github at https://immersive-web.github.io/webvr.

You can write WebVR apps in any text editor, the same way you code an HTML page or JavaScript application. However, going directly to the WebVR or WebGL specification and trying to write code against it can be a daunting task for all but the most dedicated developers. For many people looking to create WebVR content, there are far easier ways to begin developing WebVR applications.

FIGURE 9-15:
Web AR on
Google Pixel.

Coding frameworks built on top of WebVR

A number of frameworks have been created to try and take some of the pain out of creating WebVR experiences.

Before WebVR existed, a JavaScript library called three.js was conceived for creating 3D graphics in the web browser. Three.js is built using WebGL, the same JavaScript API that WebVR utilizes for rendering its visual content. With the rise of WebVR, three.js extended its capabilities to handle WebVR-based content as well, cementing three.js as a popular library for those wanting to get into WebVR-focused development. However, three.js is very code-heavy and can be intimidating for those seeking to test the waters of WebVR. With the recent growing interest in WebVR, a number of other libraries have been created to ease users into the world of VR on the web.

A-Frame is a popular library created for building VR experiences. It handles all the boilerplate code and VR setup you would otherwise have to code on your own, simplifying and speeding up the development process for browser-based VR.

A-Frame is based on HTML markup, so it's accessible to almost anyone with a small amount of coding experience. And at its core, A-Frame is built on top of three.js, which enables developers interested in diving deeper into the source to do so, providing unlimited access to the three.js library, JavaScript, WebVR, and WebGL code powering the experience. A-Frame supports several types of 3D models as well, from glTF to OBJ to COLLADA, making it easy for developers to import their preferred model types directly into A-Frame for display in the browser.

Developing 3D experiences through code alone can make visualizing the end product of that code difficult. Developers often find themselves not sure how things should be positioned, moved, or scaled through numbers on a screen alone. As A-Frame looks for further ways to simplify the world of 3D VR development on the web, it also provides a visual 3D inspector to view exactly how your experience is shaping up, and enables you to tweak and adjust values while visualizing the results. Figure 9-16 displays the A-frame inspector being used to examine an A-frame example scene.

FIGURE 9-16:
The A-Frame inspector.

AR development with A-Frame is possible, though it suffers the same issues as most other WebVR-based experiences trying to run AR. Most web AR experiences are backed by a variation of ARToolKit (see Chapter 8), which requires a fairly powerful mobile device for anything beyond very simple executions and most utilize a marker-based AR experience. For some applications, this may not be an issue, but for others this can introduce another level of friction for users, which may make it an inappropriate choice.

REMEMBER

Most executions of AR on the web are not quite as polished as web-based VR executions. This is a trend you've likely noticed across the board for all AR hardware and software in comparison to VR. In broad terms, AR is not quite at the same stage of development as VR hardware and software. With AR still in its early stages, learning and experimenting with the technology now puts you in a great position to be well ahead of the curve as AR gradually moves toward the mainstream.

Using online development environments

One of the more interesting developments following the rise of WebGL has been the rise of online game engines and editors for building VR and AR experiences. Web applications such as Amazon Sumerian and PlayCanvas contain many of the same features that game engines such as Unity or Unreal offer, but with a focus on creating online experiences. Instead of running software on the desktop and building apps that store most of their assets on the hardware device running the application, Sumerian and PlayCanvas run in your browser and store their assets online. Cost is typically based on usage. The Sumerian engine, for example, is free to use, but you pay based on the amount of storage your 3D assets consume and the volume of web traffic they receive.

Marco Argenti, vice president of technology for Amazon Web Services, had the following to say regarding Sumerian's goals:

> Customers are daunted and overwhelmed by the upfront investment in specialized skills and tools required to even get started building a VR or AR application. With Amazon Sumerian, it is now possible for any developer to create a realistic, interactive VR or AR application in a few hours.

Figure 9-17 shows the web-based Sumerian interface in use.

FIGURE 9-17: Amazon Sumerian interface.

Side-by-side, the Sumerian and PlayCanvas applications appear very similar both to one another and to other offline game engines such as Unity and Unreal. Both applications come packaged with a library of 3D objects that users are able to import directly into their scenes. Similar to desktop gaming engines, both engines have a drag-and-drop environment to let users arrange their assets within their 3D scene.

What sets Sumerian apart from PlayCanvas is its focus on visual scripting. Sumerian hopes that its visual scripting tool will enable less technical users to create simple logic for their VR and AR experiences without the need to write code. If you need to write custom code for your experience, both engines utilize JavaScript as their scripting engine. Both engines are focused on utilizing the web to deploy their VR and AR content instead of creating standalone applications to deploy to app stores or devices.

Figure 9-18 displays the PlayCanvas web-based interface in use. Note the similarities and differences between both Sumerian and PlayCanvas, as well as similarities between the desktop-based game engines Unity and Unreal previously in this chapter.

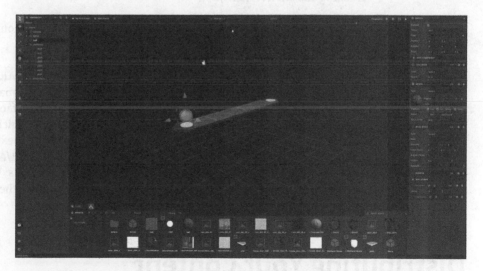

FIGURE 9-18:
The PlayCanvas
editor interface.

These online development environments can be very attractive if you plan to deploy your experiences directly to the web, and if you may not be confident in what you could capably create yourself using another WebVR library like A-Frame. The visual interface and scripting options make it relatively easy for a beginner to jump in and start developing right away.

WARNING

Sumerian and PlayCanvas do have their own limitations. If you want to export to platforms other than the web (native PC apps, mobile apps, and so on), these engines are likely not currently the choice for you. Because they're built on top of web technology, the experience will likely not reach the same visual fidelity or performance benchmarks that native desktop engines such as Unity, Unreal, or Lumberyard will be able to reach. Plus, some of those engines (such as Unity) enable users to export their experiences to WebVR, making the choice for how to build your WebVR experience more difficult.

Engines such as PlayCanvas and Sumerian are built for exporting to the web, but your user will also need a specific web browser/headset combo to run your applications. It's worth spending the time to get to know your audience's consumption habits and how they may view WebVR content to make sure your WebVR plans and their consumption needs align.

In a familiar refrain, WebVR support within PlayCanvas and Sumerian is strong, but AR support is lagging behind. PlayCanvas recently released AR support built on top of ARToolkit to build web-based AR applications. These applications are marker-based applications (requiring a physical marker for targeting and tracking the environment).

AR is not supported yet on Sumerian, though Amazon has announced upcoming support for AR to be releasing soon.

TIP

Many visual editors promise that they'll let "anyone create VR/AR applications in minutes!" Although this is generally true, the application you may have in mind could require expertise beyond the simple drag-and-drop interface or visual coding environments these apps provide. If you're looking to quickly share some simple 360-degree photos or videos, one of the options in the next section of this chapter may make more sense than learning a full-fledged VR/AR development environment. If you're interested in developing more serious VR/AR content, however, it's worth your time to take a deep dive into the programming environment/language of your choice.

Distributing Your Content

In the beginning stages of any VR or AR project, consider how you'll distribute your content to your users. Unlike websites or traditional computer applications, which can be run on a wide variety of equipment without issue, sharing your VR or AR content with users will likely be heavily dependent on the particular combination of hardware and software available to your audience.

Applications such as Unity and Unreal provide you the flexibility to export to many different platforms, while other development environments such as XCode may enable you to create content for a specific platform only. Make sure you understand the market you're trying to reach before determining how you'll be creating your application.

Virtual reality desktop headsets

You can develop standalone applications for desktop headsets (useful if creating projects that may be distributed in-house only), but most desktop head-mounted displays (HMDs) have their own distribution platform. For example, the HTC Vive's official app store is Viewport, and the Oculus Rift distributes most of its content through the Oculus Store. Windows Mixed Reality apps are distributed through the Microsoft Store. PlayStation VR games are available through traditional brick-and-mortar stores as well as the online PlayStation store. Other options such as Steam VR allow you to distribute to multiple devices, but this may not be as friction-less an experience as the "officially" supported app store for a certain device, most of which are available both while in the VR environment or in front of a 2D screen.

Each store may have a different set of requirements and regulations. If you're creating content for these devices, make sure you understand what you need to provide each store when submitting your applications and how your applications will be displayed and showcased.

Virtual reality mobile headsets

Similar to desktop headsets, mobile headsets typically have an associated store or distribution platform that most users will use to download their content. It is possible to create standalone builds for users, but most VR content you create for mobile headsets will be downloaded from the official distribution platform for each headset. The Google Play Store exposes VR content through the Daydream app, while for the Gear VR most content is accessed via the Oculus Store available through the Gear home screen.

Figure 9-19 shows the Oculus Store as seen through a Gear VR.

Google Cardboard

Google Cardboard is less tied to a specific piece of hardware or software, making its app distribution channels a bit more open. Most content will likely still be accessible from each specific device's distribution store. For Android devices, you would likely distribute your applications through the Google Play Store, while for iOS devices you would distribute content via Apple's App Store.

FIGURE 9-19:
The Oculus Store
via Gear VR.

WebVR

WebVR gives you a much broader distribution platform than the "walled gardens" of the device-specific app stores. As you would with any website, you simply need to find a web host to store your WebVR work. Doing so will enable users on the likes of Cardboard, Daydream, Gear VR, Rift, Vive, and Windows Mixed Reality to experience your content via VR-enabled web browsers.

Augmented reality headsets

AR headsets seems to be headed in the same direction as VR headsets with regard to application distribution. However, because most AR headsets are being targeted toward enterprise-level customers at this time, it will be interesting to see how these distribution methods play out. Microsoft's HoloLens applications, for example, are currently available through the Microsoft Store.

Mobile augmented reality

Mobile AR applications, much like typical mobile applications, can be found in their respective app stores. ARKit apps are available through Apple's App Store, while ARCore apps are delivered via the Google Play Store.

Web-based AR, similar to WebVR, can be accessed via a web browser on your mobile device. It's worth noting, though, that mobile AR often requires very specific hardware and software, beyond the standard mobile web browsers available to users. Be aware of which devices and software can support your experience if you intend to distribute your AR app via the web.

Other options

You may create VR content with a specific application or method of distribution in mind. Or you may want to create and share simple content, such as 360-degree photos or videos, without developing an application to do so.

Distributing 360-degree video content has become much easier, with platforms such as YouTube, Vimeo, and Facebook enabling 360-degree video on their respective platforms. The videos can play through standard browsers on 2D screens and on most major VR headsets. If you're looking for a simple way to distribute your VR video content to a large audience, a solution such as YouTube can often be the best method of doing so.

Various photo apps enable you to share your photos in VR as well. The photo-sharing site Flickr produces a Flickr VR app that allows you to share your photo content in VR. Facebook's 360 app for Gear VR enables users to browse 360-degree VR photos from their friends, and sites such as Kuula (https://kuula.co) allow users to create and share their 360-degree VR photos, as well as add 3D hotspots, videos, and links to other photos, all within the 360-degree experience. These 360-degree images can all be browsed within a standard 2D web browser.

Figure 9-20 shows the Kuula website interface displaying a 360-degree image on a desktop, as well 3D hotspots linking to other images, YouTube videos, and information.

FIGURE 9-20: The Kuula website interface.

The nature of AR and its current level of maturity can make sharing AR content a bit more limited. However, applications such as Instagram, Snapchat, and Facebook all provide their users various ways of sharing their photos and videos complete with AR filters applied to them. The "AR-ness" of these items is limited in scope (often little more than applying a filter to a user's face to make him appear to have koala ears or a butterfly crown), but these simple AR features are likely the widest current usage of consumer AR to date — they're used by millions of users daily. As AR grows in maturity, it will be interesting to see how it will evolve beyond these simple but popular filters into sharable content with more substance.

4

Virtual and Augmented Reality in the Wild

Discover some of the industries utilizing virtual and augmented reality.

Explore specific applications built in virtual and augmented reality.

Evaluate use cases of virtual and augmented reality and what they mean for industries moving forward.

Chapter 10

Exploring Virtual Reality Use Cases

A common misconception about virtual reality (VR) experiences is that they are all predominantly games or entertainment applications. Far from it. VR does allow for incredibly engaging gaming experiences, but the technology has potential that reaches far beyond the gaming world. In fact, VR will only reach its true potential as a transformative technology if users are able to step beyond treating it as a simple entertainment device and use it to create, learn, empathize, and heal.

This chapter examines some of the ways that VR is being used in various industries today. I review a number of applications that currently exist, what these current applications mean for the industries they're a part of, and what they may tell us about the future of VR within that industry.

REMEMBER

There are hundreds of industries with thousands if not millions of uses for VR technology. Use the information in this chapter to help brainstorm ways VR could be used in industries that may not be mentioned here.

Art

Art and technology have long had a tumultuous relationship. The art world has often been slow to adapt to new technologies. Computer-generated art has long been dismissed by some critics as not truly "art." But from the first time primitive people put markings on a cave wall, artists have been pushing the boundaries of what may or may not be considered art by the establishment. The rise of new hardware and software is often accompanied by groups of artists, designers, and innovators finding ways to utilize that technology to create works never before thought possible.

The experiences listed in this section represent VR's many forays in the world of art, from creation to experience.

REMEMBER

VR can facilitate more than the creation of new artworks. It's a new medium to experience art as well. And not just a way to experience works of art specifically created in VR. VR also opens up new possibilities for experiencing existing art, from ancient sculpture to paintings to architecture to industrial design and more.

Tilt Brush

Tilt Brush, at its core, isn't a 3D modeling tool like Google Blocks. It's distinctly a drawing and painting application. However, instead of drawing in two dimensions, as most drawing programs allow, Tilt Brush permits users to draw in all three dimensions, providing your drawings with width, height, and depth.

Figure 10-1 shows a user drawing in VR via Tilt Brush.

FIGURE 10-1:
The Tilt Brush
environment.

The concept sounds simple — and that simplicity may be the secret to Tilt Brush's success. Tilt Brush is intuitive — anyone of any age or any artistic skill level can pick up it up and immediately begin creating, with little instruction. In Tilt Brush, one hand holds your brush, and the other hand holds a palette of tools, similar to the way a painter would hold a palette of paint in the real world. You paint with your brush in 3D as you would in real life — in large, sweeping strokes. But beneath Tilt Brush's simple interface lies a depth that allows users to create beautiful works of art. Tilt Brush users can not only share their own creations with others, but also share the creation process as it occurs, allowing users to watch a drawing or painting come into being as if they were watching a video of the work in progress. This enables anyone to dissect his favorite images to determine how they were created, and to copy those techniques while building his own creations. Tilt Brush also lets users load in, edit, and reset users' favorite works created by others — perfect for the remix culture that exists today.

Figure 10-2 displays multiple angles of Van Gogh's *Starry Night* as re-created in Tilt Brush by user Ke Ding. Experiencing this artwork in VR enables users to move around and through a previously flat work of art. Imagine the myriad of uses an artist such as Van Gogh would have found for VR had the medium been available to him!

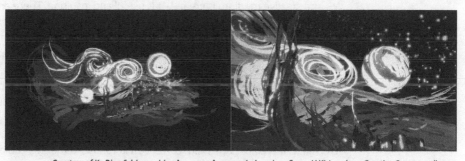

FIGURE 10-2:
Multiple views of
Starry Night
re-created in Tilt
Brush.

Tilt Brush's place in the future of the art world is unknown. But it has shown that VR can and will be used to create not just utilitarian objects but true works of art. Google has teamed up with various artists and other creators to harness the tools available via Tilt Brush with its Artists in Residence program. The purpose of this program is to help develop Tilt Brush and better understand the potential of this new form of art. Many museums and institutions, including the Royal Academy of Arts, have created exhibits displaying VR art and exploring how Tilt Brush and other VR tools will influence the art world today and in the future.

VR offers artists the ability to create works never thought possible with traditional mediums. Wherever Tilt Brush ends up, it's clear we're only at the beginning of cementing the place of VR in the world of artistic creation.

Tilt Brush is available on HTC Vive and Oculus Rift.

TIP

Even without a VR headset, you can still explore some Tilt Brush creations on Google's site for 3D artifacts, Poly (`https://poly.google.com`).

CREATING ART IN VR

Yağız Mungan is an interdisciplinary artist/developer focused on utilizing VR to facilitate creating works of art. I spoke with him regarding his latest piece, *À Quatre Mains*, a VR musical synthesizer and art piece powered by WebVR. Yağız offered up the following on his work and VR as a medium for new artwork:

> I have a varied background, and as a musician, programmer, and artist, I like creating new instruments that help me explore different aesthetics or ideas. With *À Quatre Mains*, my latest piece, I had a few things in mind. Using the digital to go beyond the limitations of the physical. Keeping the physical action to a natural interface. Exploring multi-user dynamics in a virtual medium. And creating a more immersive instrument for musicians.

> VR as a creative medium is great — it is useful and inspiring. There are things that are practically (budges, permits, etc.) or literally impossible to do in the physical realm that can be created in VR. And everything is about perception. Right now with the consumer hardware, we have vision, hearing, and some touch (haptics, physical floor, etc.). And then we have the person's head and hands. With these, you can create a very solid "presence" for the user, and once they are in your experience, their mind fills in the gaps. I think for creators and artists it is a great medium with the ability to be very personal and stimulating.

> Of course, there are issues with current VR iterations, tethering, cables, etc. But the mind is ready to ignore those if the experience is good. The most interesting thing to me is not re-creating existing things but discovering the new experiences only VR can offer. Things you can only imagine in the physical realm are a possibility within VR. In that sense, to me VR is less of the Wild West and more exploring seas and oceans for the first time. With where VR is now, I do not think we have begun to swim just yet but instead are standing on the shore in the sea and perhaps wading in the water up to our chest.

> And all that is happening on many levels; individual creators, companies, research institutes. Some are trying to build ships, some are trying to rent beach, some are building aquariums. We will see who/what stays as we traverse through the hype cycle.

Pierre Chareau exhibit

Pierre Chareau was a French architect and designer in the early to mid 1900s. He was noted for his complex and modular designs for his furniture and interiors. His furniture designs were innovative and clean, with movable parts that appealed to those who valued both form and functionality from their furniture.

One of the pieces Chareau is most famous for is the *Maison de Verre*, the glass house, located in Paris. When the Jewish Museum in New York sought to exhibit Chareau's work, they found a way to not only blend physical artifacts of Chareau's, such as furniture, fixtures, drawings, and interiors, but also utilize VR to transport museum patrons into an otherwise impossible-to-visit location, the glass house itself in Paris.

Figure 10-3 displays the *Maison de Verre* experience as presented by the Jewish Museum's website for the Chareau exhibit.

FIGURE 10-3: The *Maison de Verre* as presented by Jewish Museum 360 experience.

The exhibit, created by Diller Scofidio + Renfro (DS + R), gave patrons the chance to explore Chareau's designs, including some of the furniture they may have just seen in the exhibit gallery, brought to life in VR within the Maison de Verre as Chareau originally intended. This created a scenario that was likely the closest most patrons would get to the real home experience, short of transporting the house itself to New York.

This same VR experience was then extended to exist on the Jewish Museum's website for the digital patrons of the museum. Even though the exhibit has long been closed, visitors from around the world can still visit the museum's website and experience some of the content previously exhibited in their browsers via 360 stills. Go to http://thejewishmuseum.org to check it out for yourself.

The Pierre Chareau exhibit is an early taste of how art museums may begin to adjust their offerings to patrons. With the rise of VR for simulating physical experiences, institutions that rely on physical user presence, such as brick-and-mortar museums, will look for new ways to differentiate themselves to potential patrons. Because VR enables users to experience artifacts they may never have had a chance to experience otherwise, it may help museums present parts of a bigger story to their patrons. Imagine being placed in the same asylum as Van Gogh to see what he saw when he painted *Starry Night*. Or visiting Monet's pond depicted in *Water Lilies*. Or visiting the world's numerous sculptures and architecture with views never before seen now afforded to users by VR.

Google Arts & Culture VR

The Google Arts & Culture VR application enables users to view artworks curated by museums from around the world.

Much like a standard museum, the Arts & Culture VR app curates works of art based around certain artists or time periods. Within the Edward Hopper exhibit, for example, you may find work featured by Hooper predecessors and influences such as William Merit Chase, as well as works featured from his peers, such as Georgia O'Keefe.

Figure 10-4 shows a user exploring the Edward Hopper exhibit in the Google Arts & Culture VR app.

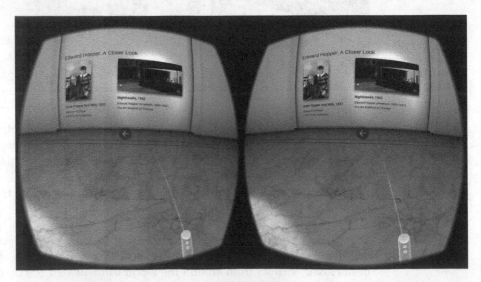

FIGURE 10-4:
Google Arts &
Culture VR in
Google
Daydream.

From early Asian artists to contemporary artists, from Manet to Van Gogh, the app lets you explore art periods and work from each time period. Works are accompanied with audio excerpts for each piece alongside textual information explaining the pieces' significance. Users are also able to zoom in to view individual brush strokes on each piece and to examine them in ways they may never be able to otherwise.

TIP

Google Arts & Culture VR is currently available only for Daydream, so you can't walk around the art as you might otherwise be able to do in a room-scale VR experience. Similarly, the addition of 3D works (sculptures, ceramics, and so on) could add another dimension to the application (no pun intended), but it would also require a flawless way of digitizing those artifacts. Google Arts & Culture VR isn't perfect, but Google's exploration of new ways to view art points to an intriguing future.

Google Arts & Culture VR is a wonderful way of enabling users to explore works they may otherwise be unable to view physically. In the near future, there may be a time when exhibits otherwise unreachable to users are replaced by VR experiences. Children in inner-city Baltimore schools could find themselves browsing the Louvre's galleries while still in school, or senior citizens in the Midwest may be able visit the Met in New York without the hassle of having to hop on a plane.

Google Arts & Culture VR is available on Google Daydream.

Education

VR and education seem like a natural fit. A recent survey of more than 1,000 teachers and educators by Samsung Electronics America, Inc., and GfK showed that while only 2 percent of teachers had used VR in the classroom, 60 percent were interested in making it a part of the learning experience, with 83 percent believing that supplementing their coursework with VR would likely improve learning outcomes. Additionally, 93 percent of educators said that their students would be excited to use VR to learn.

The VR experiences in this section exhibit a few of the many options for utilizing VR in education settings, from classroom-based educator-guided VR tours to exploratory historical simulations to VR's place in eliciting empathy through education.

TIP

Getting students excited about learning can be one of the toughest hurdles for teachers to overcome. If VR can make a student feel more connected to the material, it's far more likely that the student will retain knowledge of that subject matter. Plus, VR could help enhance learning for students with various learning challenges whose needs may not be met in a traditional classroom passive-learning setting.

Google Expeditions VR

Google Expeditions is a VR teaching tool created for taking students on virtual field trips, minus the busses and packed lunches. Expeditions has created hundreds of VR field trips, spanning the fields of arts and culture, science, the environment, current events, and more. Using 360-degree photography, audio, and video, students can visit physical locations such as the Congo to study gorillas, or the Great Barrier Reef to study biodiversity and coral types, or to Borneo to study environmental change. Students can also travel to places otherwise impossible to visit, such as a three-dimensional representation of the inside of the human respiratory system or the inside of a cell.

With Expeditions VR, teachers act as guides throughout the experience. A teacher typically will lead the expedition via an iOS or Android tablet, while students are given Google Cardboard devices to explore their 360-degree surroundings. The devices are all connected via shared Wi-Fi, and the Expedition leader (the teacher) of the experience controls the scenes that will be loaded up in the explorers' (students') headsets.

The leader is provided with a number of different facts and points of interest she can point out to students within the experience. While exploring NASA's Juno mission to Jupiter, for example, a leader may point out Jupiter's Great Red Spot. When the leader clicks the Great Red Spot, it's highlighted in all students' headsets, and arrows guide each explorer to the exact spot the teacher is discussing. The Expedition leader's tablet is also provided with a view of where each student is looking. This can help the leader guide those explorers whose attention may tend to wander. Expeditions also provides a number of questions and answers to the leader, from beginner to advanced, to pose to the explorers to ensure students are retaining the information being presented.

Far more than simply looking at a picture in a book, Expeditions VR brings life to information that students may otherwise have trouble engaging with. Reading that the Burj Khalifa in Dubai is the world's tallest artificial structure is one thing. Allowing students the experience of standing on the edge of the 153rd floor is quite another.

Figure 10-5 displays Google Expeditions as seen through a leader's tablet and an explorer's mobile phone, exploring Festivals of the World by Vida Systems. The leader is provided with various facts and points of interest to talk the explorers through each experience, as well as a view of where the explorers are currently looking.

Expeditions is available on iOS and Android devices for Google Cardboard.

Clouds Over Sidra

Clouds Over Sidra is a VR film created by Gabo Arora and Chris Milk and backed by the United Nations. It tells the story of a 12-year-old girl named Sidra, a Syrian refugee living in the Za'atari refugee camp in Jordan. It follows Sidra from her home, to school, to playing soccer, and back home again, all while filling in pieces of her experience via voiceover, video, and other shots of children throughout the refugee camp. The video ends with a group of children crowding around the viewer.

Clouds Over Sidra is an interesting study. Shot in 2015, it's one of the early forays into VR video storytelling. It isn't technically complex. There are no bells and whistles to the experience. It's a straightforward 360-degree video. It's also likely not what springs to mind when you think of VR educational applications.

And yet, it shows just what can be done with only a simple VR video. Videos such as this can be used both in and out of the classroom to educate children and adults about a real-life refugee crisis. People tend to tune out news reports or headlines covering the refugee crisis. But in VR, you aren't given that option. You're placed in the shoes of someone embedded within a refugee camp, and you can't look away.

With a rise of the availability of VR headsets, immersive storytelling videos such as this could become the de facto standard for informing students and adults alike about current events. *Clouds Over Sidra* proved that the medium can work. The 2015 fundraising conference where *Clouds Over Sidra* was shown raised over $3.8 billion, 70 percent more than projected. According to the UN, viewers shown the application by UN teams were twice as likely to donate than they were otherwise.

Figure 10-6 displays a series of the user's journey from the VR experience of *Clouds Over Sidra*.

Clouds Over Sidra is available from WITHIN on the web at `https://with.in/watch/clouds-over-sidra`. You can watch it via WebVR, Google Cardboard on iOS and Android, Samsung Gear, HTC Vive, Oculus Rift, and PlayStation VR.

FIGURE 10-6:
A series of screen captures of *Clouds Over Sidra*.

Apollo 11 VR

Apollo 11 VR is the story of the Apollo 11 spacecraft, the spaceflight that landed the first humans on the moon. The Apollo 11 VR experience seeks to enable users to experience this historic event as if they were there. The app utilizes original archived audio and video from NASA, as well as historically accurate re-creations of the spacecraft's interiors and exteriors, to place the user within the experience.

Apollo 11 is an interactive documentary of sorts, in which you will not only be able to see the events occurring as if you were there, but also take control of the command module, or land the lunar lander, or explore the moon's surface yourself.

This ability to be an active participant in events rather than simply a passive viewer mimics a trend in education today. Active learning, which has students participate in the process of their own learning, has been shown to be dramatically effective in promoting comprehension and memory.

Apollo 11's experience in providing both a passive experience as a user watches events, but also an active experience, in which a user is invited to participate in the event itself, could be a harbinger of things to come with VR in education. The Apollo 11 experience shows that VR can even provide that active learning experience within the confines of historical events.

Figure 10-7 displays some screenshots of the gameplay within Apollo 11 VR.

Apollo 11 VR is available for Vive, Rift, and PlayStation VR, with a mobile version for Daydream and Gear VR.

Entertainment

A recent report from PricewaterhouseCoopers (PwC) on the entertainment and media outlook for the next five years noted that entertainment and media growth will likely struggle to keep pace with the growth in gross domestic product (GDP). PwC singled out traditional media segments such as TV and cinema as likely to experience sluggish growth and shrink as a share of the global economy between now and 2021. The next wave of entertainment will likely come through emerging technologies such as VR. Just how quickly that wave arrives and is able to be capitalized on is a big question for VR entertainment experiences.

The VR experiences within this section show some of the ways VR is starting to affect our entertainment space. For example, some apps are designed to make us feel like we're truly at an event while we sit in the comfort of our own homes. Others are location-based experiences designed to help us experience things we never thought possible.

REMEMBER

One of the major potential issues in the entertainment space for VR is how quickly that market will be able to mature. In order to create compelling content within VR, VR creators need to be able to produce high-quality content while still being able to monetize on that content. The relatively immature VR market means many VR content creators are still experimenting with ways to develop a working business model for their content.

Intel True VR

Live sporting events and VR have had a tumultuous relationship. On the one hand, the social nature of being at an event would seem to go against the more isolating aspects of VR. On the other, VR, like no technology before it, provides its users the feeling of "being there" even when they aren't.

Enter Intel's True VR technology. True VR is Intel's platform for broadcasting live events in VR. It includes panoramic stereoscopic cameras to capture the event from views never before thought possible. Intel has utilized this technology for everything from Major League Baseball games to the National Football League to the National Basketball Association and the Olympics.

Within True VR, you can do things in VR that you couldn't currently do any other way. You can select from any number of different views from all over the field or court. At a baseball game, you might choose a view that puts you directly behind home plate. Or perhaps, after a home run, you may want to switch over to the dugout view to see players' reactions up close. Intel also makes it a point to find unique camera locations most visitors seldom experience, such as the swimming pool at Chase Field in Arizona, or behind the Green Monster at Fenway Park in Boston.

Intel has added deeper features to the technology as well. The True VR apps include live event stats, curated event views, VR-specific commentary, highlights, and more. All in all, True VR takes the normal user experience and personalizes and enhances it.

Where VR will ultimately end up in relation to live events is unknown, and True VR is a constantly evolving product. Using the technology, you can easily imagine a future where putting on a headset to watch a sporting event is just as natural as turning on your TV, and perhaps a more satisfying experience as well.

Figure 10-8 shows images captured from the NBC Olympics VR app, as well as the NBA on TNT VR app, both powered by Intel True VR technology.

The Intel TrueVR apps are available for Gear VR, Daydream, and Windows Mixed Reality.

FIGURE 10-8:
NBC Olympics and NBA on TNT, powered by True VR.

EXPLORING THE FUTURE OF LIVE-ACTION EVENTS

Kalpana Berman is a product manager at Intel in charge of the team designing and building VR applications that utilize the Intel True VR technology. As the manager in charge of executing Intel's vision for True VR technology, she was able to provide some insight concerning the road map for Intel's True VR technology, the challenges that need to be overcome, and the future of VR and live events.

While the future road map for Intel's True VR technology is confidential, Ms. Berman was able to discuss how she pictures the technology moving forward from a broad perspective:

> I think we can look forward to . . . ingesting new types of volumetric video in VR to allow users the freedom to be anywhere in the field versus fixed points-of-view. Imagine replaying the game from quite literally any possible angle. We want fans to not only feel like they're at the game, but to experience things they could not in real life.

> VR also gives you the ability to ingest and visualize information in a completely new way. We will be experimenting with ways to view that relevant data in a 3D space. We also want to create an experience that is truly personalized to you.

> Finally, we think one of the value propositions of VR could be to remotely connect with users who aren't there with you. Sports *is* a social experience for many fans. Imagine being able to experience a game with your college friends who are spread out around the world. We'll be looking at not only a shared experience within the headset but how to leverage technologies to have an experience for users that bridges across those that do not have a headset.

There are still hurdles for VR to overcome to get there. Ms. Berman adds:

> The market share of users is not where we would like it to be just yet. That could be due to any number of reasons; form factor discomfort, computational intensity, bandwidth, and [the fact that] VR can be isolating. But most importantly, we need to reach a point where the quality of live VR events is on par [with] or better than the amazing quality offered in TV broadcasts. To do so will require advances in not only the capture technology, but in the entire content delivery chain to create, produce, and distribute that content. The industry is likely still at least three to five years out from being there.

(continued)

(continued)

Regarding the future of live events and broadcast, Ms. Berman had the following to say:

> Live events and sports are one of the things holding up traditional TV/cable numbers. I think VR could transform the way people view live events if we address some of the challenges of VR in general. I can picture people putting on a headset with friends who aren't physically with them to go to a concert together and have a shared experience. I can picture a person who plays in a weekly basketball league or a Little League coach watching a game in VR and analyzing the plays in different ways to learn how to improve their performance. I can picture a sports enthusiast catching Sunday night football in his headset while viewing fantasy player updates and controlling where he can be throughout the game.

The Shard

The Shard is a 95-story skyscraper built in Southwark, London. At 1,016 feet high, the Shard is the tallest building in the United Kingdom.

As part of the viewing experience from the Shard's uppermost skydeck, two separate VR entertainment pieces were created, The Slide and Vertigo. In The Slide, users are strapped to a moving chair and sent hurtling down a virtual slide from the top of a virtual Shard to experience the London skyline as it's never been seen before.

Figure 10-9 shows a user experiencing The Slide in VR, a 360-degree ride that moves the user throughout the London skyline.

In Vertigo, users travel back in time to a virtual environment that takes place during The Shard's construction. User walk across a thin balance beam a few inches off the ground, while inside a VR headset they appear to be suspended 1,000 feet in the air walking across steel beams put in place during The Shard's construction.

Location-based experiences such as The Slide and Vertigo use VR as an attraction to entice users to experience something they can't from the comfort of home. They also often try to socialize what can often be a more solitary experience, whether it be by creating an actual multiplayer social experience or capturing the feel of multiple people observing the single participant in VR. You often find a crowd gathered around the single participant of The Slide, laughing and discussing the current rider's reaction. VR experiences such as these are a look at how VR can be utilized as attractions offering a deeper and more engaging experience in locations such as museums and tourist destinations.

FIGURE 10-9:
A user
experiencing The
Slide experience
at The Shard.

Courtesy of The View from The Shard

EXPERIENCING VIRTUAL LOCATIONS

Brad Purkey is an interactive project lead at the Museum of Pop Culture (formerly EMP) in Seattle, Washington, with experience running various location-based VR experiences, most notably the popular *Game of Thrones* Ascend the Wall exhibit. He shares his experiences here:

> Our VR experiences have all been staffed experiences to this point. We need space and someone to monitor the hardware. VR is not like an iPad, where someone can just walk up to it and know what to do. That will change as things become more ubiquitous. It's an interesting challenge: You want to provide a unique experience that draws people in, but at the same time having hardware that everyone is familiar with and may even already have on them and knows how to use is a huge advantage; there is less of a learning curve for users. Additionally, we may not have to provide the hardware, and it is less tempting for people to walk off with [it].

> To me, VR within a setting like ours becomes more powerful when it is a part of a larger experience and not the experience itself. The *Game of Thrones* exhibit, with its addition of 4D elements such as the elevator structures and fans blowing cold wind — even those simple little things pull users into the experience that much more. VR for locations should be part of a bigger whole to create an engaging experience. That's where I see VR living in spaces like museums — as a feature piece but still part of a larger experience.

(continued)

(continued)

As far as a timeline for when VR will become mainstream, you look to the evolution of something like the iPhone. The iPhone was released around ten years ago; the pace of that from then to now is just amazing. I know VR will have a similar pace. It's going to come faster than a lot of people think. Five years from now, VR will be everywhere. I can imagine ten years from now . . . something similar to a Google Glass AR device that can quickly morph into a VR headset — when that happens the content floodgates will open for content. It's all about penetration for content creators. When we talked about VR just a few years ago at the museum, the thought was, "It's so unique so people will come see it." We're already to the point where it is a regular sight at museums — it's no longer unique, now the experience needs to be a draw.

When asked about VR's potential to replicate and potentially replace the space that museums and other brick-and-mortar locations occupy, Mr. Purkey said:

In the future, I could see the immersion into the digital world we're bound to all fall into could actually create the desire to see more real, physical objects. I'm constantly surprised, when I go in and see physical artifacts, the effect they have on me. As an example, we currently are running a Jim Henson exhibit, and to see Grover in front of me, the real Grover — it's so different than just seeing a photograph. Looking at a photograph, you don't get the same feel, and there's always going to be something to that. I don't think we'll ever get to the point where it replaces reality. Rather, it will function to enhance reality.

Healthcare

To some, healthcare and VR may seem an odd couple. However, healthcare is one of the earliest explorers of the potential benefits of VR. As far back as the 1990s, medical researchers were reviewing methods for applications of VR in medicine. The technology is just now beginning to catch up to its potential uses in the healthcare field.

The experiences in this section cover several medical uses of VR, including simulating disease for the purpose of developing empathy, educating future medical professionals by creating difficult-to-replicate training scenarios, and new methods of dealing with psychological issues such as depression and post-traumatic stress disorder (PTSD). And that barely scratches the surface of what VR can do in the field of healthcare. As VR matures, even more uses will come to light.

VR in healthcare is an incredibly exciting field to be exploring at the moment, with many new ideas are being explored. The options for creating medical training scenarios for future surgeons to gain more experience on procedures can drastically improve patient outcome, and the potential patient treatment options for issues ranging from Parkinson's to amputations have offered great promise for the future of VR in healthcare scenarios.

Beatriz: A journey through Alzheimer's disease

Beatriz is the creation of Embodied Labs, a company focused on utilizing VR as a tool for training healthcare professionals in patient understanding. In Beatriz, the user embodies the title character as she progresses through early, middle, and late stage Alzheimer's disease (AD).

Each part of the experience covers ten years in the life of Beatriz, from age 62 to 72, and in each part, you, embodying Beatriz, experience her struggle with further cognitive impairment. In the early stage, you experience Beatriz coming to realize her brain is changing and dealing with these changes in both her job as a teacher and in family life. You're made to feel confused and disoriented at your job and in other locations such as the grocery store.

In the middle stage, you're made to observe how AD actually affects the brain at a macro level. You then return to embody Beatriz, who begins to experience hallucinations and becomes confused and frightened in her home, requiring assistance and outside care. You also begin to experience her family's conflict over decisions being made about her care.

In the final stage as Beatriz, you experience symptoms of late-stage AD. You see Beatriz's family struggling with their emotions related to her progressing AD and experience small moments of joy during a holiday gathering.

Beatriz is experienced through a combination of live-action 360-degree video, game-based interaction, and 3D medical animation. "The goal is to take the macro human experience and pair that with the science behind what is actually happening in our bodies," says Carrie Shaw, Embodied Labs CEO.

Beatriz is aimed toward healthcare personnel and other primary caregivers of those with AD. The goal of Beatriz is to help these audiences experience what a person with AD is actually going through. Seeing through the eyes of someone with AD enables these audiences to recognize how AD can change visual and auditory processes and how it can affect communication. By identifying these changes, users can begin to empathize more deeply with their patients and learn to become better healthcare providers.

Figure 10-10 displays a user experiencing what Beatriz experiences throughout her slow progression through the stages of Alzheimer's.

FIGURE 10-10:
A user experiencing Alzheimer's through Beatriz.

REVITALIZING HEALTHCARE

Carrie Shaw is the CEO and founder of Embodied Labs, a company focused on using VR as a tool for healthcare training and patient understanding. I talked to her about Beatriz and her personal connection to Alzheimer's disease:

When I was 19, my mother was diagnosed with early-onset Alzheimer's disease. From that point on, we were on this journey with her as her caregivers. It was something I struggled to wrap my head around. As she was changing, I couldn't understand how she now perceived the world through this new cognitive interpretation. However, I found if you could create a strong visual, it would immediately cut through language, culture, and education barriers.

I moved home with her as her primary caregiver. She had right brain atrophy at the time, and that caused her to have a left visual field deficit. I made a simple pair of goggles with parts of the field of vision blocked off to try and explain to her caregivers what she was experiencing. Rather than myself just explaining her impairment to them, having the caregivers simulate that impairment, they could immediately understand what she was going through. It intuitively made sense to them once they put on this basic pair of goggles.

Embodied Labs' applications focus on simulating for healthcare professionals what their patients are experiencing in their everyday lives, with the thought that by simulating these experiences, healthcare providers develop a better understanding of their patients' worlds and become both better communicators and develop better understanding of the life of a patient and what they're going through.

Ms. Shaw continues:

> VR allows us to simulate more than a simple vision impairment. It lets us simulate these patients' worlds. Our goal is that experiences like these will help people connect with the disease and not treat it as this mysterious unapproachable thing.
>
> VR has shown to reduce negative stereotypes to different groups, so while most nursing students are white, we decided to make Beatriz a member of a minority group in the U.S. (Latina). We've measured ageism and reduction of stereotype in the elderly after using our applications, and we saw very good pre and post change during the pilots and analytics we've done.
>
> Finally, we are also tracking caregiver impact pre- and post-usage. Our assessments have been able to track data and correlate what happens with our VR experience to align with better healthcare practices, higher safety ratings, and higher retention rates for healthcare employees.

Virtual operating room

VR has great potential as a teaching medium in the medical field as well. Within the medical field, getting proper training in the fields you want to study can be difficult. Doctors or other medical professionals can be held back by lack of access to potential patients or colleagues to learn from or study with.

Medical Realities is a company focused on delivering surgical training using VR. It seeks to extend surgery observation from an on-location event to one that can be viewed from anywhere in the world via VR. Co-founder Dr. Shafi Ahmed was the first to give VR access to his operating theater in 2016 when he removed cancerous cells from a patient in London. Nearly 55,000 people tuned in to the three-hour procedure.

The goal of Medical Realities is to make users feel as if they are in the operating room during the procedure, with the ability to change views to what interests them the most. The current Medical Realities platform also includes the ability to toggle to different camera feeds, such as laparoscopic or microscopic feeds, as well as 3D close-up feeds of the area being operated on. The teaching modules inside Medical Realities also include VR anatomy for each module, as well as a list of questions for each module that allow viewers to test themselves before and after each module to ensure the material is being learned.

VR allows for more than just a new way to observe operations. A company called 3D Systems has created surgical simulation modules to replicate the surgical environment. The LAP Mentor VR system is intended to act as a fully immersive laparoscopic training experience, enabling users to experience a virtual operating room, complete with audio distractions and the stress of working within an operating room atmosphere. And instead of utilizing traditional VR motion controls, the 3D Systems experience also utilizes the LAP Mentor, a set of controls created to provide realistic tactile experience for a simulated experience of tissue resistance during actual surgery.

Psychological therapy

PTSD is a mental health issue often thought of in conjunction with the military, but it can occur in anyone after experiencing a life-threatening event such as combat, a car crash, or sexual assault. There is no medical consensus on the cause or treatment of the issue. However, one treatment area that has shown promise is exposure therapy. Exposure therapy is the psychological treatment developed to help people confront their fears. It has been demonstrated to be a helpful treatment component for things ranging from phobias to generalized anxiety disorder.

Exposure therapy has several variations, from vividly imagining and describing the feared object or trauma to directly facing a feared object. But often it is not practical or possible to directly face a feared object under therapist supervision. VR adds a new dynamic to exposure therapy. Instead of relying on a patient's imagination to confront his trauma, VR can create controlled simulations in which both patient and therapist can experience the virtual scenario together. As the experience is fully simulated, the therapist is able to control the scenario to the appropriate amount for the patient, while the patient can talk through the scenario as he experiences it with his therapist.

The psychological treatments do not stop at PTSD alone. A study published in the *British Journal of Psychiatry Open* suggested that VR therapy could reduce depression symptoms by combating levels of self-criticism and increasing levels of self-compassion. In the study, adults with depression underwent sessions where they were told to calm a digital avatar of a crying child. As they did so, the child would gradually cease crying. Next, the patients were embodied in the child's figure, and they were able to listen to their adult selves being compassionate toward their avatars. The findings were preliminary, but the majority of patients reported reduced depression symptoms and found themselves becoming less self-critical in real-life situations after undergoing the therapy.

VR is also being studied for its potential effects in improving eating disorders and *body dysmorphia* (obsessive thinking that the body is deeply flawed). A recent study invited women to estimate various widths and circumferences of their body parts; then they entered into VR where they were body swapped with an avatar image of themselves with a slightly flatter stomach. The women then were asked again to estimate their body parts' widths and circumferences. The findings revealed that after the participants had embodied the virtual body, they were more likely to estimate their body size correctly as compared to women who were shown an exact virtual replica of their body. In essence, VR was able to provide the participants a better sense of what they truly looked like. This could make VR a very effective treatment method for those suffering through eating disorders or body dysmorphia, who often incorrectly view their body sizes and shapes and adjust their behavior in unhealthy ways. By helping body dysmorphia sufferers establish a true picture of themselves, VR can instill healthier habits in patients.

Gaming

VR has very obvious alignment with the gaming industry. Gamers tend to be a fairly technically savvy group, and gaming was one of the first industries to embrace VR's potential and help push the VR industry forward.

The VR executions discussed in this section step a bit outside traditional VR gaming scenarios. There are hundreds, if not thousands, of impressive VR gaming titles available to explore, from simple puzzle games such as Land's End, to horror games such as Resident Evil 7, to shoot-'em-up games like SuperHot or Robo Recall. You don't have to search far to find amazing VR game content. Instead, the pieces discussed in this section focus around gaming experiences with less exposure in the VR space: social gaming and VR arcades.

REMEMBER

Perhaps in part because of gaming's "early adoption" of VR, VR's biggest question in the gaming market is whether the hype of VR can meet the expectations of gaming consumers. Gamers' embrace of VR early on means they've been with VR since the Oculus DK1 Kickstarter in 2012. Massive improvements to the technology have occurred since then, but VR has yet to reach mass consumer level, and some within the gaming industry find themselves growing impatient to see when VR finally will have its breakthrough moment for everyday consumers.

Rec Room

Rec Room has often been called the "Wii Sports of VR," a title not bestowed lightly. Wii Sports was widely considered one of the best titles for the immensely popular Nintendo Wii system, and it achieved that without fancy graphics or even any real storyline. Wii Sports focused simply on gameplay and allowing users to learn the capabilities of their new Wii system's motion controls.

In that way, Rec Room is quite similar to Wii Sports. Rec Room features a series of simple mini-games such as paintball, dodge ball, charades, and other adventures that allow users to explore the basic control schemes of VR. Each mini game offers simple controls; for the most part, the games are light experiences without much depth, but they're more than fun enough to keep you entertained for hours.

Where Rec Room shines is the social interaction with other players. Rec Room is a wide open space where you can interact with other players, toss Frisbees and darts, and so on. Microphones enable voice chatting with other users and their simple avatars, and you can join parties to play in various game rooms with you. There are other additional features (Quests, Private Rooms, and so on), but they all work in service of and are benefited by the social component of multiple users within a shared VR experience.

Figure 10-11 shows screen shots of the multiplayer game Rec Room, which includes a number of different mini games to play against real-life opponents, such as paintball, laser tag, and paddleball (shown in the figure).

FIGURE 10-11: Screen shots from the multiplayer Rec Room.

TIP

The beauty of Rec Room lies in its simplicity, and VR game developers should take note. A game does *not* have to be graphically over-the-top or feature massive storylines to be successful. By focusing on what actually makes multi-user experiences fun in VR (simple games played with friends and strangers), the developers at Against Gravity were able to turn a basic concept into hours of enjoyable gameplay.

VR arcades

Some iterations of VR look to find ways to view events from the comfort of your own home, but others seek to do the exact opposite. VR arcade experiences have started to pop up in shopping centers across the United States. VR theme parks and arcades have also begun to appear throughout Japan, and China is getting into location-based VR as well, looking to launch the East Valley of Science and Fantasy park, a massive VR theme park in Guiyang, China.

Another such arcade is the Adores VR Park in Tokyo. Originally opened in December 2016 as an experiment, during busy periods the park operators even today find themselves having to turn customers away. The arcade artfully combines various technologies to enhance the VR experience. On a magic carpet ride, for example, users stand on a platform that moves with the action while fans are triggered to give users the feeling of flying. Interestingly, the core VR technology is often little more than headsets that users could purchase for use at home, the HTC Vive and Samsung Gear.

What the arcade does well is in turning the sometimes isolating experience of playing VR and making it a social event; some of the games are multiplayer, and almost all invite friends to watch your gameplay on a big screen as you battle monsters or robots inside your headset. Adores takes an experience that could be isolating and makes it social.

Also in Tokyo, game developers Bandai and Namco have teamed up to create the VR Zone, a VR arcade with a number of different VR experiences available. Most of the titles here are multiplayer experiences, all with custom hardware to enhance the user's VR experience. For example, the extremely popular Mario Kart VR experience includes a physical go-kart that turns and rattles along with the gameplay, immersing you within the racing experience. Similar to Adores, the HTC Vive headset powers most of these experiences as well.

VR arcades have proved the public interest in the market for VR. Where the more costly VR headsets have proven prohibitively expensive for some consumers, the massive interest in these VR arcades has shown that the public is wildly interested in VR, and large companies are looking for way to capitalize on that experience. The VR industry is still figuring out the correct cost point for home-based VR experiences, but in the meantime VR arcades are cashing in on consumers' interest in VR. Perhaps even with VR reaching a critical mass with consumer headsets, VR arcades will look to stay viable by offering up-leveled social and interactive experiences that can't be replicated with your setup at home.

Chapter 11

Exploring Augmented Reality Use Cases

M any consumers were first introduced to augmented reality (AR) via Pokémon Go in 2016. The game provided users a rudimentary AR experience, where a Pokémon could appear to inhabit your environment via a 3D overlay of your mobile device's video feed. AR technology has been around far longer than that, though, with many uses in industrial fields such as manufacturing and maintenance. And although consumers' introduction to AR may have been via a game, AR has often been regarded as the technology consumers of the future will utilize to get work done, whereas its relative VR will be used mainly for entertainment.

Manufacturers such as Microsoft and Meta have thus far seemed to target their headsets more towards this idea of getting work done. The more open nature of AR seemingly lends itself better to collaborative environments where you work alongside coworkers, whereas VR experiences have been more solitary. And because of VR's closed-off nature, implementing it in most workplaces would require a total sea change for the way work is currently accomplished — including developing entirely new systems of hardware and software.

But thinking about VR and AR only in terms of these strict silos is far too simplistic. VR has a number of uses for work and getting things done (see Chapter 10), and AR has just as many uses in the gaming and entertainment fields. On a long enough timeline, both fields will likely see a convergence of work and play.

In this chapter, I examine some of the ways AR is being utilized today. Because AR is still an emerging field, many of these use cases may not be available for consumers just yet. However, I also discuss a few applications that you can view today with your mobile device.

REMEMBER

Try not to concentrate on the specific AR application being discussed. Instead, allow each usage of AR to be a springboard for your own ideas on what an AR app could be. In fact, because AR is still such a young technology, the application being discussed may not even be the optimal use case or form factor. Try to review each application critically and ask yourself: What is it that makes this experience unique? Could the app be better executed in a different form factor (for example, if currently in a mobile device, how would it perform as an AR wearable)? What does this execution of AR mean for the future of this technology?

Art

In the same way that the VR world has begun making various forays into the art world (see Chapter 10), AR has as well. And, just as in the VR world, art in AR has a number of detractors questioning the legitimacy of AR artwork.

The art world has always been a constant battleground between those arguing for what is and what isn't art. AR in the art world is no different. In fact, the nature of AR may even be exacerbating the issue. Often considered an inaccessible world for many, with true "artwork" only visible at galleries or museums, AR has started to push forward the question of the nature of art in the same way graffiti artists have been for the past few decades. AR can make art far more accessible to those who may not typically spend their time at galleries or art shows. With AR, art can be everywhere — if you know how to find it.

Facebook Building 20

While walking in Facebook's Frank Gehry–designed Building 20, you may come across any number of people staring through their cameras at what appears to be nothing more than a large white wall. To the naked eye, there is nothing there. However, equipped with the Facebook Camera app, users are treated to an installation created for the entirely new medium of AR-based art.

Heather Day is the artist responsible for the installation. Ms. Day is an artist living and working in California. Her physical work is featured at a number of high-profile tech companies, from Dropbox to Airbnb. She primarily works with paint and other nontraditional materials to create abstract murals.

Facebook approached Ms. Day about collaborating for the project based on her previous artwork. While Ms. Day utilized her normal painting techniques, Facebook video crews recorded her entire process. They then were able to create a digital library of her animated painting techniques. Combined with a 3D model of the space, Facebook and Ms. Day worked together to map out how these animated marks could interact and animate within the environment via AR.

The final installation can be viewed at Facebook's headquarters in California. Facebook's Mark Zuckerberg unveiled the art at the F8 developer conference, "With augmented reality, you're going to be able to create and discover art all throughout your city," Zuckerberg said.

In reference to Ms. Day's installation, due to the nature of the piece's interaction with its surroundings, Zuckerberg proclaimed, "It's something that would be impossible to build in reality. . . . One thing that is a funny side effect of this is that, at Facebook, we have people gathering around looking at blank walls. This is going to be a thing in the future."

Figure 11-1 displays a screen capture of what a user sees when viewing Ms. Day's mural in AR.

FIGURE 11-1: A screen shot of Heather Day's AR mural at Facebook.

Source: https://vimeo.com/215573899

Jeff Koons and Snapchat

Snapchat followed a similar approach to Facebook in creating AR art targeted at a more public audience.

For a few weeks in the fall of 2017, Snapchat teamed up with artist Jeff Koons to create an AR Snapchat World Lens based on Koons's artwork. Users of the popular Snapchat app in one of a number of cities (including Chicago, New York, Paris, and London) could unlock some of Koons's most famous works to display in AR. To view the installation, a user had to be within 300 meters of the location where the piece was being "displayed," with the Snapchat application opened on her mobile device. If a user were close enough to one of the art pieces, an indicator would guide her to the place to look, at which point the artwork would be displayed in the environment as a 3D World Lens on the user's phone.

3D World Lenses in Snapchat are AR filters that are applied to the environment around you when using the Snapchat app. Users typically use these AR filters to put simple holograms in their environment, like a dancing hot dog or Bitmoji. Brands such as Bud Light and Warner Bros. have also experimented with creating their own "sponsored" Lenses, enabling users to add a virtual beer vendor or futuristic vehicle to their environment.

Figure 11-2 depicts users exploring the AR artwork in the real world, and how it appeared to users in AR on their mobile devices.

FIGURE 11-2:
Jeff Koons's
Snapchat
installation
promo.

Source: https://youtu.be/d5z9-JLIuis

In an interesting turn of events, there was a backlash by those in the community who felt that this was just an instance of a corporation being allowed to push themselves into a public space. The artist and designer Sebastian Errazuriz went so far as to mock up a digitally vandalized version of Koons's Snapchat artwork.

"We're moving very quickly to an augmented reality life," Mr. Errazuriz stated on Instagram. "For a company to have the freedom to GPS tag whatever they want is an enormous luxury we should not be giving out for free. The virtual public space belongs to us." Errazuriz said that we should be able to charge these companies rent, and we should be able to approve what can and cannot be geotagged in our public and private digital spaces.

Figure 11-3 displays Sebastian Errazuriz's mockup of Jeff Koons's Snapchat installation, virtually graffiti-tagged.

FIGURE 11-3:
Sebastian
Errazuriz's digital
alteration of Jeff
Koons's AR work.

The public space may have only been affected digitally, but it does bring up interesting questions about the nature of AR and how public spaces should be treated in this new world. This may seem to have a simple solution for now: "You don't like it? Turn off the app!" However, in the future, things may not be so simple. In a decade's time, is it possible that while wearing your AR glasses you'll be inundated with digital advertising scattered throughout the public space?

It's hard to say if that rather dystopian outlook is the future of AR, but the time for having these conversations regarding the nature of AR is *now*, as opposed to waiting until that future is already upon us.

Education

Educators are constantly on the lookout for methods to help engage students. The more engaged students are with the material, the more likely that they will retain the information presented. AR can help facilitate learning by helping students with that engagement. Professional environments can also benefit from increasing engagement when training employees and technicians.

The experiences in this section reveal a few of the ways that AR can be utilized in traditional and nontraditional educational settings.

Google Expeditions

Google Expeditions is an immersive education platform released in 2015 as a way for Google to deliver low-cost virtual field trips for classrooms. Google Expeditions already has a VR component powered by Google Cardboard (see Chapter 10). Expeditions AR looks to expand Google Expeditions VR into the AR world via smartphone-powered AR experiences.

Expeditions AR maps the physical classroom and uses that digital mapping to place 3D holograms around the environment. Students are given supported mobile devices and can then walk around the digital holograms, explore them up close to look at details, or step away to get an overarching view of the holograms. The teachers leading the Expedition can walk the students through what to look for within each digital hologram or allow the students to explore at their own leisure.

Where Expeditions shines is when it enables children to explore in ways they wouldn't otherwise be able to. Not every student learns the same way, and letting students walk around and explore a volcano or a DNA strand at their own pace is far different from lecturing them on the subject or even showing them a video. Expeditions AR hopes to help trigger those engaging moments for students.

Figure 11-4 shows students using AR to explore a digital hologram of a volcano via Google Expeditions.

FIGURE 11-4:
Students explore a volcano via AR and Google Expeditions.

Source: https://youtu.be/-DYq1aMWTVg

AR in the classroom may not be totally ready for primetime. It can still be a costly proposition for schools to have the necessary hardware available for each student. However, computers in the classroom were once a rare sight as well. Nowadays it's a requirement for many students past a certain grade level to have a computer or tablet. Many students have their own mobile devices as well.

As headset prices come down, it's possible that, like computers, AR hardware could quickly become so common in the classroom that students may not be able to recall a time without it.

Major League Soccer Replay

Major League Soccer (MLS) and POP, a digital agency in Seattle, recently explored the possibilities of combining AR within a professional sports training environment. The MLS Replay application was created to enable coaches and players to review set pieces in a completely new way.

The MLS Replay app allows users to select from any number of highlights throughout a match. Selecting a highlight projects the highlight as a 3D hologram onto a real-world surface, complete with game and player statistics. Using the HoloLens, players and coaches can then view the replay from any angle, from down on the field to a bird's-eye view of the action.

This ability to view plays from literally any angle can provide new information to both players and coaches about the match, allowing deeper analysis of player decisions and how plays develop, because the view on the field can be drastically different from what a coach saw from the sidelines.

Analyzing video replays is nothing new for sports teams. And getting yelled at by your coach for something they saw from the sidelines that you did not see is a rite of passage for athletes playing sports at any level. The ability of VR and AR devices to give users a completely new perspective on the action is something quite different. The NFL recently unveiled a similar twist on this theme. They put forth a vision of how fans could consume football content using AR in the near future (see Chapter 15).

Most coaches will likely be sticking to clipboards for now, but apps such as MLS Replay illustrate that that may not always be the case. There may be a time soon when coaches, players, and fans at all levels of sports are all analyzing action via AR.

Healthcare education

Similar to VR, AR will likely see inroads into the healthcare industry on a number of fronts, both from a student/education standpoint and usage directly in the operating theater.

DESIGNING AUGMENTED EXPERIENCES

Di Dang is a senior user experience (UX) designer at POP, a digital agency in Seattle. I sat down with her to discuss how to establish best practices for designing experiences in a rapidly developing industry. Here's what she had to say:

> To establish best practices, technology needs users. We have started to see the beginning of consumer-facing AR on mobile devices, but adoption in other form factors will likely be slow on the consumer side for some time. Mobile AR is where we can expect to see the most investment over the next two years at least.
>
> AR is in an interesting spot. Unlike VR, the form factor is not decided upon. It's still a blank slate. You have headsets such as the Meta 2 and HoloLens. You have goggles from Magic Leap. You have Android and iOS phones and tablets and heads-up displays in smart glasses. We, as an industry, haven't decided how consumers will consume AR. The best practices for each of those form factors will likely be very different. Designing for AR headsets versus glasses versus mobile form factors are vastly different experiences.
>
> With traditional user interfaces [UIs], such as web and mobile experiences, we're almost always presented with a 2D UI. As a UX designer in AR, there are a number of situational concerns that have no boundary. Where is a user going to be using this? On their couch? Outside? On the street? Who are they with? Are they by themselves? Using it during the day? At night? VR is constrained and you do not have to take these factors into account, [but] with AR you have to consider all these options.
>
> As a UX designer, I try and approach all of these questions with a user-centered mind-set. It can be difficult to try and combat all those scenarios at once. It's best to start small. Don't try to solve for too many use cases at once. Instead, narrow your focus to a single use case, solve it, and work outward from there.
>
> The place I like to start is to figure out the user journey. You have to ask yourself, "Why is a user using this application in the first place?" and ensure that all your decisions are based on that premise. Otherwise, it's too easy to get caught up in what ifs: "What if our app did this?" "What if our app did that?"
>
> As a user-centered designer, I try to counter those what ifs with "Why?" Asking why over and over and over again to find out just what is in it for the user.
>
> While AR's form factor is not yet decided, we still have to find ways to intelligently work with each form factor or new scenario. What I have found works across these experiences is making sure to prototype these experiences regardless of the platform you are designing for. In-person prototyping [acting out situations in the 3D area of the phone or headset], as well as software prototyping in 3D, combine to help account for the varying spatial relationships that exist in AR.

Almost all doctors have gone through the rigors of dissecting a cadaver. Anatomy has been taught in this same way for hundreds of years without an update. Dissection labs help medical students understand the human body and how its systems work together. There is often little substitute for the hands-on experience students can gain in these laboratories.

However, labs often suffer from a number of issues. They can be expensive for universities to keep up, and every student may not get the same hands-on experience due to a limited number of cadavers. Case Western, in collaboration with Cleveland Clinic, is looking to upend this traditional way of teaching anatomy.

Students starting at the new Case Western health education campus learn anatomy through the HoloLens. Case Western's developers are building out virtual human subjects — teachers now guide students through a virtual human hologram rather than a traditional cadaver. The university held trial lessons utilizing these AR anatomy lessons, comparing them against students who utilized traditional lab-based lessons. One hundred percent of the students who utilized the HoloLens said they would use it again, with many claiming they were able to see things via the HoloLens that they could not see in a traditional human cadaver.

These studies point toward a digital future and raise interesting discussion points around where AR can supplement education and training, and when hands-on training is required. A hologram will likely never fully provide the same experience that hands-on training allows for, but it can fill in (or augment) many of the gaps hands-on training may lack.

Outside of college campuses, AR is being used to educate surgeons preparing for healthcare procedures in the operating theater. Dr. Maksymilian Opolski of the Warsaw Institute of Cardiology has long been a proponent of finding ways of bringing new technology to the operating room. Dr. Opolski has run a 15-patient pilot program utilizing Google Glass to project images of a patient's heart onto head-mounted AR glasses donned by surgeons. (These images would traditionally be shown on monitors within the lab.) Cardiologists were given the ability to navigate through these AR holograms via voice command, freeing up their hands for the multitude of other tasks that surgery requires. Surgeons within the pilot reported a high level of satisfaction with the technology and reported they would like to use it in their regular work. Additionally, surgeons utilizing the AR headsets tended to use less contrasting dye on patients and were able to better choose the proper type of guide wire to use during surgery.

There are still questions to answer around AR's usage within the medical space. The field of healthcare is very sensitive to making sure changes are not change just for change's sake, but lead to better patient results. These studies show that AR will likely soon find its way into the field of mainstream healthcare.

Industry and Commerce

Industrial applications are one of the areas in which AR has made the biggest headway. The cost of enterprise-level headsets has been prohibitive for most consumers thus far, but it isn't as large a barrier for modern manufacturing.

On an industrial scale, anything that saves even a little time, be it per engine built or per smartphone produced, can quickly work out to huge savings overall. Companies such as Boeing, General Electric, and Volvo have all experimented with AR on their assembly lines or factory floors to determine where these technologies could be utilized to save time and money.

REMEMBER

Many experts predict that AR will see massive growth in the industrial sector. Headset and software cost can easily be justified in the savings generated by creating a better trained and more accurate workforce.

The items in this section touch on how some companies today are utilizing AR in construction and manufacturing for communication, maintenance, and training.

thyssenkrupp

thyssenkrupp's name may not be immediately recognizable to you. However, you may use their products every day, perhaps even multiple times a day. thyssenkrupp is an industrial engineering company known for developing elevators, escalators, and moving sidewalks.

thyssenkrupp has developed multiple HoloLens application scenarios focused around ways to improve the speed and efficiency of their technicians out in the field. In one of thyssenkrupp's AR scenarios, a field technician is called to do maintenance on an elevator out in the field. When out in the field, the technician is able to place the HoloLens on his head and pull up historical data for the elevator's past maintenance schedule. The technician is also able to pull up a 3D view of the elevator within his headset to find which part is causing issues.

Previously, technicians in the field would carry laptops for many of these functions. With AR headsets such as the HoloLens, the ability to be hands-free gives the technician the ability to keep this data pulled up as he needs it, while leaving his hands free to work on the elevator itself. The HoloLens also allows the technician to trigger a call to a remote subject-matter expert. The off-site expert is shown a live video feed of what the technician on-site is seeing. This allows the off-site expert to walk the field technician through any potential changes or fixes that may need to take place via holographic annotations that appear in the field tech's 3D world space of the HoloLens.

thyssenkrupp's testing of this scenario has shown a significant savings of time and effort. Jobs that previously took two hours and required arranging travel for subject-matter experts now could be completed with a subject-matter expert off-site in 20 minutes. "The introduction of HoloLens into our operations will empower the over 20,000 field service engineers in doing their job better and more efficiently," claims Andreas Schierenbeck, CEO, in thyssenkrupp's new vision for elevator maintenance promo video touting one of their AR use cases.

Figure 11-5 displays how thyssenkrupp envisions its operators working out in the field.

FIGURE 11-5: thyssenkrupp's take on a field technician's use of AR.

Source: https://youtu.be/80WhGiyR4Ns

WorkLink

Scope AR is an AR company focused on providing guidance and support for industrial industries to help improve their cost and efficiency. Its product, WorkLink, enables users without any coding knowledge to create AR Smart instructions and training materials for operators out in the field. These Smart instructions can project digital holograms directly onto industrial machinery to walk operators through completing tasks or training on a new piece of machinery.

By moving away from traditional, paper-based instructions into AR-based instructions, Scope AR hopes to help improve the comprehension and knowledge retention of operators, which should lead to higher-quality results. Studies have shown that, when compared to a control group using traditional paper-based manuals, AR-based instructions have led to fewer mistakes overall.

Users of the WorkLink software do not need any prior coding knowledge. A user can import 3D model data from computer-aided design (CAD) to create 3D animations of instructions, breaking down complex tasks into simpler steps. A content creator can also add in text and reference images or videos to help make the task more understandable to the end user.

These instructions can then be distributed wirelessly to iOS or Android devices, or even HoloLens, for operators' consumption in the field or on the manufacturing floor. Transferring these instructions from paper-based to an augmented form factor means the digital holograms can be projected directly onto an operator's work area to walk them through the task.

Figure 11-6 shows the WorkLink app using AR to take users step-by-step through training materials.

Source: https://youtu.be/8950ZPSSNkI

FIGURE 11-6:
Scope AR's
WorkLink
application
in use.

MANUFACTURING REALITY

David Varela is a senior research engineer at the Manufacturing Technology Centre in the UK. He recently sat down to speak with me on how VR and AR technologies were changing the landscape of manufacturing. Here's what Mr. Varela had to say:

We develop both VR and AR apps for the enterprise industry and focus mainly on high-value manufacturing. We've done work in both the VR and AR space. Though we have done a number of VR experiences, we're finding AR tends to work the best with the companies we work for, specifically [with] the Microsoft HoloLens.

AR/MR provides this blended real/virtual scenario that suits use cases for appearing in the shop floor, on-site, and so on. As we work closer with these groups, we tend to find AR/MR solutions more plausible than VR, as they allow interaction with the physical environment. For our requirements, we find the average quality of the visualization experience in the HoloLens (considering graphics, field of view, stability of holograms, tracking and positioning, sight obstruction) provides the most useful AR experience.

The biggest challenge for us in the industrial space is data reuse. In the industrial environment, it is critical how you create and manage existing data. Companies are already spending a huge amount of effort and cost in designing their product. They don't want to be redoing that work just for the sake of putting it in AR.

Imagine a car. The car goes through the design process and is approved by the manufacturer or design experts and is pushed down to production. If you want to start developing an AR application for that vehicle, you would likely take that car's CAD model, import it into your AR environment, modify it by making it low poly so it can run well within AR, and so on. You would need to get artists to do the optimization or utilize various automated tools to do it for you. Then you'd need to pull it into your development environment such as Unity or Unreal, then export to deliver it to the operator.

But what happens if there is a change to the model? What if the manufacturer started to produce the car but found by changing to a different bracket they could save cost? Suddenly, the AR app you already deployed is obsolete. What is most important for manufacturers is finding a way to reuse the data that they already have — developing a single source of truth and thinking about how you can talk directly to the core models and data that already exist. But these are all problems that can be solved.

(continued)

(continued)

Mr. Varela closed with his thoughts on the near future for AR:

I think manufacturing is where AR will start to pick up adoption. It will be slow at first. Three years out, the adoption at industrial scale will start to scale up. These industries are slow, and implementing things take time. It's not like consumer-level consumption where something can get popular and pick up immediately. In manufacturing, there are IT departments, security, ergonomics, existing infrastructure, a lot of factors to work with. So it will start in manufacturing, and you'll see steady adoption from there.

Challenges aside, manufacturers, service providers, and the overall B2B market are the ones that will see the biggest return on investment. You can see up to 50 percent reduction in assembly time utilizing these technologies. For a company such as Rolls-Royce, that can work out to multi-million dollar savings per engine — those are big figures. And that is without taking into account quality improvements. In addition to reducing assembly time by 50 percent, you can see up to a 90 percent improvement in the right-first-time quality rate using these technologies. Those are figures Boeing has validated with AR on tablets; utilizing headsets is going to take those numbers even higher. Other benefits will come from faster and more efficient training, knowledge transfer across generations of workers, enablement of flexible work force, increased collaboration across teams, augmented remote site support, etc. The technology will enable workers to access the data and resources they need when they need them.

Entertainment

Although AR headsets and glasses have seen use in manufacturing industries for some time, AR has also seen a good deal of use in the entertainment industry, though not in a form factor you may think of.

As I explain in Chapter 1, when watching a football game on TV, you may see the yellow first-down marker appear on the field or even player graphics and stats displayed as if they're part of the stadium. When watching racing heats in the Olympics, you may see a "ghost" line or racer, indicating the first-place time that heat is competing against. News broadcasts and weather stations have also regularly made use of AR graphics to display further information on certain topics.

Figure 11-7 displays some of news outlet Al Jazeera's coverage of the 2018 Winter Olympics using AR graphics to spell out various points of interest to its viewers.

FIGURE 11-7:
Al Jazeera's 2018
Winter Olympics
coverage
utilizing AR.

Source: https://youtu.be/aMoxhqrB-pQ

Similar to VR, gaming is an obvious area for AR applications, as evidenced by the multitude of games already utilizing ARKit and ARCore. This section shines a light on a few of the more unique uses of AR in gaming and entertainment and what they could mean for the future of AR in our entertainment experiences.

REMEMBER

AR/MR is not just headsets, glasses, and mobile devices. AR is anything that augments a user's reality with digital information on top of real-world environments.

Star Wars: Jedi Challenges

Star Wars: Jedi Challenges is a mobile-based AR headset system created by Lenovo. It may hold claim to being one of the first mass-consumer AR headsets, after the early forays like the Nintendo Virtual Boy (see Chapter 1). The system is designed to enable users to play a number of *Star Wars*–inspired games, such as dueling Darth Maul in a lightsaber battle or facing off with an opponent in a game of holographic chess.

Star Wars: Jedi Challenges comes equipped with everything you need to create an AR-based *Star Wars* experience: the AR headset hardware, a tracking device, and a lightsaber hilt. As the user, you're required to provide a supported mobile device to complete the experience. Luckily, Lenovo made it a priority to support a number of older mobile devices, claiming that most phones dating back two years should work. If you have a moderately new mobile device, your phone is likely supported.

The smartphone-powered experience allows you to play in one of three modes: Lightsaber Battle, Strategic Combat, or Holochess. The latter two games are enjoyable, but the system stands out in Lightsaber Battle. In that game mode, you can step through various combat stages, fight a swarm of battle droids, or take on Darth Maul in lightsaber combat.

Your mobile device is the brains of the operation. Download the associated Jedi Challenges app onto your smartphone and place it within the headset. The headset then projects the images from your smartphone via a series of mirrors to make the characters appear to be in the room with you. Your lightsaber pairs with your mobile device via Bluetooth, and the tracking beacon is placed on the floor to track against. It all adds up to a very compelling experience. This is the closest you can get to feeling like a Jedi Knight!

Star Wars: Jedi Challenges is not without flaws. The setup can be tedious. The tracking on both the lightsaber and the tracking device can be loose. And the cost for a one-off headset experience may price many consumers out of the market. However, when viewed as the first foray of toys into AR, it's actually a compelling experience. The tracking is good enough that most players won't complain. The tedious setup is not enough to take away from the experience. And the cost, though high, is arguably not out of line for an experience that is the first of its kind. Already, Star Wars is helping to justify the cost by updating the experience with new content from The Last Jedi.

It's hard to say whether other companies will follow suit in producing their own branded AR headset experiences. Star Wars exists in that rarified space with massive consumer recognition and rabid fans, many with deep enough pockets to justify the cost of something like Star Wars: Jedi Challenges. Few other brands would be able to pull off the same feat.

It is hard to imagine users purchasing multiple standalone AR headsets such as the one included in Star Wars: Jedi Challenges. A more likely future scenario is a standard AR headset that consumers only have to purchase once, with various brands creating content for that headset, similar to gaming consoles of today.

Figure 11-8 shows a user in the Lenovo-powered Star Wars: Jedi Challenges AR experience.

FIGURE 11-8: Star Wars: Jedi Challenges AR headset and lightsaber.

The New York Times Winter Olympics AR

For the 2018 Winter Olympics in South Korea, the *New York Times* rolled out an AR campaign featuring athletes from four different sports: figure skater Nathan Chen, speed skater J.R. Celski, hockey goalie Alex Rigsby, and snowboarder Anna Gasser.

Using AR within their standard *New York Times* application for iOS (a not quite full-featured version was available for Android), the NYT Winter Olympics AR campaign enabled you to place a digital hologram of any one of these four Olympians in 3D space in your home, and explore these holograms by walking around them, getting up close and personal or backing far up to capture the entire hologram. As you explored each hologram, more information rose to the surface. Exploring figure skater Nathan Chen from the front may have given you information on how he generates spin, whereas stepping back and behind him may have given you information and visuals on the distance his jumps cover. Moving behind goalie Alex Rigsby illustrated her point of view and the speed of the shots she faces, and from the front you could see how her pads cover as much of the goal as possible.

The campaign was part of the *New York Times*'s push to introduce AR capabilities within its mobile app. It succeeded as a simple illustration of what AR can do well: making connections to users to engage more deeply with their content than a simple photograph may otherwise accomplish.

Here's how the *New York Times* described this set of experiences in the launch announcement:

> . . . by using your smartphone as a "window," we are extending stories beyond the inches of a screen, by digitally adding objects into your space at real scale. And those objects — a border wall or a work of art — can have provocative explanatory value, because you can get close to them. This technology also allows us to explore the evolving nature of how we share ideas and tell stories.

AR usage within traditional media is not new (see Chapter 8). However, the *New York Times*'s take feels different from earlier experiments. Launching as part of the main *New York Times* news app is a much more frictionless experience for users. They have also (in the case of the Olympics) chosen a subject that lends itself well to AR. This AR experience, focused around marveling at Olympians and seeing their physicality at a real-world scale, offers a unique consumption experience.

It remains to be seen just how many AR-based news stories we can expect from the *New York Times* or others in the near future. What may be most telling is how quickly advertisers become interested in creating AR-based ads to support the space. The *New York Times* Winter Olympics AR campaign illustrates that there is a place for this type of experience, and we can likely expect more and more similar experiences cropping up in the future.

Figure 11-9 shows a view of the *New York Times* coverage of the 2018 Winter Olympics utilizing ARKit on an iPhone. Users could explore 3D representations of Olympians in their own homes.

Look closely at Chen's form. From this view, you can see his arms and legs are tight to his axis of rotation, which helps him spin faster than 400 r.p.m.

FIGURE 11-9:
A *New York Times* 2018 Winter Olympics story in AR.

Kinect Sandbox

The Kinect Sandbox is an example of AR that exists outside of typical AR experiences constrained to headsets or mobile devices. The Kinect Sandbox consists of a standard sandbox similar to sandboxes you may find in any regular playground. However, this sandbox utilizes 3D vision (typically provided by a Microsoft Kinect or similar device) to create a topographical view of the structures a user would create. It then uses this information to digitally project a map back onto the sand consisting of snow-capped mountains (the high points of sand), rivers and lakes (the low points of a user's sand environment), and everything in between.

TECHNICAL STUFF

The Microsoft Kinect is a motion-sensing device originally created for the Microsoft Xbox. It contains an RGB camera, as well as an infrared sensor for detecting depth, making it a popular low-cost 3D sensor. It was released in 2010 and discontinued in 2016.

The Kinect Sandbox idea is actually not new. In technology terms, it's a fairly old execution of AR. One of the first instances of a Kinect-powered sandbox can be found as far back as 2011, when students Peter Altman and Robert Eckstein created what they dubbed the "SandyStation."

Figure 11-10 displays a user building at various stages using the SandyStation. As the user creates different shapes in the sand (trenches and hills), the SandyStation detects these changes and projects different visuals onto the scene depending on the topography changes to the sandbox.

FIGURE 11-10:
The SandyStation
in use.

Source: https://youtu.be/E9aL3HjZbcw

The SandyStation consists of special software written by Altman and Eckstein, a Kinect, a projector, and a box of sand. The Kinect detects changes to the sand's height and depth. That information is parsed via the associated software, and the projector is fed the information to be displayed. Users can pile sand into mounds to create projections of mountains or carve out rivers and watch digital water appear to flow from a high point down to the lowest points of their sandbox. Users can even dig holes into the tops of their mountains to create volcanoes that erupt with lava flowing down the sides to low points on the map.

The SandyStation is a notable example of combining the physical world with digital information without the use of a headset or glasses. This is an idea that goes far beyond that of just a sandbox.

In another example of non-wearable AR, the Future Interfaces Group at Carnegie Mellon University has created an AR projector that can project interactive displays onto any surface. Called Desktopography, the system uses a compact projector and a depth camera small enough to plug into a light socket. In a video demonstration, Desktopography holograms are summoned via simple hand gestures. Working maps, calculators, and more are all shown as examples of digital interfaces projected onto physical surfaces via Desktopography.

Further, Desktopography allows fairly complex interactions between physical objects and the virtual artifacts. Projected digital objects are shown snapping to and releasing from physical objects. In one example, a user "attaches" a digitally projected calculator to a physical computer. When moving the physical computer, the holographic calculator moves along with it. Desktopography also intelligently fits its digital projected artifacts into the physical space you have available on your desk. Holograms may be occluded by physical objects and will attempt to move out of the way of the physical objects or resize in order to save space.

Figure 11-11 shows stills from a promo video for Desktopography. Desktopography augments the physical world by intelligently sizing and displaying representations of digital utility applications in a user's real-world space.

Source: https://youtu.be/L5mCxfjk6hc

FIGURE 11-11:
Desktopography-
projected AR.

Similarly, Lightform (https://lightform.com) is a computer vision and hardware startup that has created a computer specifically built for projected AR content. The Lightform computer uses depth sensors to scan its environment and, when paired with a projector, projects digital holograms on top of physical objects, effectively creating AR without a headset. This projected AR is known as projection mapping, and the Lightform computer makes creating this once-complicated process of projection mapping simple, enabling a seamless blend of digitally projected content with physical objects.

TECHNICAL STUFF

Projection mapping is the use of projected images to turn any object into a display surface for video projection. This technique can create optical illusions and make static objects appear to be in motion.

The Lightform content is not currently interactive "out of the box," but combining the real-world sensors of the Lightform with the interactivity of Desktopography could lead to interesting AR results. With projectors consistently getting smaller, cheaper, and brighter, projected AR offers a picture of one direction non-headset AR could be headed.

Figure 11-12 depicts a simplified example of Lightform's usage. In it, the projector has detected the menu board and vase shapes and is able to adjust its projections for each accordingly.

FIGURE 11-12:
Lightform's
projection onto
physical objects.

Courtesy of Lightform

Utilities

Part of AR's reputation for "getting work done" is the number of utility applications that the technology lends itself to. The nature of the technology is predicated on its openness to the outside world, so augmenting the physical with the digital can lead to a number of utilitarian applications. These range from simple ruler/measuring applications you can download today (see Chapter 15) to the more complex applications discussed next.

This section focuses on a few utility apps whose features will likely break into the AR space in one form or another.

Perinno-Uno

Perinno-Uno is a remote collaboration platform with AR capabilities. It's built on top of two applications: Uno, a browser-based app that allows communication via WebRTC, and Perinno, an AR application currently available for the Microsoft HoloLens.

TECHNICAL STUFF

WebRTC stands for *Web Real-Time Communication*. WebRTC is an open-source project that enables real-time communication over the web via application programming interfaces (APIs). In short, it offers a free way to enable audio and video communication over the web without a user needing to install extra plugins or applications.

The Perinno-Uno application enables peer-to-peer collaboration with audio and video. A user at a desktop computer running the Uno web application can communicate directly with a user in a HoloLens running the Perinno application. The user on the web application side receives a direct feed of video from what a user in the HoloLens is seeing, while a user on the HoloLens side will receive a webcam video from a user on the web application side (if available). The web application user also has the ability to share her screen if desired.

Where Perinno-Uno excels is in its ability to enable deeper collaboration between users. Users on the web application side can annotate on top of a HoloLens user's feed, sending images, text messages, and 3D holograms to users on the HoloLens, which will then appear in 3D space within the HoloLens. Web application users can also draw on top of the live video feed, pointing users on the HoloLens to areas of interest. These sketches will appear in 3D space within the HoloLens as well. Finally, users of the web app and HoloLens app can manipulate 3D CAD models, selecting and moving items in 3D space, with those changes reflected in the shared space.

The Perinno-Uno app is one of many applications looking to conquer the field of remote communication in AR. A strong use case for AR right now is the ability to send headsets out into the field or factory floor to allow employees direct communication and troubleshooting with others off-site. Today, this is often accomplished via video chat over the phone, which can be a clunky experience, especially if the problem you're looking to fix requires more than a single hand to accomplish. The hands-free approach of applications such as Perinno-Uno, combined with the ability to collaboratively edit 3D models and annotate in 3D space, is an attractive solution.

The uses in fields such as manufacturing or construction are many: Supervisors or other employees can assist in troubleshooting issues that arise out in the field, saving time and money by providing clear instructions to users in the field wearing the headset. Having trouble with a particular piece of machinery? A supervisor can overlay a building information model (BIM) 3D image in an operator's headset and direct an employee to exactly what part she needs to fix and how. Home usage may see just as many potential applications. Changing the oil on your car or hanging drywall and don't know where to start? Call your parents and have them walk you through all the steps via your AR headset.

TECHNICAL STUFF

Building Information Modeling (BIM) is a digital 3D model representation of a physical space. BIM files are often used by architects, engineers, and construction workers to maintain an accurate digital representation of construction or engineering projects. The recent rise in interest and availability of BIM models is providing an unprecedented level of information availability to the construction sector, perfect for usage within VR and AR.

The application is still in beta, but the promise for advancing collaboration runs through numerous AR applications and will undoubtedly be an early area of opportunity for AR.

Who Is It?

The Who Is It? application is a small proof-of-concept utility application developed by Cubera, an agency in Switzerland. Utilizing a HoloLens and face detection, the Who Is It? app detects the faces of those around you and displays digital information about that person "locked" to his physical location. The information displayed can vary depending on the particular use case scenario.

Dominik Brumm, the head of development at Cubera, spoke to a few of the project's uses:

> We created two versions of the application. One that utilizes the Microsoft Face API for facial recognition, and another face recognition we developed on our own that could work offline. We first built out an application with the HoloLens that can recognize people at Cubera and provide your information such as name and role within the company. We then did the same with parliament in Switzerland, where we took images from a newspaper and entered them into our database, and it was able to recognize politicians in the HoloLens. Finally, we built a proof-of-concept in a nearby coffee shop where the HoloLens recognizes frequent customers and their preferences. This person wants a cappuccino, this person wants a newspaper with his coffee, and so on. It was great for new employees to immediately know customers as they walked in. Simple things, but it demonstrates what could be possible in the future.

The beauty of an app like Who Is It? lies in its simplicity. Put on a pair of AR glasses, and suddenly your space is augmented with information about everyone around you. It shows the utility of AR when combined with other technologies. As prices of AR headsets come down and their form factor gets smaller, a future where everyone's data (at a surface level at least) is immediately available to everyone else is not out of the question.

An app like this raises interesting questions. Some people may hail an application like this as a technological marvel. Others may point to the potential lack of privacy that technology like this may encourage. Similar to the questions raised with AR advertising, what's most important is staying ahead of the technological curve and asking ourselves what may or may not be appropriate in the brave new world technology has us racing toward.

5

The Future of Virtual and Augmented Reality

IN THIS CHAPTER

» Analyzing near-future changes for virtual reality

» Evaluating the potential market

» Predicting the impact of future updates

Chapter **12**

Assessing the Future of Virtual Reality

Virtual reality (VR) has been a red-hot industry since the Oculus DK1 Kickstarter in 2013, and many of the advances since then have been powered by the momentum that that initial spark provided. With the release of second-generation hardware, the momentum of the first generation will have fully dissipated and the reality of VR will be setting in.

Will this second generation continue on the same explosive trajectory as the first? Or will the hype begin to cool as early adopters drop out, attracted by some newer tech object to obsess over? Or will reality fall somewhere in between, as VR moves past the hype and settles into the Slope of Enlightenment (see Chapter 1), slowly gaining adoption as more and more use cases for the technology are revealed.

In this chapter, I take a look at some of the changes we can expect in the near future, for better or for worse, for VR. I explore the market and provide some information on what you might expect in that area. I also discuss how you may be able to prepare for these upcoming changes.

Anticipating the Near-Future Changes

The best way to prepare for future unknowns is to review what you know. Analyzing the second generation of VR headsets (see Chapter 4), evaluating upcoming trends, reviewing new hardware accessories, and paying attention to the direction of some of the more bleeding-edge startups can all help paint a picture of just where the market might move next.

Evaluating the market

One criticism of the current VR market was the rate of adoption for first-generation headsets. Some feel that for the amount of money and attention that the VR field had been receiving, there was not an equal amount of return on investment. Critics point to slower adoption rates on the consumer side as a failure of VR. That may be a fair critique — but it's also likely that it may be more a matter of unrealistic expectations than a failure of the technology itself. It's easy to get caught up in the hype of VR and expect immediate results.

This slower adoption rate can also be frustrating for those working in the VR industry. These innovators and creators can't wait to share their work with the world — but first the world has to catch up to them. VR has seen decent adoption numbers for a first-generation device (see Chapter 2). However, a good concentration of those numbers has been lower-tier devices. There is nothing wrong with those devices, but the true transformative nature of VR is based on just how immersive an experience it can provide. And generally, the higher-end (and more expensive) VR devices provide higher-end (and more immersive) VR experiences.

That can lead to a chicken-and-egg scenario. Everyday consumers may find themselves waiting for the most immersive VR headsets to come down in cost. Content creators, meanwhile, are waiting for the most immersive VR headsets to establish a larger audience base. This can create a feedback loop: The high-end devices have a smaller market share of users, which leads to fewer applications being developed for the high end, leading to a smaller market share of users. The loop can be tricky to escape.

REMEMBER

Technologies go through periods of growing pains. The awkward product teenage years help form well-adjusted adults. Consumer-grade VR is only on its first generation of devices, and it has proved it can put forth compelling experiences. The second generation appears to be poised to make leaps ahead in user experience.

Now it's just a matter of VR finding its market fit. What sort of features does the market want? What price level will the market bear? Or, most likely, are there numerous markets, each of which can be addressed at different levels of experience?

TIP

It might be a bit odd to think of VR as a product still searching for its market fit. After all, millions of first-generation devices have been sold and are used every day. But keep in mind that VR is a product that Facebook CEO Mark Zuckerberg wants a billion people to experience. Those lofty goals come with lofty expectations. Reaching that many users definitely requires VR to figure out what its market(s) might be.

Looking at upcoming hardware and software

The next generation of headset hardware has been documented (see Chapter 4), but what about the next generation of software, accessories, and other options for VR experiences? And how will they affect consumers?

The rise of VR facilitated an explosion of companies focused on making VR more immersive, and as VR headsets have become more refined and advanced, so have the software and accessories. With so many industries arising in VR's wake, it's impossible to say which will last and prosper. Some of the features that third-party companies developed (for example, wireless adapters) have been popular enough that hardware manufacturers are incorporating them directly into the next generation of headsets. Other features, such as eye tracking, appear to be on the VR headset road map, but they'll likely continue to be provided by third-party vendors for the near future. And still other features, such as smell in VR, will likely stay as third-party accessories for a long while.

Most of the features described in the following sections probably won't appear as a direct part of the second generation of headsets, but they're poised to make big waves in the near future.

Haptics

The sense of touch may well be the next field VR looks to conquer, having put its stake in the ground for audio and visual experiences. Companies like HaptX, GoTouch VR, and UltraHaptics all offer totally different methods of experiencing haptics in VR and could point to VR's next big leap in updating its level of immersion for users.

Figure 12-1 depicts a user utilizing the HaptX Gloves in conjunction with a VR headset.

FIGURE 12-1:
The HaptX
Gloves.

Courtesy of HaptX

TOUCHING THE FUTURE

Jake Rubin is the founder and CEO of HaptX, a haptics company concerned with bringing the sense of touch to the digital world. The company has a grand vision and "won't stop until you can't tell what is real from what's virtual." The company's current main product is the HaptX Gloves, designed to bring realistic touch and force feedback to VR. However, HaptX's technology could work in almost any form factor, including full-body suits. HaptX's smart textiles can provide a realistic sense of texture, size, and shape through embedded microfluidic air channels. An optional second layer can deliver thermal feedback through variations of hot and cold water.

Mr. Rubin had the following to say about HaptX and the future of haptics:

> Haptics is actually much larger than VR alone. Haptics involves merging the analog and digital, so it should not be tied to just VR or just AR. It can apply to either. But both benefit from it. Right now there is a concerted effort to get haptics into VR. Users in VR can have their minds blown initially, but after five minutes, can turn around and say "Alright, what's next?"
>
> That is where haptics comes in. The audio/visual piece of VR and AR was already going to be solved. But implementing touch for fully immersive experiences was not. That is what we zeroed in on.

Most current haptics companies have been following the same path — vibrating tactile feedback. The main issue here is the haptic version of the "uncanny valley." There is no technology right now that can do decent haptics at a sub-$1,000 price point. Vibration alone is not sufficient to trick the brain. You also end up with poor tracking in most of these products, finger tracking that does not quite align.

Our strategy was a different approach. To start from the high end and work our way down in price. Essentially create a device that is limited volume, limited accessibility, and get it right. We'll begin shipping gloves to customers this year [2018], and we'll be focusing on the enterprise market initially. There is a lot of interest in medical, defense, industrial, and first-responder applications, and design and manufacturing.

We are just getting to the point technologically where we can cross the tactile uncanny valley. The field feels as if it is about five years out from mass consumer adoption. It's a slow and steady approach. But if you make the time frame long enough, full immersion is the only logical endpoint. In the midterm, you'll likely have to go outside your home to a VR arcade or something location-based where there will be a haptic station with VR/AR. Hop in, do your thing, and hop back out. Within ten years, it might start making sense for the average users to have systems in their homes.

Note: The *uncanny valley* is a term used to reference the phenomenon where a computer-generated character or robot is nearly identical to an actual human. However, their differences are just enough from that of a real human that they trigger a negative emotional response from real people. Consider a very realistic mannequin with expressive face and eyes or a ventriloquist's dummy. These attempts at getting close to a human are often met with unease. The uncanny valley in technology is often used to refer to any problem attempting to simulate an existing, "real" experience.

Eye tracking

In Chapter 2, I discuss eye tracking and the benefits that might be gained with this feature. An increase in the expressiveness of avatars, gains in speed and accuracy of item selection, and vastly more efficient graphics via foveated rendering are some of the potential gains that eye tracking will bring about.

Eye tracking could be built into headsets, but most headset manufacturers likely will not address that feature directly in their second-generation headsets. Within the following generation or two, however, it is almost a guarantee this feature will eventually be integrated into VR headsets. The upsides are just too great.

In the meantime, look to third-party companies such as Tobii and 7Invensun to continue to carry this feature forward as one of VR's next big technological leaps.

Social/communication

Even with the release of a number of different social apps for VR, social interaction still feels like VR's missing feature. Game applications like Against Gravity's Rec Room (see Chapter 10) do a wonderful job of finding the right balance between a "purely social" app and a game, and force some socialization on its users. By forcing users into games with other users, Rec Room removes much of the potential awkwardness of meeting strangers in VR.

Other apps, such as Pluto VR, seek to enable users to connect in VR in ways that are not tied to a dedicated experience. Pluto can communicate with others in VR while using any VR app. By running as an overlay on top of your current VR experience, Pluto can turn any VR experience into an area to meet friends. But the makers of Pluto don't consider it a social application per se. "We are not a social application," said Forest Gibson, co-founder at Pluto VR. "We consider ourselves a direct communication app."

You can contact your friends in Pluto while in any VR app. They then appear as floating avatars to chat inside whatever VR environment you currently reside. Regardless of what apps you choose to launch, your friends' avatars inside Pluto will continue to stay with you.

Figure 12-2 shows Pluto VR on top of the Vive home environment.

CONNECTING THE VIRTUAL WORLD

Forest Gibson and Jared Cheshier are co-founders at Pluto VR. They sat down (virtually, of course) to talk with me about Pluto VR and the future of communication in a mixed-reality world.

Regarding Pluto's goals, Mr. Gibson said, "We're building the next generation of communication. If you can do things virtually like commute to work and school, it opens up a new world and breaks down a lot of barriers. We want to help humanity transcend physical location."

Mr. Cheshier added, "The idea is that you shouldn't have the location you're at impact your ability to communicate as if they are in the room with you."

Mr. Gibson touched on some of the challenges for communication in VR: "One of the bigger challenges with where VR is now is the single application focus, where only one app runs at a time. If you have a single application focus, people expect that single application will meet all their needs. I have a need for connection with other people. I have a need for activity and fun and play. I have a need for productivity and working. Suddenly every single application has to meet all of those needs. We've taken a very direct communication focus for Pluto."

"Pluto runs on top of other VR applications by rendering as an overlay," said Mr. Cheshier. "The analogy we usually use to describe it to people is to have them consider traditional 2D applications such as Skype. If I was using Skype to chat with you, I wouldn't see the other applications you have running."

Mr. Cheshier continued, "We are one of the first VR applications that work alongside other applications. That's how we imagine the ecosystem of mixed reality in the future. Rather than being limited to a single application at a time, Pluto works alongside other applications so you can run it alongside other applications as needed. We believe that is the future. We're hoping to contribute back to standards such as OpenXR about the way we're doing things. Not just for full-environmental apps, but discrete apps as well. Imagine a VR watch, just a simple app that stays with you all the time that works alongside your other VR applications. That's how we handle things and how we picture things going in the future with open standards like that of OpenXR."

Regarding the future of communication in VR, Mr. Gibson said, "Hopefully, in the next year or two we have something appropriate for the earliest of early adopters. The mainstream market is not really in VR yet. We're starting to get ideas for the foundation and what makes our perception of the world what it is in regards to communication. One of the things we locked onto early on is positional tracking. So much of what makes our own physical perception of the world is based on how we move. It's so key to how

(continued)

(continued)

we perceive the world that any hardware platform that does not have that positional tracking falls below our primary threshold of what we think the future of computing is. The ability to naturally perceive the world as we move is so important."

Mr. Cheshier added, "There's a certain threshold that, once it's met, things feel more human. It's such a big leap for people to get there. But the trajectory for devices is there. We are seeing it now, as platforms begin to support multiple applications and as VR apps begin to provide some of the things physical devices provide now."

"It takes a long time for people to absorb something brand new and so fundamentally different from what they're used to," closed Mr. Gibson. "It's going to be a slow churn of adoption. But ultimately we imagine a future where the ability to communicate with someone else virtually is almost indistinguishable from talking to someone in person. We have rudimentary avatars now, but as the technology continues to get better, it's going to be closer and closer to just short of teleportation. We believe in a world where physical location is no longer relevant."

Note: OpenXR is a group of VR/AR/MR/XR experts and companies aiming to design a set of standards for VR and AR. These standards should make it simpler to create and develop VR and AR hardware and software that works across multiple devices.

Social interaction and communication will be an important factor affecting the future of VR. Although headset manufacturers can find ways to encourage this interaction among users both co-located and far away, they won't be able to solve the problem alone. Software developers will need to take up the cause of determining the direction of social interaction in VR.

We'll likely see major growth in social VR within the next few years. In the near future, look for VR software developers to continue to work on cracking the social interaction nut.

Considering Virtual Reality's "Killer App"

You may often hear pundits wonder what the "killer app" will be for VR. What, they ask, is that feature or software that will suddenly propel VR to the stratospheric heights most enthusiasts hope for it? After all, reaching a billion users can be tough without a killer app that drives its engagement forward.

TECHNICAL STUFF

Killer app is a term used to describe any application or accessory that is so desirable that it propels its parent hardware or software into the mainstream for customers, ensuring the parent technology's success. Spreadsheet applications such as Lotus 1-2-3 and Microsoft Excel were often considered the killer app in the early days of the personal computer in the office world, while the web browser was considered the killer app for the Internet.

It is nice to imagine a single killer app that immediately proves VR's worth to all consumers and immediately drives adoption to the fabled billion users. And a number of features will likely propel VR forward in the next few years. The inclusion of inside-out tracking on headsets will enable headsets to become much less frictionless to wear. Better motion controls will help drive VR forward. A better experience at a lower cost will open VR up to new consumers. A strong social experience will help make VR less solitary. Various development studios will output never previously imagined experiences, which will help surge adoption forward.

But the truth is there is likely no one single killer app that will cause a wave of VR adoption. Instead, all these features will be enough of a reason for VR to continue to slowly be adopted by both businesses and individuals. The app that is a killer app for Person A will be different for Person B. VR will start leaking more and more into everyday life in different ways. Through use for work or education, or friends that have purchased VR headsets, or location-based experiences that are starting to pop up nearby, VR will likely just become fairly ubiquitous without ever triggering a big "aha" moment for every consumer at once. It will just start appearing in spots until you can't remember a time when it wasn't around.

Predicting the Impact

Throughout this book, I refer to the Gartner Hype Cycle to try to determine VR's placement in the cycle. As the dust has settled on the first generation of VR, the VR hype, while perhaps not totally dead, has died down to a dull murmur.

And that is a good thing. In the tech world, hype comes easily. Tech products and perhaps entire tech industries have been propped up based on hype alone. These products burn brightly for a short time, and often they're reduced to ashes just as quickly.

Hype can affect both good and bad products. The Segway and Google Glass both experienced so much hype ahead of their release to the public that it's doubtful *any* product could have satiated the hype built around them. No less a tech authority than Apple CEO Steve Jobs had claimed about the Segway ahead of its launch,

"If enough people see the machine, you won't have to convince them to architect cities around it. It'll just happen."

Comparing VR to those products may be worrisome for some people. After all, the Segway didn't achieve anywhere near the expected level of adoption. And Google Glass struggled to gain adopters and was eventually taken off the market for retooling. Similar to both the Segway and Google Glass, VR has attracted praise from tech visionaries, touting the "future potential" of the product, regardless of the technology's present state. But that's where the similarities end.

With the hype around VR dying down, what you're left with is actual, proven results and usage of a product. Rather than the promises of what a product could be, you begin to see what a product actually *is*. And although VR is not currently the *Star Trek* holodeck many may have hoped it would immediately become, it's still an incredible product, even more so considering we're still only experiencing the first generation of devices.

In the near future, you can expect likely more of the same from VR's advances. So far, VR's biggest gains in traction have relied on the entertainment and gaming industries. But many industries have begun to see VR's potential and are working on adopting VR for their own uses. Education, healthcare, and industrial uses have all begun to emerge (see Chapter 10), pushing VR use cases further into the limelight. These industries and more will continue their adoption as VR's quality improves and its technology becomes less costly.

Location-based experiences are emerging as a surprising introduction to VR for many users. Some envision the rise of VR to mean you may no longer need to leave your house but can experience everything virtually! Instead, mass consumers have thus far hesitated to go all in on purchasing the most immersive VR hardware for their homes, content for the time being to pay to experience cutting-edge VR onsite elsewhere. Likely, this trend will continue for the next few years, as location-based experiences will find ways to outperform what a user may be able to replicate at home.

Manufacturers focusing on more mobile, standalone headsets point to consumers wanting a portable, low-cost device, though it may not necessarily be the most powerful or immersive. There will, of course, always be a group of consumers pushing for the most cutting-edge experiences possible, and there will be devices built for that group as well.

However, the mid-tier standalone headsets appear to be where manufacturers are turning their main focus. It will be interesting to see if this push toward standalone devices continues. If Moore's Law holds, our mobile devices might soon become powerful enough to run very immersive VR experiences on their own.

With the next generation's focus on standalone headsets, however, it appears the days of cellphone–based VR, while currently the most popular way of experiencing VR, could be numbered in favor of standalone devices.

AUGMENTING VR'S REALITY

Jeff Ludwyck is the founder of Hyperspace XR, a Seattle-based tech startup creating an extended reality (XR) experience that takes your standard VR experience and brings it into the XR space by layering further physical interaction with real-world objects into VR. Mr. Ludwyck said, "We're working on an experience that goes far deeper than what you'll get with at-home VR. We want to push the edge on immersion, merging the virtual with the physical."

Hyperspace is focused on building large-scale XR experiences where users can move around a physical set built specifically for the VR experience the player is being shown in the headset. The VR headset provides the visuals, and the physical environment provides the rest. Touch, sound, smell, and elemental effects such as wind, heat, and cold are all carefully manufactured to align with the VR visuals. If the virtual environment you see is a forest, you'll be able to reach out and feel the moss on a tree. Walking up to a campfire, you'll smell the smoke.

"VR has had an adoption problem so far," Mr. Ludwyck said. "The form factor in which most people have been experiencing it just isn't right. Many see it through lower-quality headsets, and even most current location-based experiences are small 10-foot-by-10-foot experiences that just aren't impressive. We want to change that."

"Immersion into a reality requires stimulating all the senses, and that's what we want to do with Hyperspace. Home VR can do audio and visuals fairly well, but the experience stops there. We want to be able to stimulate all the senses. Rumbling, heat, cold, wind, smells are all part of our experience. It will be a long way off for home VR to get to the level of immersion that these types of location-based experiences can offer."

Only a handful of companies are working in this large-scale, location-based XR space, but even amongst those few, Mr. Ludwyck believes Hyperspace stands out. "We take a slightly different approach from most other companies. All our environment tracking is done via inside-out tracking, rather than having to worry about external sensors to track users in space — everything is tracked via a system on the players themselves. Our use of inside-out tracking just makes setup/install/changes to the experience so much easier, and more portable to move to new locations."

"Though we're currently staged at the Pacific Science Center, our goal is to have our experiences set up in four new locations by next year [2019]. And our inside-out

(continued)

(continued)

tracking should make it easy to expand to new locations. Theaters, theme parks, museums, there are lots of places that could benefit from this type of walkthrough experience.

"In-home VR will always be playing catch-up. And location-based experiences like ours will need to keep working to offer up something new to stay ahead of the curve. It might be a wider field-of-view headset, or appendage tracking, or a tactile suit they may not have access to at home. There will always be something new to add to these walk-through experiences to keep ahead of what you might experience at home."

"In five years, experiences like these could be so deep I could see people staying in them for days at a time. Right now, our experience requires a wearable backpack to power the experience. But I can picture an experience like this where the VR headset and computer form factor is much smaller, and you just become immersed for long periods of time, potentially for days. A big part of VR is social, and home VR hasn't quite gotten that just yet. That's something we can do really well. If you could travel to a location and go visit Mars in VR with your family or friends for a couple days, how cool would that be?"

TECHNICAL STUFF

Moore's Law is an observation that was made by Intel co-founder Gordon Moore. He noted that the number of transistors in an integrated circuit doubled nearly every two years. In general terms, it predicts that the processing power of computers will double every two years. This was more applicable in the past and may not exactly hold true today, but it's still considered a rule of thumb. For more information, visit www.mooreslaw.org.

In the end, the customer may not always be right, but they'll always be the customer. Manufacturers may be able to lead them to water, but they can't make them drink. Consumers will be the ones driving adoption. The most telling factor of where VR will likely be concentrated in the near future will be the adoption rate of the second-generation of VR devices. If it's focused around mid-tier headsets, expect developers making applications to reflect that same focus, with more of an emphasis on mid-tier consumable experiences.

Expanding the timeline out for far-future predictions, it's easy to imagine a form factor that merges both VR and AR into a single device. Such a device could turn fully opaque and closed off to display VR experiences or turn transparent with overlays to allow AR experiences. It would be small enough to be portable, yet powerful enough to deliver an amazing graphic experience. That device is just a pipe dream for now, but so were immersive consumer VR headsets only five years ago. And look where we are today.

For content creators and many consumers, this second generation of devices is the perfect time to enter the market. VR headsets haven't reached their ultimate potential, but they already offer an incredible experience for consumers. Jumping in now offers distinct advantages for both creators and customers. Creators will still be in the market early enough to experiment and make the inevitable missteps and course corrections, solidifying their product before the true mass consumer wave occurs. Consumers will be in the market late enough that many of the first-generation issues will have been ironed out and addressed, and with a healthy marketplace of hardware and software in place, driven by the first-generation devices.

Chapter **13**

Assessing the Future of Augmented Reality

Whereas virtual reality (VR) is quickly driving toward the second generation of consumer devices, with many second-generation devices seeing a release in 2018 and 2019, most augmented reality (AR) hardware devices have yet to see a first-generation mass consumer release. Many devices still release in "developer preview" mode, with devices targeted to developers to ensure that a market is created before releasing to consumers. And some companies are currently only taking preorders for their yet-released AR hardware.

We won't be able to accurately assess AR's potential hardware adoption until AR headsets begin to see larger-scale rollouts and consumer releases. In fact, AR headset manufacturers themselves likely are still studying just what a mass consumer rollout of AR hardware could look like.

In this chapter, I use what we *do* know to determine what AR might look like in the future. With much of AR still existing in the "hype" phase, I look to see if that hype is justified and try to determine what it means for the future. Finally, I discuss what the future of AR could mean for you as either a content creator or a consumer.

Analyzing Near Future Changes

The near future of AR is hard to predict. Future items exist on a spectrum ranging from near certain to be released to wild speculation, making AR both an exciting and a frustrating market. Analyzing the future of the AR market is as much an art as it is a science; it takes some research and guesswork to know what to take seriously and what to ignore.

TIP

Evaluating the AR market can be a difficult task. There are a lot of predictions and a lot of promises to sort through. Keeping abreast of changes in the industry and potential upcoming hardware and software is a good idea, but don't let rumors and speculation distract you. Focusing on actual released hardware and software will help you filter out a lot of otherwise distracting noise.

Evaluating the market

The near future market for AR will likely fall into two categories: mainstream mobile AR experiences and enterprise-level AR experiences. These can potentially run on any number of form factors, but likely will lean toward some type of headset or glasses.

Additionally, AR is a totally new paradigm for most users to acclimate to. The introduction of smartphones is a good example of new technology that came with an appreciably large consumer learning curve. It took years before a majority of consumers were comfortable with this new form factor. Even then, the jump was essentially from a large 2D screen to a smaller 2D screen. Many users may not have used a touchscreen device themselves up to that point, but they had at least passing familiarity with how to interact with one.

AR, on the other hand, is a completely new method of interacting with the world around us. Even if an inexpensive mass-consumer AR device were to release tomorrow, it would undoubtedly take some time before consumers felt comfortable with how to interact with this new way of consuming content. Manufacturers themselves have yet to agree on best practices or standardized interactions. Things we take for granted on our computers (click and drag, copy, paste) or mobile devices (pinch to zoom, tap and hold to select) are still being determined for AR.

Couple this learning curve with a lack of consumer hardware (compounded with a lack of consumer software), and AR headsets for mass consumers is still a ways out. Without a new competitor unexpectedly throwing a hat in the ring (such as Google or Apple, perhaps), it's easy to imagine mass-consumer-adopted AR headset hardware being at least two to four years out.

There are hopeful signs for the eventual adoption of headset AR. Apple's release of ARKit and Google's release of ARCore have led to consumers starting to experience AR and given developers ways to test the AR waters on a larger audience. Mobile devices may not provide the perfect AR experience, but this early introduction to AR will go a long way toward starting consumers on the AR learning curve. When a mass consumer AR headset is introduced, there will be a much smaller mental hurdle for most users to leap over.

AR in the enterprise world is picking up steam quickly, especially in certain sectors. In Chapter 11, I explore a number of industrial use cases. Industrial use is one area in which AR could be adopted very rapidly. Industrial use cases vary broadly, but many focus on methods of cutting production or maintenance time and errors. While the cost of a HoloLens or Meta 2 might be high for an everyday consumer right now, for industrial use they can pay for themselves almost immediately, where even small improvements in worker productivity add up rapidly over time.

TECHNICAL STUFF

There are numerous case studies on the efficiency of AR in industry. In one example, factory workers at General Electric utilizing Skylight, an AR platform for smart glasses, saw a 46 percent increase in productivity and reduction in errors compared to the paper-based process. The Skylight system provided real-time information for item location to floor workers, leading to far quicker order fulfillment (https://upskill.io/landing/ge-healthcare-case-study).

Considering AR's "Killer App"

You may hear Pokémon Go, the successful location-based Pokémon mobile phone game, referred to as AR's "killer app." The debate over whether Pokémon Go is "true" AR aside, it never met the criteria of "killer app" for me. A killer app is one that immediately drives consumers to purchase or proves the worth of their purchase of hardware or software.

While Pokémon Go is a brilliantly thought-out and executed mobile game, it didn't drive massive adoption or purchases of new mobile devices. In fact, Pokémon Go was successful largely because mobile phone adoption was already so high. The prevalence of existing hardware gave the software the potential to be massively successful.

AR hardware (that is, AR outside of mobile devices) will likely have a much different mountain to climb when it releases at consumer level. The apps will need to be compelling enough to drive consumers to purchase the hardware. It is not an easy challenge, especially for the user-experience paradigm shift AR promises to be.

AR will probably not have one killer app that immediately proves its worth to consumers and has them rushing out the door to purchase their first AR device. More likely, AR will just start to fill various niches, and users' reasons for purchasing will be that it fulfilled the need of their particular niche.

If there were to be a killer app for AR, it likely would not be a single application, but could be its many industrial applications. The rapid growth of AR at the enterprise level is a seemingly different path than that of VR, which (past iterations aside) jumped fairly directly to consumers. This initial focus on industrial applications could be a good thing for consumers in the long run. Releasing for mass consumption becomes a delicate balancing act as you try to encompass all the possible needs of your consumers: solid technology, not too expensive, production scaled to millions, need for supporting software, usage learning curve, and so on. Mass consumer releases will also come under increased scrutiny and the inflated expectations of millions of customers, unlike smaller, enterprise-level releases.

Figure 13-1 displays one of the Meta 2's many commercial usages, in this case depicting architectural plans in 3D space.

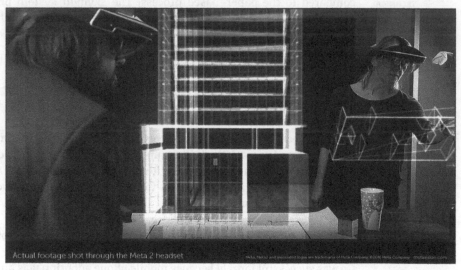

Actual footage shot through the Meta 2 headset

Courtesy of Meta

FIGURE 13-1:
Footage of the
Meta 2 utilized
for architecture.

AR's concentration on headsets and glasses for enterprise ahead of a mass consumer release minimizes a number of those potential issues. A higher price tag is less likely to scare off enterprise-level consumers. Production does not need to be scaled as rapidly, software is typically bespoke (made to order) for industries, and extras like training are typically included as part of the enterprise package. This will allow AR to experiment and refine what works within certain markets before making its way down to the consumer.

Predicting the Impact

As previously mentioned, AR's near-future fate is in an awkward place to predict. With manufacturers still very much in early release, pre-first-consumer generation mode, it makes the future a bit hazy. After all, how can we predict the future if we aren't even sure about the present?

Revisiting the Gartner Hype Cycle (see Chapter 1), you find that Gartner analysis of AR has placed mass-scale adoption at around five to ten years out. With the current state of AR, that feels like an appropriate prediction.

Hype is easy to come by. It's easy, cheap, and quick to drum up excitement around potential hardware or software releases. Where the rubber hits the road is where actual products out in the field see usage in real-world scenarios. The greatest products in the world don't mean a thing if they never see the light of day and real world usage.

WARNING

Don't get sucked in by the hype around a product (any product). Almost every product will market itself as "the next big thing." On the flip side, don't let the fact that a product is hyped immediately discount it in your mind either! Sometimes hype is justified, and sometimes it's just hype.

Consumers are also a wild card in the AR scenario. Sometimes driven by marketing, sometimes driven by other desires, consumers can inadvertently drive the direction of entire industries, and they don't always respond in ways you might expect.

That is one of the reasons that VR, while still early in its life cycle, is easier to predict the future of than AR. VR has at least seen a large-scale consumer release of a number of products. This, in turn, led to the ability of headset manufacturers to see what consumers were responding to: what worked and what didn't. This led to further refinements and a better idea of where things are headed.

AR has yet to have that luxury. It has taken some steps out from the safety of backroom laboratories and research centers, but it still has yet to take much of a real step beyond its own front door. Mobile AR and the various enterprise-focused AR form factors have been a trial balloon for AR, akin to sticking your hand out the window to see what the weather is like.

It's a wide world out there. It's time for AR to step off the front porch and start to experience it!

INCUBATING THE FUTURE

Elizabeth Scallon leads CoMotion Labs at the University of Washington, an incubator system for high-tech, high growth startups, and part of UW CoMotion. CoMotion Labs opened a space specifically dedicated to VR/AR startups in 2016.

Ms. Scallon sat down to speak with me about where VR and AR are headed in the future, and the issues we might face to get there. As an incubator for VR/AR startups, CoMotion is on the frontlines of seeing what ideas are and are not being adopted by the industry. I asked Ms. Scallon what the industry seemed to be receptive to currently. "With VR/AR at this point, it's too early in the market to show success or not," she said. "Our startup members are still testing their market. With VR/AR, the industry is still so immature that even a larger startup can still be pretty vulnerable to the market. We'll have another three years before we can definitively say what ideas seem like they are going to succeed and what ideas might not."

"The great thing you see right now is a lot of strong partnerships," Ms. Scallon continued. "When you have nascent technologies like this, you see the entire community rally around each other. HTC, Valve, Microsoft, Magic Leap, Oculus. They need developers and innovation on their platform, so we are seeing lots of good partnerships with those companies."

With regards to some of the issues of adoption for headsets, Ms. Scallon said, "Every headset needs killer content. And investors have shown that they are interested in hardware, in 'picks and shovels,' but not necessarily software just yet. We as an industry need to figure that out. Who is creating that content? Where is the funding coming from? And how do you showcase it? Those are big questions. And that's why you see a lot of B2B work currently; companies are happy to hire developers to create content for them. But for the consumers, we're still waiting for more and better content."

"But we will get there. Creating content is getting easier. The world is going screenless. And every industry is going to be impacted. I think the AR transition will happen first. I think cellphones are going away, and it will make the transition to AR easier. What we use cellphones for currently will be incorporated into AR devices. And looking at a 2D screen is going to be so yesterday. The generation of children growing up now is going to be laughing at us and our primitive cellphone technology."

Finally, Ms. Scallon touched upon the importance of inclusion for VR and AR. "We need to make sure we provide opportunities for every person to engage in this ecosystem so we no longer have user groups who are left behind by this technology. We need to make sure we don't create archetypes of investible looking people, that we bring forward all groups and have diversity and multiple voices around the table determining the future of VR/AR. I want to make sure we don't have pockets or groups of people left behind by this technological transformation. It is not just for the elite."

"With this new technology, we have the power to create the world we want to experience. Let's be as inclusive as possible."

AR has had some promising signs for adoption. Consumers have gotten a small taste of AR via mobile AR and have reacted positively. Proven technology companies like Microsoft, Amazon, and Apple have thrown resources behind AR, new technology companies like Magic Leap and Meta are finding a reason to jump in in a big way, and general investment in the technology has yet to slow.

With AR development still in its early stages, it can be somewhat irresponsible to make any sort of guess as to just where we'll end up both in the near and far future. But let's live a little dangerously here and speculate!

The near future for AR adoption looks promising but slow (at least, in tech time, where every year can feel like seven years). Expect further advances in both form factor and software, as companies work to put together hardware that they feel is acceptable to mass consumers.

We are likely at least a hardware generation or two out from a time when an everyday consumer might consider purchasing an AR headset, as most first-generation devices will continue to focus on enterprise-level releases and/or developer-based releases. What that works out to in real-world time can be tough to say for certain, but Gartner's prediction of at least five years wouldn't be a surprise. But no one knows for sure. Anyone making time-based predictions in the tech world is bound to be made to look silly eventually.

On a long enough timeline (as discussed in Chapter 12) it is easy to imagine a device that merges our VR and AR experiences into a single hardware form factor. After all, most AR devices are already being asked to do the same tasks VR devices accomplish (3D visuals, audio, motion tracking, and so on). AR just adds additional complexity. If a device can pull off a convincing AR experience (that is, truly make it feel like 3D holograms inhabit your physical world), that same device is likely powerful enough to pull off a convincing VR experience.

There are, of course, still many challenges for such a "combined" headset to solve. (For example, how will visuals work, especially as many AR images are projected reflections? How does the headset toggle between opaque VR and transparent AR?) But what was quite literally the stuff of science fiction as recently as a few years ago is now on our doorstep as a distinct possibility.

Figure 13-2 depicts the Microsoft HoloLens in use in a design scenario. A designer making changes to a model on a 2D screen may see those changes updated on the fly in 3D real-world space.

Used with permission from Microsoft

FIGURE 13-2:
The Microsoft
HoloLens in a
design scenario.

The promise of AR is there. As is the feeling that AR could potentially be an even larger market than that of VR. AR's ability to mix the real world with the digital would definitely seems to lend itself more toward supporting how most of us currently work, whereas working fully in VR would require a total adjustment in how we currently approach the workplace. Both are possible, though AR may find itself more easily adapted to our current workflow, which could be a massive boon to adoption.

With AR's long adoption cycle, now is a good time for content creators to enter the market, but make sure you understand what you're getting into. Be aware of the market you're entering; outside of mobile AR, the mass consumer market of headsets is not there yet and is likely a few years out. There are still plenty of opportunities to create for mobile AR or for creating applications for use at the enterprise level. Just be sure you understand what sort of market you may be targeting.

WARNING

With AR, as with any tech, know your market. If you expect to become an AR millionaire within the next year by selling 99-cent holographic widgets in a headset app store, your market may not exist quite yet.

Everyday consumers are likely still a few years off from entering the market in large numbers. You may start to see AR headsets find their way into your workplace in the next few years. If you're in charge of making those sorts of decisions, now can be a great time to evaluate how your industry could integrate this technology into your workflow. You may find that it's appropriate to start to integrate now, or you may not, but these technologies will be here quicker than you think.

That said, if you have interest in the technology, especially as a content creator, there is no time like the present to throw yourself into AR. Getting in early enough will allow you to take chances and risks, learning and adjusting your course along the way. Early entry into the market will allow you to build up your experience and will also increase the potential for you to corner the market in the vertical you are working in.

With AR, you're in a unique position to invest your time or talents in a life-altering technology. But AR is still young. Its maturity is likely similar to very early days of the Internet. And if you could go back in time and be one of the first to invest your time and talents into a technology as life-changing as the Internet, wouldn't you?

6
The Part of Tens

IN THIS PART . . .

Find answers to ten common questions new users have regarding virtual and augmented reality.

Check out ten industries that could experience a major upheaval via virtual and augmented reality.

Explore ten augmented reality applications that can be downloaded on a mobile device today and review what their future implementation could look like.

Chapter **14**

Ten Questions about Virtual and Augmented Reality

I f you're interested in virtual reality (VR) and augmented reality (AR), you've likely asked yourself one or more of the questions in this chapter. In many cases, there aren't definitive answers available, but I tell you what I think and what many of the leading experts in the fields of VR and AR have said.

How Will Virtual and Augmented Reality Affect Me?

Wondering how VR and AR technologies are going to affect your life? You're not alone. Many are wondering the same thing, and the future is uncertain, so any answer to this question is going to involve some guesswork.

The good news: Neither VR nor AR will likely be thrust upon you unwillingly in the near future. Do not expect to come to work tomorrow and find that your PC has been completely replaced by a pair of AR glasses.

VR will likely start to seep into your life around the edges. A VR arcade may spring up at your local mall, or a tech-minded friend may have a headset for you to experience. As the lower-cost headsets start to arrive, you may even decide to purchase one yourself. A lot depends on the industry you work in, but VR seems unlikely to *force* its way into your life as much as gradually work its way in through location-based experiences, entertainment, and gaming.

AR has the potential to be more disruptive, and its strengths make it a contender to be implemented in the workplace before VR. Similar to the early days of the personal computer, that may be many user's first exposure to the technology. However, full-scale industry usage is likely some time off. Barring a large leap forward for AR (and depending on your industry), you're likely still at least five years from passing colleagues sporting AR glasses in lieu of a PC.

WARNING

The VR and AR industries are anything but static, and growth can come in leaps and bounds. It would be foolish to make a prediction about either industry without constantly revisiting that prediction to realign with reality. Oculus turned the VR world on its head in 2013 with the DK1. HTC did it again with the Vive in 2016. Google and Apple flipped the AR world upside down with ARCore and ARKit in 2017. Magic Leap hopes to do the same with the Creator Edition in 2018. That's a lot of turns and flips. The only constant is change, so keeping abreast of changes is vitally important if you don't want to be left behind.

Which Technology Will Win?

A popular question now that both VR and AR have risen in public awareness is which technology will win the battle of the fourth wave of technologies — VR or AR? From a business point of view, you may want to know which technology to throw your development resources behind. From a consumer point of view, you may want to know which devices you should consider purchasing.

A realistic answer is that, in the long run, both are likely to win (that is, become an integral part of our technological lives). VR and AR are different technologies. Although they exist in the same sphere, they aren't in direct competition with one another. There likely won't be one winner and one loser. They both have different sets of strengths and weaknesses. In the future, a user may wear her AR glasses on the job to complete her workday tasks, and then come home and don her VR headset for some evening entertainment.

Having said that, the ultimate form factor may be a headset that can merge the two technologies. No current device has offered this option, though many VR headsets have multiple front-facing cameras on them that could conceivably be used for AR experiences. Microsoft even went so far as to name its VR headsets Windows Mixed Reality, leading many to speculate that Microsoft sees the technologies merging to a single device in the future. (For its part, Microsoft has claimed that the name is due to its headsets belonging to its Windows Mixed Reality platform, which includes the HoloLens.)

A wireless headset that offers the ability to switch between the full immersion of VR and the mixed worlds of AR could be a solution consumers flock to.

REMEMBER

VR and AR are not necessarily competitors! Each has its own set of strengths, and each technology's strengths actually serve to shore up the other's weaknesses.

What If I Don't Have a Headset?

Some websites utilize WebVR (a way to experience VR in a browser), and some applications enable you to use your computer or phone without a headset. YouTube, for example, has a number of videos that let you look around and explore in 360 degrees. However, in those applications, you aren't really experiencing VR. You're just viewing a 360-degree world via a two-dimensional screen.

To truly experience VR, a headset is required. A number of basic headsets, such as Google Cardboard, allow you to experience VR at very low cost (often less than $20). Having said that, I encourage you to seek out the highest VR experience you can. You don't need to rush out and buy the most expensive VR headset you can find. But find a location-based VR experience, or even try your local mall or big-box retailer that has VR demo areas. The difference in quality between a simple Google Cardboard viewer and the high-end headsets is massive. If you've yet to experience high-quality VR, it is an amazing experience that is not to be missed.

To experience a slimmed down version of AR, often all you need is a recent version of an Apple or Android mobile phone or tablet. iOS and Android have released ARKit and ARCore, versions of AR specifically created for their respective mobile devices. A number of applications exist in the App Store and Google Play Store tailored to those technologies. You can read about some of the more compelling AR experiences available for download in Chapter 16.

How Large Will the Virtual and Augmented Reality Consumer Markets Get?

It's difficult to pin down the current market sizes of VR and AR today, let alone know what will happen to those markets in the future. Market size is difficult to determine for many reasons, including lack of availability of precise market analytics, various form factor executions, and market fragmentation. However, we can look at some products and technologies to help with some rough estimates.

For VR, now is the perfect time to take stock of the direction the markets are headed. The first generation of devices has had ample amount of time in consumer hands. A number of second-generation VR devices are becoming available. More details will also have emerged around manufacturers' plans for the future, and how they're adjusting to where the markets seem to be headed.

All of this should add up to informative years for VR. Manufacturers appear to be planning for a sharp uptick in VR headset sales, with sales likely concentrated around the midrange headsets. The sales of these second-generation devices should help predict the size of the consumer base for VR. There may or may not be a massive explosion of VR adoption, but most hope that a steady increase over time in the quality of headsets and experiences should bolster the market.

AR will likely not see much of a consumer jump for a few years, outside of executions within mobile devices. Most AR devices are targeted toward enterprise businesses instead of consumers. If your dream was to sell a billion headset-based AR apps in the next few years, you're likely to be disappointed. But fear not! What headset-based AR will lack in market size, it will make up for in enterprise-level executions. There will likely be a large influx of companies looking to utilize AR within the next few years.

WARNING

You can typically extrapolate predictions based on existing markets, consumer price point comfort, and ability to scale to mass-consumption level. Generally, those data points give you enough information to make a reasonable guess at market size within the next year or two. However, there will always be the potential for a game-breaking technology to appear. A company could release a mass-produced AR headset tomorrow that immediately blows these predictions out of the water.

When Should I Enter the Market as a Consumer?

There is no "right" or "wrong" time to enter the VR or AR marketplace. Evaluate each technology on its merits and decide what is right for you.

VR is, at present, a more mature market on the consumer side than AR. There is more competition among headset manufacturers and more content available via various manufacturers' app stores. There are also a number of choices at various levels of quality and price points.

AR, on the other hand, lags behind in the consumer space. Only one or two headset/glasses manufacturers seem to be in any sort of position to produce hardware at anywhere near mass consumer scale, and the price points of these devices are far beyond what most consumers are willing to pay. However, users can also get a taste of AR via applications for their mobile devices.

In the end, this is a decision you must make on your own, considering how you plan to use the hardware and software. Are you looking for the highest-quality immersive experience for gaming or entertainment? A higher-end VR headset may be a good choice. Are you looking for a bleeding-edge, early adopter glance at how we could be working in the near future? Perhaps one of the AR headsets is your best bet.

For most of the general population, AR headsets at consumer scale is probably a few years out. Experiencing AR via your mobile device will likely suffice for most consumers for the time being.

VR, however, is readily available for public consumption now. If you have an interest in experiencing VR in the comfort of your own home, there is no reason to hold back any longer from purchasing a device. As with most tech hardware, at this point it's just a matter of evaluating the hardware and upcoming choices and deciding what's right for you.

TIP

When choosing a VR/AR device (or any technology), evaluate not only the current choices, but the upcoming choices as well. For example, a user looking for a VR device may be focused on the current generation of devices. As with many technologies, these devices are likely refreshed and improved upon every few years. Be sure to evaluate your current choices versus all upcoming choices to help avoid any buyer's remorse.

When Should My Company Enter the Market?

There is no right or wrong time to enter the emerging technology market as a consumer, but there *can* be a right or wrong time to enter it as a company. Enter too early or without a strong direction, and you risk being so far out on the bleeding edge that the market hasn't built itself to sustain your entry. Enter too late, and you risk the market having passed you by.

Now is definitely a good time to be evaluating both technologies to determine how they fit within your organization's long-term growth and development. VR is fast maturing as a market. In the next two years, you can expect to see rapid growth in this space at mass consumer and enterprise scale.

AR is lagging behind slightly in availability for mass consumer adoption. Mobile AR will play a large role for the next few years, with AR wearables likely a few years beyond that. However, AR is already catching on within enterprise lines of business. AR in the enterprise will likely see very steady growth, with the potential for extreme spikes in certain enterprises such as medical, industrial, design, and manufacturing fields.

TIP

In general, the drawbacks of incorporating technology within your market too early pale in comparison to those of entering a market too late. Although you may jump the gun and find yourself with a smaller market by entering too early, you may find your market cornered by competitors if you enter too late.

You should already be evaluating how these technologies could shake up your particular industry. If you still aren't sure how these technologies may fit within your industry, running one or two small pilot projects or ideation labs utilizing VR or AR within your company walls could help you decide where VR or AR adoption within your industry could take place in the future.

REMEMBER

William Shakespeare wrote, "Better three hours too soon than a minute late." The penalty your company will pay for entering the market too early is rarely higher than the steep price it could pay for entering the market too late. We all would love the ability to time the market just right, but that's impossible. Err on the side of being proactive instead of reactive.

Which Virtual Reality Headset Is Right for Me?

Deciding upon a VR headset is a question with a number of variables involved — there is no one right answer that will work for everyone. Chapter 2 can provide a good reference for you to review comparisons of some of the current options available. At a high level, there are three different tiers of VR hardware:

>> **High-end "desktop" headsets:** If you're looking for the most immersive VR experience and have external hardware ready to power your headset, one of the high-end headsets is likely appropriate for you. These headsets offer the most immersive VR experience consumers can purchase today. They typically run on external hardware such as a desktop computer. Offloading the processing work to a desktop computer allows for a graphically intense experience because of the desktop PC's powerful processor and memory availability. High-end headsets can also allow for freedom of motion with room-scale tracking and feature-rich external controllers. Most have a very strong selection of immersive games and entertainment selections.

The drawbacks of the higher-level headsets include price and the reliance on an external computer to power these experiences.

Current examples of high-level headsets include the Oculus Rift, HTC Vive Pro, and Windows Mixed Reality headsets.

>> **Mid-tier mobile headsets:** The mid-tier (or mobile-powered) headsets offer a solid VR experience at a much lower price than the high-level experiences. Most of these headsets do require external hardware, but only a mobile phone that adheres to the VR device's requirements, many of which consumers may already have. (The upcoming generation of mid-tier headsets include devices such as the HTC Vive Focus or Oculus Santa Cruz, which will be standalone and not require an external device.) Because these devices do not require a desktop computer, these headsets are far more portable. Without a reliance on tethering to an external piece of hardware or any extra sensors, these devices can be carted anywhere.

The drawback of these mobile experiences is the level of experience offered. With the limited computational power of mobile devices, the level of immersiveness can be less than that of the high-end headsets. The first generation of mid-tier devices does not offer the same fidelity of tracking the user, and the controllers are often fairly simplistic compared to the high-end options.

The mid-tier headset is often a good starter level for users intrigued by VR but not yet willing to go all in on a high-end device. They enable users to experience a taste of VR at a lower price point.

Current examples at this tier include the Samsung Gear VR and Google Daydream.

>> **Low-end mobile headsets:** Low-level headsets consist mainly of Google Cardboard and devices built around the Google Cardboard specification. These low-end devices are powered with separate mobile hardware, which makes them easily portable.

Unlike the mid-tier devices, most of these low-end devices do away with niceties like controllers or other separate hardware and software integrations. The hardware and software experience is as bare bones as you can get while still remaining "VR." These devices are often referred to as "viewers" — a good name for them, because they're mainly built for viewing VR experiences and worlds, with very little interactivity.

Current examples include Google Cardboard, View-Master VR, and SMARTvr.

These low-level headsets are good as a way of democratizing VR experiences. Cardboards are relatively inexpensive, so they can be branded and shipped to consumers at a low cost. *The New York Times* did just that, shipping out over a million branded Google Cardboards and access to their NYT VR app to their customers. Similarly, Cardboard hardware may be a good choice where replacement cost or user damage is an issue, such as within elementary schools looking to experience VR without breaking the bank.

REMEMBER

There is no "wrong" choice of VR headset. Just as your mobile phone is different from your TV, the mid-tier headsets have a different set of strengths and weaknesses than the high-end headsets. As a simple analogy, you may love watching a football game on your 60-inch flat-screen TV at home, but you can't carry your 60-inch flat-screen everywhere you go. The portability your mobile phone offers can be a huge benefit, and you may find you end up spending even more time on your phone than in front of your TV, even though your TV offers an arguably "better" experience.

As the saying goes, "You get what you pay for." VR in Google Cardboard is a great, low-cost introduction to VR, but don't think that if you've used a Google Cardboard you've experienced the level of immersiveness VR can offer. The difference in experience from a Google Cardboard to a high-end VR experience can be the difference between watching a feature film on your mobile phone and watching it in a theater with full surround sound.

For AR experiences, there is little reason to purchase a headset right now for consumer consumption. The market for consumer-based AR applications and use cases outside of mobile AR aren't yet at a critical mass. However, there are plenty of reasons to purchase AR headsets to create applications targeted toward enterprise-level consumption. For example, if you're tasked with building an AR application for commercial or industrial usage. These fields will likely experience tremendous growth in usage of AR. You should evaluate the specific customer needs within that space and find the AR headset that aligns most closely with the requirements of that task.

TIP

With both Oculus and HTC releasing dedicated untethered devices in 2018, and Magic Leap scheduled to release hardware within that same timespan, make sure to compare the latest set of apples to apples when purchasing any VR or AR devices. The market is constantly in flux, so make sure to find the device whose strengths align with your project's needs.

What Could Impede the Growth of Virtual and Augmented Reality?

The growth of these two technologies seems inevitable, but there are potential bumps in the road you should be aware of that could potentially throw one or the other off track.

VR seems to have made it through its Trough of Disillusionment (see Chapter 1). Short of studies finding massive health risks within VR, there is likely little to impede its growth at this point. The worst-case scenario for VR would seem to be sluggish growth. If the second generation of headsets gets a lukewarm consumer reception, or if the headset and application market becomes more fragmented and confusing, VR's growth as a mass consumer device could slow down. It wouldn't be the death knell for VR, but sluggish market growth can mean less investment capital. Less investment capital can create a feedback cycle of slower improvements, leading to sluggish growth, which leads back to slower improvements.

AR's growth, outside of executions on mobile, is more constrained at the moment. Limited availability of hardware to developers can create lack of development resources, which can lead to lack of depth of content. The high price point of headsets, nonexistent content ecosystem, and no standardization of experience expectations when using AR are all things AR will struggle with over the next few years.

Are There Lasting Physical Effects?

Many emerging technologies have faced the prospect of potential medical questions. When computers were quickly becoming mass consumer devices, medical experts questioned the effects staring at computer screens all day could have on us long term. When mobile devices began their ascent into the public consciousness, worries about electromagnetic radiation from the phones themselves and cellphone towers had medical researchers studying the relationship between mobile phone radiation and cancer rates.

The same sorts of questions currently exist for VR and AR. Will having a screen so close to our eyes cause lasting damage to our eyesight? Could working long term in VR cause lasting nausea? Could there be lasting behavioral effects from staying in these virtual worlds for an extended period of time?

Many of these medical effects are believed to be little more than short-term issues, but there have yet to be long-term studies evaluating the usage of VR or AR.

Most experts agree that for the time being, you can be cautious and sensible about the potential risks, but that caution should not prevent you from utilizing the technology as you see fit. Take off the headset if you're feeling nauseated, and take "screen breaks" every half-hour to give your eyesight time to readjust to the real world. These are all standard rules you should already be following in regards to any screen time (VR headsets, computer screens, or mobile devices).

What Is the Future of Virtual and Augmented Reality?

All transformative technologies have positive and negative potential. Because of its ability to be immersive, VR will likely suffer from many of the same issues other technologies experience today, but to a greater degree. Some of the potential issues of this new technology include VR addiction; users checking out of the real world and spending far too much time in the virtual. The potential to desensitize users to their actions in the real world due to the lack of consequences of their actions in the virtual world is an issue that has been cited as well.

AR could suffer from some of the same issues VR may struggle with. It also could grapple with a few issues of its own. Who owns the rights to the digital world? Should anyone have the ability to display AR content anywhere? Could our AR experiences become too lifelike? Could we become incapable of distinguishing the real world from the virtual enhancements?

These are interesting concerns or thought projects, but they're massively outweighed by the enormous potential of these technologies.

VR has the ability to reach across boundaries and borders. The Internet connected people like never before. VR takes that power and adds in the ability to form a truly empathetic global social space. It has the capability to completely revolutionize how we learn and how we play, and perhaps most importantly how we connect with one another.

AR has the ability to enhance our everyday actions within the real world. It has the potential to help people make smarter decisions via information availability. It can make the world around us interactive. It can facilitate creating new connections with others via shared experiences and change the ways we currently work. You name the industry, and within ten years, AR may have massively transformed that industry as we know it.

Chapter 15

Ten Industries That Will Be Transformed by Virtual and Augmented Reality

Major technological changes such as virtual reality (VR) and augmented reality (AR) rarely take place without disrupting a number of existing industries. Some of the industries that will be affected are obvious (such as gaming and entertainment). But many more industries may not even have VR or AR on their radar today, to their detriment. VR and AR could cause a massive upheaval in the industry as they now know it.

TIP

All industries should take stock of how VR or AR could end up affecting them. The last thing any industry wants to be is slow to react to upcoming changes. Even if you don't see your current industry on this list, that doesn't mean it'll be free from change. When you consider the future of VR and AR, cast a wide net and think of every possibility, no matter how unlikely it may seem based on current technology.

In this chapter, I evaluate how VR and AR will shape ten industries in the future. I look at where the technology is now and what the future could look like at the more extreme ends.

REMEMBER

Letting your mind wander and consider ideas that may seem crazy today is far less expensive than *not* considering a possibility and having that possibility brought to life by another company while you're left flat-footed, unprepared for change.

Travel

The travel industry is one of the sleeper industries that could see the greatest amount of upheaval because of VR and AR. And it can be difficult to pinpoint just which way the wave will break for the travel industry. The VR and AR revolution could become a huge boon to the industry — or its greatest threat.

On the upside, VR and AR are opening up a world to potential customers like never before. VR can give users glimpses of places throughout the world, inspiring them to want to visit the real-world versions of the locations they've only experienced a small taste of in VR.

AR applications are already helping expose users to information when they're out and about in unfamiliar places. For example, the social review app Yelp has long had a built-in feature called Monocle, which provides users overlays of information about nearby businesses in AR, as shown in Figure 15-1. Other apps, such as England's Historic Cities, serve as virtual tour guides, superimposing information about various tourist destinations and artifacts for users to explore while in the locations themselves.

On the flipside, could VR or AR applications remove people's desire to travel at all? In Chapter 10, I discuss VR applications such as Google Earth that let you teleport to almost any major tourist destination in the world to soar above mountains or dive to street level and stroll around the city. Google Earth is currently a poor replacement for the experience of actually being there, but who's to say that future generations that incorporate VR or AR won't be dramatically better?

AR applications such as HoloTour allow any user with a Microsoft HoloLens to tour locations such as Rome or Machu Picchu via panoramic video, holographic scenery, and spatial sound, all without leaving the couch. HoloTour includes a virtual travel guide, serving up historical information along with visuals. And in certain locations, such as the Colosseum in Rome, you can travel back in time to experience historical events in ways unavailable to you even if you were to travel there in the real world.

FIGURE 15-1:
Yelp's Monocle feature.

Experiences such as these will only serve to get better as VR and AR solve more of their existing issues with fidelity and locomotion. At a fraction of the price of a single trip to these locations, headsets may eventually replicate the fidelity of travel "close enough" for many users. Or it may not. The travel industry should evaluate these upcoming changes now to stay ahead of the curve.

TRAVELING WITHOUT MOVING

You may think that the virtual worlds created via VR could never provide the same fidelity of experience as being there in person. That may be true, but companies are already capitalizing on the potential of VR and AR to simulate that experience. Rendever is a startup focused on providing this sort of experience to senior citizens who may no longer be tolerant of cramped plane rides or long bus trips. Utilizing 360-degree imagery and video, users in senior living communities are able to explore the French countryside or ocean depths without ever leaving their armchairs.

Museums

Similar to the tourism industry, museums rely on providing an experience to their visitors that they can't receive while sitting at home. The rise of personal computers and the Internet has seen museums grow and change along with the differing needs of their visitors. Now that the entire knowledge of mankind is a touch away on any mobile phone, museums have looked for angles to bring a deeper experience to their patrons, finding new and interesting ways to incorporate digital technology alongside physical experiences. Many museums have created exhibits that do just that, combining technology and physical interaction in new and interesting ways that patrons could not otherwise experience on their own.

VR and AR introduce a new twist on the old technological challenges. How can museums stay relevant in a world where VR or AR provides the sense of presence to users, a niche currently filled by museums?

The Skin & Bones exhibit at the Smithsonian National Museum of Natural History may provide a glimpse of potential future uses as museums seek to embrace VR and AR alongside physical exhibits. The Bone Hall opened in 1881 and is the Smithsonian's oldest. The exhibit still contains many of the original skeletons that the hall opened with more than 100 years ago, but now guests can utilize an AR app to overlay animal skin and motion onto the bones themselves. The exhibit is given new life as guests can watch a bat form from a skeleton and fly out of the exhibit, and see a rattlesnake latch onto a virtual rodent.

Figure 15-2 shows the view of a visitor both without AR and with AR through the museum's Skin & Bones application, to be used when at the museum to augment the exhibits. Even better, the museum has allowed a select number of the exhibits to be viewable at home. Not only is AR giving old exhibits new life, but it's serving as marketing material for the museum outside the museum, enticing users with an interesting look at a current exhibit and the promise of a deeper experience on-site.

REMEMBER

Museums are constantly looking to stay ahead of the curve in how to handle incoming technological changes. The combination of a physical exhibit experience augmented with extrasensory digital information points to how museums could work to keep up with ever-advancing technology.

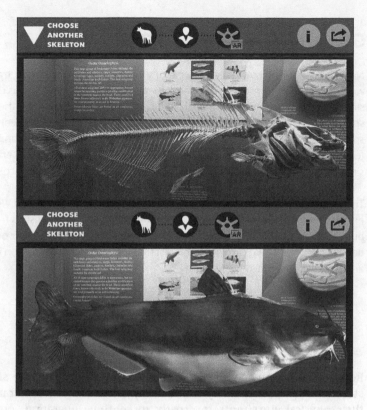

CHOOSE
ANOTHER
SKELETON

FIGURE 15-2:
The Smithson-
ian's Skin & Bones
app without AR
(top) and with AR
(bottom).

Aerospace

Space exploration is currently at a crossroads. On the one hand, national organizations such as NASA have seen a steady decline in their budgets as a percentage of the federal budget for the last two decades. On the other, a new breed of entrepreneurs is stepping in to fill the void left by NASA. New companies such as Blue Origin, SpaceX, Orbital, and Virgin Galactic are looking to make space mining, space tourism, and even trips to Mars viable in the near future.

SpaceVR is looking to align itself with the space tourism movement. The platform, billed as the first of its kind in creating "live, virtual space tourism," is planning to launch a satellite capable of capturing high-resolution, fully-immersive live video and beam it back to any current VR device, ranging from mobile VR headsets up to the Oculus Rift. Depending on level of interest, an entire cottage industry could be created from virtual space tourism.

It's possible to imagine one of the space tourism companies, years from now, landing on Mars while millions watch from here on Earth. Not huddled around a television set as we were in 1969, but instead with our VR/AR headsets on, a fully immersed 360-degree live video feed of what the first astronauts see upon landing on Mars.

GROUND CONTROL TO VR

NASA, with its falling budget, is finding that VR can be a replacement for training that would otherwise be costly. An early adopter of the technology, NASA has used VR in simulating virtual spacewalks for astronauts, enabling them to practice their exact spacewalk scenario hundreds of times before actually performing the real thing in space. NASA also has invested in various VR modules used to train astronauts on how to operate their SAFER jetpacks in the unlikely event of an emergency scenario; VR can simulate the situation extremely realistically, over and over, at no extra cost.

The future of VR within NASA's walls seems clear. Heavier investment in VR technology enables them to better train astronauts, getting more and better results from smaller budgets. This holds true for many industries where training is otherwise prohibitively dangerous or costly. VR can simulate most training scenarios at a fraction of the price and danger of the real thing.

Retail

Retail is already undergoing its own dramatic shift. Malls are struggling to fill storefront space, and many traditionally brick-and-mortar brands are finding their physical storefronts too costly to continue operation, opting instead to maintain only their online properties.

Malls may meet with an unlikely savior in the form of VR. Large-scale free-roaming VR experiences as location-based experiences, or "VRcades," are currently being rolled out to malls and other brick-and-mortar locations everywhere. These types of experiences can't be duplicated within most users' homes, so malls may be the perfect places for many users to experience high-end VR for the time being. HTC has announced plans to open up 5,000 VRcades in the near future, and companies such as the VOID and Hyperspace XR are also exploring location-based extended reality experiences. This sort of location-based entertainment likely won't sustain malls indefinitely, but it may offer a stay of execution for a short while.

Large retailers such as IKEA, Amazon, and Target have already begun using AR to allow customers to see how furniture could look when placed in users' homes. Find the product you want, and place it virtually in your own space!

AR has made its way into the fashion world as well. Major retailer Gap unveiled a pilot app called DressingRoom, which utilizes AR to help users "try on" clothing through their smartphones, placing a 3D avatar of a user in her physical space to view how the clothing may look on her.

AR applications such as these make you think: Could AR eventually be the downfall of brick-and-mortar stores? If the fidelity of the visuals in VR or AR reaches a point where the realism is close enough to the real world, will there be a reason for users to go to these physical storefronts at all?

REMEMBER

The Internet changed the way that people and businesses buy and sell products. Companies that were able to adapt to this new reality were wildly successful; those that were unable to adapt were left behind. Perhaps hard to imagine now, VR and AR could be the impetus of a similar technological leap in the retail space, making it vital for those in the retail industry to consider their positioning and how they plan on adapting to this changing retail landscape.

Military

The military has long been a supporter of evaluating cutting-edge technology. They have always looked for ways to incorporate technology in order to cut costs or improve the way departments are run. This openness to new technology and willingness to experiment should serve the military well moving forward. It could provide a blueprint for other industries, laying out the proper way to address emerging technologies.

Though few businesses may have the time or budget that most militaries do, any business can emulate the experimental mind-set the military has adopted concerning emerging technologies. Rapid experimentation and prototyping is important. Choosing a solution, testing it, keeping what works, and discarding what doesn't can be done by any company, large or small.

HISTORICAL HEADSIGHT

The military industry is no stranger to funding emerging technologies in an attempt to better departments. Military spending brought about what is now considered the very first head-mounted display (HMD) equipped with user motion tracking. In 1961, the Philco Corporation created the HMD for a military project. Labeled the "Headsight," the HMD incorporated a video screen for each eye along with a custom magnetic tracking system linked to remote closed-circuit televisions.

The Headsight was intended for use by the military to enable natural viewing of remote situations. A user could move his head naturally, and the remote cameras would respond in kind to his movements.

This willingness of the military to experiment could pay off dividends in the long run at getting things done better, cheaper, and faster.

Today, the military has already incorporated VR into its training protocols. Companies such as Cubic Global Defense are creating VR military training experiences such as the Immersive Virtual Shipboard Environment (IVSE), which places trainees in simulated "real-life" experiences, simulating scenarios that would be prohibitively expensive to replicate in real life.

But the greatest change VR and AR could bring to the military is only tangentially related to the military itself. VR is often referred to as an "empathy machine." It offers an intimacy to viewers that no other medium can match. As such, could VR help nations better understand one another? Could it serve to help end conflicts between countries? Some entrepreneurs believe so. Karim Ben Khelifa, a wartime photojournalist, had long questioned whether his photographs conveyed the reality he was experiencing on the ground. "What is the point of images of war if they don't change people's attitudes towards armed conflicts, violence, and the suffering they produce?" Khelifa asked. "What is the point if they don't change anyone's mind? What is the point if they don't help create peace?" (Go to https://arts.mit.edu/artists/karim-ben-khelifa/#about-the-residency to read more.)

With these questions in mind, Khelifa set out to create "The Enemy," an experience combining both VR and AR, aiming to inform users about a number of conflicts throughout the world. Users can don a VR headset and explore a digital environment where combatants on both sides of a conflict share their stories and experiences. They can download an AR app and listen to one combatant share his story; then they can turn 180 degrees and find that combatant's "enemy" standing there, waiting to tell his side of the story.

Some people may say that counting on VR or AR to end conflicts is a pipe dream. But technology and the dissemination of information has long been a powerful tool for breaking down barriers. By nearly any measure, we live in a far more peaceful and inclusive time than any of our ancestors, and technology has played no small part in accomplishing that. As Khelifa's experiment claims on the project website (http://theenemyishere.org), "The Enemy is always invisible. When he becomes visible, he ceases to be the Enemy." VR and AR can help bring visibility to opposing sides.

Education

VR and AR companies are already targeting the business of education. And with good reason. The functions VR and AR do well — presenting a plethora of information in new and engaging ways — align perfectly with the needs of educators looking to inform an increasingly tech-savvy generation of students. What may start off as a traditional lecture on a historical event such as the sinking of the *Titanic* could instantly be transformed as the lecturer turns the classroom itself into a virtual setting of the ship colliding with an iceberg. Or perhaps the lecturer changes the view to one of a submarine, exploring the depths of the wreckage in a realistic virtual setting.

On a larger scale, entire classrooms could now take place virtually. Children who couldn't attend school for various reasons (illness, distance) could attend these same classes virtually. Class size and school location could play much less a factor in what school a child attends. The virtual experience could also offer a far deeper experience than the one currently offered by books or computers alone.

REMEMBER

As we move forward with technologies such as VR and AR, it's important that as a society we consider ways to ensure these technologies are accessible to all, regardless of ability or socioeconomic status. The ability for all to experience VR was one of the tenets of Google Cardboard. Finding ways for VR and AR to make it into classrooms, libraries, and other public settings to ensure everyone can experience these technologies should be something to consider as we progress.

Within the realm of AR, it's easy to imagine AR taking the place of many online lessons that are currently paired with textbooks. Put on your AR headset and watch a World War II history lesson come alive on the pages of your textbook. The proliferation of AR on mobile devices means that, within the next few years, this type of experience may become the most common way students experience interactive textbook content. Point your mobile device to a tracking marker in your textbook and an interactive experience appears.

Taking things further, is it possible that books could be eliminated entirely and replaced by a pair of AR glasses? Many schools already require students to purchase laptops as early as middle school. It isn't farfetched to imagine, within the next decade or so, students being required to buy AR or VR/AR-hybrid glasses. These glasses could present information in engaging ways far surpassing that of traditional printed material, with the added benefit of removing the need to purchase textbooks for each class or area of study. A single pair of AR glasses could be all a student needs, and each course could provide lessons formatted for that device.

Entertainment

Entertainment is an industry in which the tie-ins to both VR and AR seem obvious. The usage of VR in gaming is currently overrepresented compared to its presence in most other industries, and VR in film is just another tool in filmmakers' toolbox for presenting the stories they want to tell.

A number of VR film studios have popped up in the wake of the release of the Oculus DK1 in 2013, such as Kite & Lightning and Limitless. These studios push the boundaries of traditional storytelling, not only by subverting 2D filmmaking for 360-degree 3D films, but also by beginning to explore a level of interactivity within these experiences, taking the experience a step beyond more passively consumed 2D films.

Similarly, AR games and entertainment are already somewhat pervasive throughout the AR market. The most widely downloaded AR app was the game Pokémon Go. Many other AR games and entertainment apps exist, with large brands such as the Harry Potter franchise looking into how they can use AR to keep fans engaged with their franchise outside the walls of traditional media.

But aside from these more "traditional" uses, what sort of seismic shifts could the future of entertainment undergo with these technologies? For one, live entertainment could soon see an upheaval thanks to VR. A number of potential customers for live events have already traded in the experience and hassle of attending a live event for the comfort of their own couches and big-screen TVs. What happens to these live events when VR takes its next big technological leap forward?

Will attending these live events become a relic of the past? Instead of a stadium packed with 50,000 fans, will stadiums instead be packed with 360-degree cameras, each offering a different ticket "package" for viewers to subscribe to? Some people theorize that with enough cameras and enough data, you'll be able to extract enough information from the scene to virtually view from locations where no cameras even exist and watch from literally any angle you like.

AR also has application for live sporting events. Microsoft put together an impressive vision of the future football fan experience using the HoloLens in conjunction with the NFL. Alongside the game on TV, users with a HoloLens are treated to a second screen experience using AR. The game is extended beyond a fan's TV set, with Marshawn Lynch's latest rushing statistics projected on the wall or an overhead view of Russell Wilson's latest miraculous evasion of a sack projected on the coffee table.

Figure 15-3 shows a screenshot of how Microsoft envisions the future of experiencing football games could be with the Microsoft HoloLens. The standard user experience of just watching on TV is now augmented into the user's physical environment digitally with extra data and visual holograms, all configurable by the user.

FIGURE 15-3: A screen capture of Microsoft's take on the future of football and AR.

Perhaps there are even broader implications here. Could the TV itself be disappearing? As AR glasses become commonplace or, even farther out, AR contact lenses or even brain-computer interfaces begin to arrive, the need for a stand-alone device to display video could disappear. Want a 100-inch TV for displaying video on your wall? Pop on your AR glasses, spread out your hands to make it so. Want the image to appear instead in a small out-of-the-way corner? Not a problem — just "grab" the image and scale it down or slide it over. The constraints of a standard 2D screen for viewing video may be abolished sooner than you think.

It's entirely possible that the current generation of children could be the last that actually experiences 2D TV as we know it. The TV may survive to see its 100th birthday in 2027, but don't be surprised if it's unable to make it much past that, its demise hurried along by AR.

A *brain-computer interface* (BCI) is the establishment of a communication pathway between the brain and a computer. A BCI could have the ability to augment your cognitive functions directly via your brain and remove the need for extra hardware such as glasses in order to augment your reality. It has the potential to change everything we know about what it means to be human. We're likely decades away from even considering BCIs as a remote possibility.

Real Estate

Real estate's core mantra has always been "Location, location, location." A run-down one-bedroom condominium in a desirable location such as New York or San Francisco can run you hundreds of thousands if not millions of dollars. Meanwhile, a beautiful seven-bedroom mansion in rural North Dakota may cost only a fraction of that price. However, if VR becomes convincing enough, is it possible that it could make everything we know about real estate obsolete?

It seems far-fetched to think that anyone would abandon a beach-front property anytime soon. And certainly some locations will never be able to offer the same amenities or activities as others. But the Internet has already started this trend. When hiring, companies in large cities are no longer limiting themselves by hiring employees within commuting distance of their office. Distributed teams and telecommuting are commonplace, and they'll only become more so. Companies such as Pluto are exploring ways to enhance meetings and communication between distributed users in VR. Although still very early technology, these VR communication tools offer a sense of presence beyond that of even current video conferencing levels.

If VR can deliver a realistic enough experience to a user without the need to leave his home, could some users choose to leave the high-priced, "desired" locations of today in favor of larger, cheaper accommodations elsewhere, where they can virtualize their reality as they see fit?

Similarly, will the size of a space no longer matter as much? If someone can put on a VR headset and haptic gloves or an exoskeleton for virtualizing movement and feel as if she has the space of a mansion, will that experience be strong enough for her to ignore her real-world surroundings, regardless of how small they are?

These ideas may stretch credibility today. But these questions have long been explored in media such as Ernest Cline's *Ready Player One.* In a world that's becoming more and more virtual, an industry very much based on physical location should take a hard look at itself and question where it may fall in this new virtual world order.

Advertising and Marketing

Advertisers and marketers are often quick to jump on the bandwagon of what could be the next big thing. Whatever new technology is adopted at mass-consumer level, marketers want to have a plan in place to use this new platform to advertise and sell to consumers.

It's no surprise that Google, with its reliance on advertising income, has already begun experiments on what a native VR ad format could look like. Similar to banner ads on websites, the current Google iteration displays ads as small 3D objects in a scene. If a user engages with the ad either via direct interaction or gaze, a video player opens in 3D space that can be closed out. Similarly, technology company Unity has begun its own explorations of advertising in VR, suggesting creating "Virtual Rooms." A Virtual Room would be a new VR location a user could access via a portal from the main experience, leaving the current VR application and entering into a brand's Virtual Room experience.

You can picture similar types of advertisements playing out in virtual environments. Virtual ad space could be sold to advertisers to do with what they will, and handle as they want, with static ads, motion ads, or even ads that allow user interaction. VR advertising could be aimed at fans viewing a live concert or sporting event through VR. This advertising could enable much deeper interaction for the viewer than ads aimed at those attending the event or viewing the event on TV.

Perhaps more interesting (and potentially nefarious) is the thought of AR advertising. As AR glasses or contacts reach critical mass, the AR advertising industry will explode. Think of the possibilities: When literally any and all surfaces in the physical world can become a potential area to display advertisements, companies will fight tooth and nail to display their brands in front of users.

Figure 15-4 shows a still from Keiichi Matsuda's dystopian short, *Hyper-Reality*, where every surface of a user's reality is digitally bombarded with extrasensory data. Shown through the protagonist's point-of-view via an AR device, every surface of the real world appears to be covered with digital advertisements. Everywhere the protagonist travels is an exhausting menagerie of flashing videos, infographics, and static ads. Even the interior of the grocery store offers no respite — ads for coconuts and weight loss supplements pop up, and the entire interior of the store lights up with virtual billboards like Times Square. In the film, when the intensely colorful AR experience malfunctions for a few moments, you see the real-world as it is, drab, gray, and covered with AR tracking markers.

FIGURE 15-4:
A still from Keiichi Matsuda's short *Hyper-Reality*.

This dystopian view of the future is heightened to jar the viewer, but in the near future you can count on advertisers looking to get their brands in front of potential customers using this new technology in any way possible. If we aren't careful and don't demand that advertisers and marketers use this newfound power responsibly, a view of the future similar to this may not be far off.

The Unknown

Every large-scale technological revolution or technology wave has inadvertently created entirely new industries. Some examples:

>> The rise of personal computers led to the creation of innumerable hardware and software companies, from Microsoft to Apple to gaming companies to applications and utilities.

>> The Internet's invention provided a plethora of new industries and companies as well, from Amazon to eBay to Facebook, from e-commerce to social media and social websites to blogging, from online file sharing to digital music, podcasts, and video streaming services.

>> Mobile phones' rise in popularity created an entire industry of app developers and re-birthed the popularity of microtransactions. It gave way to the rise of numerous social networking companies and applications, all based on the ability of users to connect on the go.

Predicting the industries that VR and AR will create is next to impossible. Henry Ford is often quoted as saying, "If I had asked customers what they wanted, they would have said faster horses." This quote illustrates just how difficult it can be for us to imagine the unknown. We can be limited by our knowledge, and we'll almost always ground our predictions within those known boundaries, which can make it difficult to imagine those truly great leaps forward that change the way we understand the world.

The one thing I can say for sure is, with the rise of VR and AR, new industries will be birthed alongside them — industries we may not even fathom at the moment. Perhaps years from now, it won't be out of the ordinary to see "VR environment repairperson" or "AR brain technician" as job titles. The possibilities are endless!

Chapter **16**

Ten (Or So) Mobile Apps for Experiencing Augmented Reality Today

One of the biggest challenges that virtual reality (VR) and augmented reality (AR) face today is the lack of consumer device availability. This is especially true for AR, where the best form factor experiences (glasses or headsets) are out of reach for all but the most dedicated early-adopter tech enthusiasts. Luckily, the rise of mobile AR has given way to a number of AR apps for mobile devices. These apps may not provide the optimal hardware form factor, but they can start to paint a picture for users about what sorts of problems AR will be able to solve.

This chapter looks at ten (or so) AR apps you can experience today with little more than an iOS or Android device. Due to the mobile form factor, some of these apps may not be the idealized form factor for AR. However, the engineers at Apple and

Google have done an incredible job of shoehorning AR into devices that were not originally built for AR experiences. As you review these apps, imagine how these experiences could be delivered to you in the future: in high fidelity via a pair of unobtrusive AR glasses. Consider what benefits that change in form factor could offer, how it could improve these already interesting executions. That's the promise of near-future AR.

REMEMBER

Mobile AR is an amazing feat of engineering, and it has many intriguing use cases. However, AR's ultimate form factor is likely an execution that feels less obtrusive and can be used hands-free. Keep this in mind when reviewing any mobile AR experiences. What may feel a bit awkward or strange to use today may only be a form factor upgraded version or two away from incredible.

Google Translate

Google Translate is a wonderful example of the power of AR. And not because it stretches AR to its visual technical limits — it doesn't. Its visuals are simple, but its inner workings are technically complex.

Google Translate can translate signs, menus, and other text-based items in more than 30 different languages. Simply open the app and aim the device's camera at the text you want to translate and — *voilà!* — you get an instant translation digitally placed on top of the original block of text.

Figure 16-1 shows a screenshot of Google Translate in use. A sign written in Spanish is seamlessly translated to English on the fly via the Google Translate app, which replaces the Spanish characters on the sign with a similar English font.

Imagine traveling in a foreign country equipped with a pair of AR glasses powered by Google Translate. Signs and menus that previously were nothing but strings of unrecognizable characters become instantly readable in the language of your choice. The same Google Translate includes automatic audio translation, too. Imagine those same AR glasses paired with unobtrusive headphones (which, unsurprisingly, Google also manufactures) translating foreign language audio on the fly. Both the audio and visuals "augment" your current reality and make language barriers a thing of the past.

Google Translate is available for both iOS and Android devices.

FIGURE 16-1:
A screenshot of a
sign before and
after translation
in Google
Translate.

Amazon AR View

One of the obvious questions that AR can help answer is: "How does this item look in real life?" A number of companies have attempted AR implementations of their physical catalogs, but it has generally been confined to larger items such as furniture. Furniture and other large pieces can be notoriously difficult to shop for online — picturing how these large items may look in your home can be tough.

Retail giant Amazon recently added an AR feature to its Amazon standard shopping app called *AR View*. Amazon's AR View enables you to preview thousands of products in AR — not just larger furniture pieces, but toys, electronics, toasters, coffee makers, and more. Open the Amazon app, select AR View, navigate to the product you want to view, and place it in your space via AR. You can then walk around it in three dimensions, check out the sizing, and get an idea of the object's look and feel within your living space.

Figure 16-2 shows Amazon's AR View in action, displaying a digital Amazon Echo Look via AR in a real environment.

FIGURE 16-2:
An Amazon Echo
Look in AR.

Only a small subset of Amazon's offerings are currently available in AR View, but that will likely change soon. The main drawback of Amazon being an online-only store has meant that customers can't experience the physical products as they would at brick-and-mortar locations. AR might allow Amazon to help alleviate that issue. You can imagine Amazon requesting that a majority of its vendors' catalogs be digitized in order for users to be able to experience their product listings digitally via AR.

Amazon AR View is available for iOS devices and is coming soon to Android.

Blippar

Blippar is a company with a lofty goal: to be *the* company that bridges the gap between the digital and physical world via AR. Blippar envisions a world where *blipp* becomes a part of our everyday lexicon in the same way you may use *Google* as a verb today: "Just Google it!"

To Blippar, a *blipp* (noun) is digital content added to an object in the real world. And *to blipp* (verb) means to unlock Blippar's digital content via one of Blippar's applications in order to recognize the object and display the content on your mobile, tablet, or wearable AR device.

TECHNICAL STUFF

Blippar is not just an AR execution — it's a clever mix of many technologies. Blending many technologies such as AR, artificial intelligence, and computer vision, the Blippar application can recognize and provide information about millions of real-world objects and even people.

After you download the Blippar app and point your mobile phone at an item, such as your laptop, Blippar scans the device, recognizes the item, and offers information about it. For example, for a laptop, it may show you facts about laptop via Wikipedia, let you know where to buy laptops online, and point to YouTube videos of laptop reviews. If you aim your Blippar application at a famous person, such as the chancellor of Germany, Blippar tells you her name and offers up various bits of information and news about her.

Blippar also offers branded experiences. Companies that want to provide AR data about their products can work with Blippar to create their own branded AR executions. For example, Nestlé may request that whenever a user blipps an image of one of its candy bars, the Blippar app delivers an AR game to the user. Universal Pictures may request that whenever a user blipps any of its posters for *Jurassic Park*, a dinosaur pops out of the poster in AR and provides a trailer link for the movie. Or, as Figure 16-3 shows, Heinz may request that any time a user blipps an image of its ketchup bottles, the app displays an AR recipe book.

FIGURE 16-3:
Blippar
recognizing and
augmenting
a Heinz
Ketchup bottle.

REMEMBER

Unlike many of the AR applications available today on mobile devices for consumer use, Blippar's use of computer vision offers functionality beyond just placing a model in 3D space. Blippar's ability to recognize objects and utilize AR alongside those objects may be a sign of where AR will end up next.

It remains to be seen whether one day we'll be telling our coworkers, "Just blipp it," but Blippar's future looks bright.

Blippar is available for both iOS and Android devices.

AR City

AR maps are an application whose time has long been coming. The ability to project directional arrows leading to your destination onto your car's windshield or a pair of wearable glasses has long been a goal.

Created by Blippar (yes, the same Blippar I mention in the preceding section), AR City enables you to navigate and explore more than 300 cities worldwide using AR. As you travel to your destination, AR City visualizes your route on top of the real-world view via 3D overlays of your surroundings. In certain larger cities and metropolitan areas, enhanced map content provides further information about the places around you, including street names, building names, and other local points of interest. Figure 16-4 shows an example of AR City in use.

FIGURE 16-4:
The AR City app augmenting directions into a user's reality.

TECHNICAL STUFF

In a select few cities, Blippar further utilizes what it has termed its *urban visual positioning* (UVP) *system*. Blippar claims that UVP enables the company to get up to twice the accuracy of GPS, the current technology behind standard mobile phone mapping applications. Using UVP, Blippar claims it can get data so precise that it could begin placing virtual menus on walls in front of restaurants or interactive guides on famous monuments, with pinpoint accuracy.

As with the other items on this list, the ultimate form factor of AR navigation as shown in AR City is likely not within a mobile phone. A similar navigation system embedded in glasses or projected on your windshield may sound like something from the far future, but AR City proves that that future is fast approaching.

ARCity is available for iOS devices.

ARise

ARise is a departure from many of the AR game apps currently in the Apple App Store and Google Play Store. Unlike many games that feature AR as an add-on to the main gameplay mechanic, ARise is designed specifically to make use of AR features.

In ARise, your goal is simple: to guide your hero to his target. However, you're provided with few controls for doing so. You never touch the screen or swipe to solve the puzzles. Line of sight and perspective are your only methods of navigating these virtual worlds.

Figure 16-5 shows ARise being projected into a user's environment for gameplay.

FIGURE 16-5:
The ARise game board projected onto a table.

The goal and gameplay are both relatively simple. What makes ARise a good example of AR for beginners is its requirements for users to get up and move around the game board in order to accomplish their goals. The levels within ARise are fairly large and complex. In order to correctly align your perspective to reach your goal, you'll have to navigate around the digital holographic world by moving around in the real world.

By no means should every AR game require the same amount of physical interaction that an experience like ARise requires. There are plenty of instances where gamers would prefer to sit on their couches instead of having to constantly move around a digital hologram in physical space. However, for beginning users unfamiliar with what AR can do, a game such as ARise strikes the right balance between tech demo and full-blown gaming experience, serving as a basic introduction for what AR can do.

ARise is available for iOS devices.

Ingress and Pokémon Go

It would be difficult to make a list of AR applications you should try out and leave off two of the apps that launched interest in AR and location-based gaming.

The gameplay in Ingress is fairly simple. Users choose a team ("the Enlightened" or "the Resistance") and try to capture *portals*, locations scattered throughout the globe at places of interest, such as public art, landmarks, parks, monuments, and so on. The user's map within the game displays her location in the real world and the portals closest to her. In order to capture a portal, a user must be within a 40-meter radius of the portal, making Ingress a great game for getting users to walk around and explore within the real world.

Pokémon Go is cut from a similar cloth. The gameplay of Pokémon Go aligns with its slogan: "Gotta Catch 'Em All." The user is cast as a Pokémon trainer and shown a digital representation of himself on a map, as well as the location of nearby Pokémon. As with Ingress, users playing Pokémon Go have to travel to a real-world location close enough to the Pokémon in order to capture it. When a user is within range of the Pokémon, the user can try to capture it by throwing Pokéballs at it in either a fully digital or AR environment. A trainer can use his captured Pokémon to battle rival teams at virtual gyms throughout the world.

Ingress and Pokémon Go were both very early entries into the AR space. And purists may argue that the lack of digital visual holograms interacting with the real world means neither is a true AR game. (Pokémon Go does allow you to try to catch a Pokémon as if it were visually in the "real" world, but with no interaction with the real-world environment.) However, AR can be more than just a visual display. AR can mean any method of digitally enhancing the real world. Both Ingress and Pokémon Go augment the real world with digital data and artifacts.

The debate over what is and isn't "AR" may be best left for the terminology purists to decide. In the meantime, both games are worth exploring if for no other reason than to decide for yourself what you think makes an AR experience "augmented reality."

Ingress and Pokémon Go are available on both iOS and Android devices.

MeasureKit and Measure

MeasureKit and Measure are two apps that can introduce users to the power of AR through simple utilities. MeasureKit is the iOS version, and Measure is a similar Android version. The concept of both applications is simple: Using the live video feed from the camera on your mobile device, you point at a spot in the real world. Target the spot you'd like to start measuring from and click to begin measuring. Then target a second spot and click to stop measuring. It's not the flashiest use of AR, but the apps are a good example of utility AR applications for the real world.

With MeasureKit and Measure, you can measure length, width, height, and even volume of objects, all while building a virtual outline of the space your measurements take up in the real world. Plus, the types of measurements the apps can capture, such as volumetric measurements, are often much easier to capture and visualize within AR.

As with AR in general, both apps have some work to do before they're ready for prime time. However, you can easily envision the utility these types of applications could provide for workers on a factory floor or contractors on construction sites, especially combined with the form factor of AR glasses. Virtual measurements could be shared among all workers on a construction site between each pair of AR glasses, displaying entire lists of virtual measurements overlaid on top of an unframed room, removing the possibility for errors or mixups during construction.

MeasureKit is available for iOS devices, and Measure is available for Android devices.

InkHunter

InkHunter is an application enabling you to try on virtual tattoos via AR before they're inked onto your skin for eternity. Simply download the app, draw a marker for where you would like the tattoo to appear, and select a tattoo you'd like to see visualized virtually on your skin. The inner workings of the app will detect the marker and keep the tattoo mapped onto your body, even as you move around in space, allowing you to "try on" and evaluate any number of tattoos, even tattoos made up of your own photos.

TECHNICAL STUFF

The ultimate goal of most AR applications is to function marker-less — that is, with no fixed reference point in the real world. In the case of InkHunter, however, although it can use AR and computer vision to detect surfaces around you, it would have no way of knowing what surface to apply the tattoo onto. The marker serves as a way to allow InkHunter to determine the surface and direction on which to overlay the tattoo.

InkHunter is available for both iOS and Android devices.

Sketch AR

Sketch AR enables users to virtually project images onto a surface, and then trace over the virtual images with real-world drawings. It's similar to illustrators' use of light boxes or projectors to transfer artwork onto various surfaces.

Choose a drawing surface, bring up the various sketches available to trace, select the image to trace, and then hold the camera in front of your drawing surface. The image will now appear mapped to your piece of paper, so you can trace over the lines to create your image. Although its utility for practicing sketching on a piece of paper with your mobile device is limited, a more intriguing use case is the use of Sketch AR within the Microsoft HoloLens, which enables users to transfer small sketches onto much larger murals.

Like many current mobile AR-powered applications, the ultimate form factor of Sketch AR is not your mobile device. When illustrating, you want your hands as free to move as possible. With one hand busy trying to hold your device steady at all times, the experience isn't a perfect one. Seeing that the app has been built for not only mobile devices but HoloLens as well is heartening. Most (if not all) of the AR applications described in this chapter would benefit from the form factor of a headset or glasses. As more AR headsets and glasses are released at a consumer level, companies will hopefully follow suit in bringing their mobile AR experiences to these various wearable AR form factors.

Sketch AR is available for iOS and Android devices, as well as Microsoft HoloLens.

TIP

It has been speculated that Apple's reasoning for releasing ARKit to mobile devices now was to provide a glimpse of the future while allowing developers to access the sort of application program interface (API) that will be available to them if Apple's long-rumored AR glasses come to fruition.

Find Your Car and Car Finder AR

AR car finder applications are available today, and they work well, but similar technology has broader implications for future applications. Both Find Your Car (for iOS) and Car Finder AR (for Android) are simple applications that work in similar ways. Park your car (or whatever you want to find a way back to), drop a pin, and then when you're returning to your car, a compass arrow will guide you back, providing distance and direction to where you left it.

Being able to drop a pin and be guided back to your misplaced vehicle via overlaid directions solves a problem many people struggle with, but apps to locate your car via a dropped pin have existed in some form or another for a while. Certainly AR improves the experience, but what if it went even further?

A proof-of-concept app, Neon, is looking to do just that. Billing itself as the "world's first social augmented reality platform," Neon allows users to leave 3D AR holographic messages in the real world for friends to view, which they can find by following Neon's mapping system. Plus, Neon plans to enable you to locate friends who also have the Neon app in a crowded stadium, festival, or anywhere that might necessitate the usage of the app. (Neon is not yet released to any app stores.)

With a pair of AR glasses, parents could track their children at crowded playgrounds down to the direction and distance they are apart. You could be alerted that a friend or acquaintance in your social network is nearby. Or simply never forget a name or face again — your AR glasses could recognize a user via computer vision and serve up his profile information to you via AR directly to your glasses.

Find Your Car is available on iOS devices. Car Finder AR is available on Android devices. Neon is currently in beta.

Index

Numbers

L

Land's End (VR game), 223
LAP Mentor virtual reality (VR) system, 221–222
LAP Mentor VR system, 221–222
Lasater, Zeke, 188
latency, 17, 48, 70–71
Leap Motion, 43
LEGO Digital Box, 145
Lenovo Mirage Solo, 86
Lightform (company), 246
lighthouse sensors, 31–32, 80
Lightpack, defined, 101
Lightwear, defined, 101
limited extra hardware, 120
limited immersion, 121
Limitless (VR film studio), 298
locomotion, defining, 134–136
Logitech, 39
Looxid Labs, 90
Lotus 1-2-3 (spreadsheet application), 261
low-end devices, 82–83
low-latency, 18
Luckey, Palmer, 17–18, 36
Ludwyck, Jeff, 263
Lumberyard, 188–189

M

Magic Leap
  AR headsets and, 58–60
  consumer-grade, 100–101
  example, 73–74
  new developments from, 18
  schedules releases, 285
  voice control, demoed, 65
mainstream adoption, 21
Maison de Verre (Chareau), 207
Major League Soccer (MLS) Replay, 233
ManoMotion, 66, 156
Manufacturing Technology Centre, 239
marker-based tracking, 70–71
marketing industry, effect of AR and VR on, 301–302

markets
  Chinese, 85–86
  consumer, entering, 282–284
  evaluating, 268–269
  price and, 51–52
  sizes of, 282
Markman, Michael, 168
mass consumer adoption, 146
mass consumer models, 175–176
mass consumer-scale release, 83
mass market share, 119, 121, 124
Matsuda, Keiichi, 301
Mattel View-Master virtual reality (VR), 27
Matterport Pro, 180
Maya, animation in, 170
Measure, 313
MeasureKit, 313
Medical Realities, 221
Meier, Gabriella, 103
merged reality. See augmented virtuality (AV)
Meta 2, 58–60, 98–100
Microsoft Excel (spreadsheet application), 261
mid-tier devices, 81–82
Milgram, Paul, 14
military, effect of AR and VR on, 295–297
Mira Prism, consumer-grade, 101–102
Mitchell, Nate, 52
mixed reality (MR), 9–13, 105
Mizell, David, 16, 17
MLS (Major League Soccer) Replay, 233
mobile applications (apps), AR and
  Amazon AR View, 306–307
  AR City, 310–311
  ARise, 311–312
  Blippar, 307–310
  Car Finder AR, 315
  development, 189–190
  Find Your Car, 315
  Google Translate, 306–307
  Ingress and Pokémon Go, 312–313
  InkHunter, 314
  MeasureKit and Measure, 313
  overviews, 305–306

About the Author

Paul Mealy is a technology leader/evangelist working within the emerging technology field of virtual reality (VR) and augmented/mixed reality (AR/MR). As director of interactive at POP, an agency in Seattle, Washington, Paul is charged with setting the course for the Interactive Development team, an international multidisciplinary team of creative engineers consisting of web, mobile, game, and VR and AR developers.

Paul has been involved in the fields of VR, AR, and MR since the Kickstarter release of the Oculus DK1. Since that time, he has been busy producing VR/AR experiences for various Fortune 500 companies. In his spare time, you can find Paul tinkering with emerging technologies at `http://insidedown.com`.

Dedication

To my wife and best friend, Kara, for her support, understanding, and willingness to listen to me babble on and on explaining various technologies well after her interest has waned. To Toshiko and Martha for always being inspiring. Touch the sky and dream big dreams!

Author's Acknowledgments

This book wouldn't have been possible without a number of people acting behind the scenes to help get it to the finish line. I'm especially grateful to Executive Editor Katie Mohr for helping to bring the project to life in the first place; to Jim Minatel, who helped connect me to the right people at the right time; to editors Elizabeth Kuball and Faithe Wempen for their veteran guidance and editorial chops, and for putting up with the multitude of ridiculous questions I had for them; and to my technical editor, Russ Mullen for his thoughts and making sure I didn't say anything too ridiculous.

Thanks also to my mom, Lynn Mealy, who helped turn a loose collection of thoughts into something understandable; to the number of interviewees throughout the book who were willing to spend their time and offer their opinions; and to the creators in the VR/AR industry whose hardware and software are featured throughout the book — their dedication to their craft has resulted in experiences that were only dreamed about but a few years ago.

Finally, a big thanks to all my family, friends, and everyone in the VR, AR, and MR communities who willingly shared their thoughts and encouragement. You're all a constant source of inspiration. I hope this book inspires you to go out and create whatever you may be imagining.

Publisher's Acknowledgments

Executive Editor: Katie Mohr

Project Editor: Elizabeth Kuball

Copy Editor: Elizabeth Kuball

Technical Editor: Russ Mullen

Production Editor: Tamilmani Varadharaj

Cover Photos: © Petar Chernaev/iStockphoto

Leverage the power

Dummies is the global leader in the reference category and one of the most trusted and highly regarded brands in the world. No longer just focused on books, customers now have access to the dummies content they need in the format they want. Together we'll craft a solution that engages your customers, stands out from the competition, and helps you meet your goals.

Advertising & Sponsorships

Connect with an engaged audience on a powerful multimedia site, and position your message alongside expert how-to content. Dummies.com is a one-stop shop for free, online information and know-how curated by a team of experts.

- Targeted ads
- Video
- Email Marketing
- Microsites
- Sweepstakes sponsorship

20 MILLION PAGE VIEWS EVERY SINGLE MONTH

15 MILLION UNIQUE VISITORS PER MONTH

43% OF ALL VISITORS ACCESS THE SITE VIA THEIR MOBILE DEVICES

700,000 NEWSLETTER SUBSCRIPTIONS TO THE INBOXES OF

300,000 UNIQUE INDIVIDUALS EVERY WEEK

PERSONAL ENRICHMENT

Staying Sharp	Facebook	Guitar	Investing	Beekeeping	Digital Photography
9781119187790	9781119179030	9781119293354	9781119293347	9781119310068	9781119235606
USA $26.00	USA $21.99	USA $24.99	USA $22.99	USA $22.99	USA $24.99
CAN $31.99	CAN $25.99	CAN $29.99	CAN $27.99	CAN $27.99	CAN $29.99
UK £19.99	UK £16.99	UK £17.99	UK £16.99	UK £16.99	UK £17.99

Meditation	Pregnancy	Samsung Galaxy S7	iPhone	Crocheting	Nutrition
9781119251163	9781119235491	9781119279952	9781119283133	9781119287117	9781119130246
USA $24.99	USA $26.99	USA $24.99	USA $24.99	USA $24.99	USA $22.99
CAN $29.99	CAN $31.99	CAN $29.99	CAN $29.99	CAN $29.99	CAN $27.99
UK £17.99	UK £19.99	UK £17.99	UK £17.99	UK £16.99	UK £16.99

PROFESSIONAL DEVELOPMENT

Windows 10	AutoCAD	Excel 2016	QuickBooks 2017	macOS Sierra	LinkedIn	Windows 10
9781119311041	9781119255796	9781119293439	9781119281467	9781119280651	9781119251132	9781119310563
USA $24.99	USA $39.99	USA $26.99	USA $26.99	USA $29.99	USA $24.99	USA $34.00
CAN $29.99	CAN $47.99	CAN $31.99	CAN $31.99	CAN $35.99	CAN $29.99	CAN $41.99
UK £17.99	UK £27.99	UK £19.99	UK £19.99	UK £21.99	UK £17.99	UK £24.99

SharePoint 2016	Fundamental Analysis	Networking	Office 2016	Office 365	Salesforce.com	Coding
9781119181705	9781119263593	9781119257769	9781119293477	9781119265313	9781119239314	9781119293323
USA $29.99	USA $26.99	USA $29.99	USA $26.99	USA $24.99	USA $29.99	USA $29.99
CAN $35.99	CAN $31.99	CAN $35.99	CAN $31.99	CAN $29.99	CAN $35.99	CAN $35.99
UK £21.99	UK £19.99	UK £21.99	UK £19.99	UK £17.99	UK £21.99	UK £21.99

dummies.com

dummies
A Wiley Brand

Learning Made Easy

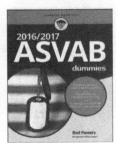

Small books for big imaginations

GETTING STARTED WITH Coding
Get Creative with Code!
Camille McCue, PhD

9781119177173
USA $9.99
CAN $9.99
UK £8.99

MODDING Minecraft™
Build Your Own Minecraft Mods!
Sarah Guthals, PhD
Stephen Foster PhD
Lindsey Handley, PhD

9781119177272
USA $9.99
CAN $9.99
UK £8.99

MAKING YouTube® VIDEOS
Star in Your Own Video!
Nick Willoughby

9781119177241
USA $9.99
CAN $9.99
UK £8.99

DESIGNING Digital Games
Create Games with Scratch™!
Derek Breen

9781119177210
USA $9.99
CAN $9.99
UK £8.99

GETTING STARTED WITH Raspberry Pi®
Program Your Raspberry Pi®
Richard Wentk

9781119262657
USA $9.99
CAN $9.99
UK £6.99

EXPERIMENTING WITH Science
Think, Test, and Learn!

9781119291336
USA $9.99
CAN $9.99
UK £6.99

CREATING Digital Animations
Animate Stories with Scratch™!
Derek Breen

9781119233527
USA $9.99
CAN $9.99
UK £6.99

GETTING STARTED WITH Engineering
Think Like an Engineer!

9781119291220
USA $9.99
CAN $9.99
UK £6.99

WRITING Computer Code
Learn the Language of Computers!
Chris Minnick and Eva Holland

9781119177302
USA $9.99
CAN $9.99
UK £8.99

Unleash Their Creativity

dummies.com

dummies
A Wiley Brand